The Ethics of Cultural

The Ethics of Cultural Appropriation

Edited by *James O. Young* and *Conrad G. Brunk*

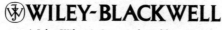

WILEY-BLACKWELL

A John Wiley & Sons, Ltd., Publication

This edition first published 2012
© 2012 Blackwell Publishing Ltd

Edition history: Blackwell Publishing Ltd (hardback, 2009)

Blackwell Publishing was acquired by John Wiley & Sons in February 2007. Blackwell's publishing program has been merged with Wiley's global Scientific, Technical, and Medical business to form Wiley-Blackwell.

Registered Office
John Wiley & Sons Ltd, The Atrium, Southern Gate, Chichester, West Sussex, PO19 8SQ, UK

Editorial Offices
350 Main Street, Malden, MA 02148-5020, USA
9600 Garsington Road, Oxford, OX4 2DQ, UK
The Atrium, Southern Gate, Chichester, West Sussex, PO19 8SQ, UK

For details of our global editorial offices, for customer services, and for information about how to apply for permission to reuse the copyright material in this book please see our website at www.wiley.com/wiley-blackwell.

The right of James O. Young and Conrad G. Brunk to be identified as the authors of the editorial material in this work has been asserted in accordance with the UK Copyright, Designs and Patents Act 1988.

Library of Congress Cataloging-in-Publication Data

The Ethics of cultural appropriation / edited by James O. Young and Conrad G. Brunk.
p. cm.
Includes bibliographical references and index.
ISBN 978-1-4051-6159-6 (hardcover : alk. paper) – ISBN 978-1-4443-5083-8 (paperback)
1. Ethnic relations. I. Young, James O. II. Brunk, Conrad G. III. Title: Ethics of cultural appropriation.
GN496 .E835 2009

2009000091

A catalogue record for this book is available from the British Library.

This book is published in the following electronic formats: ePDFs 9781444311082; Wiley Online Library 9781444311099; ePub 9781444345391; Mobi 9781444394245

Set in 10.5 on 13 pt Minion by Toppan Best-set Premedia Limited
Printed in Malaysia by Ho Printing (M) Sdn Bhd

1   2012

To Leslie Kenny
With the editors' gratitude for all of
her assistance in producing this volume

Table of Contents

Ethics of Cultural Appropriation Research Group Members

Laura Arbour is a clinical geneticist and associate professor in the Department of Medical Genetics at the University of British Columbia, based in Victoria, BC. Her research is focused on addressing genetic conditions that disproportionately affect Canadian Aboriginal people and understanding culturally acceptable ways to carry out the research.

Kelly Bannister holds a doctorate in botany from the University of British Columbia. She is an adjunct professor in the Studies in Policy and Practice Program and director of the POLIS Project on Ecological Governance at the University of Victoria. She has published in journals such as *Current Anthropology* and *Cultural Survival Quarterly* on ethnobotany and the appropriation of Indigenous cultural knowledge.

Conrad G. Brunk is Emeritus Professor of Philosophy and former Director of the Centre for Studies in Religion and Society at the University of Victoria. He is the author of numerous articles and texts on ethical issues relating to technology, the environment, law, and professional practice. Dr. Brunk consults regularly for governments and international organizations on environmental and health risk management and technology policy issues.

Elizabeth Burns Coleman holds a doctorate in philosophy from Australian National University and is a Postdoctoral Fellow in the Communications and Philosophy sections of Monash University. She is the author of *Aboriginal Art, Identity and Appropriation* (2005) and other works on cultural appropriation.

Rosemary J. Coombe holds a PhD in law with a minor in anthropology from Stanford University. She has taught law, anthropology and communication and cultural studies at the University of Toronto, York University, Harvard University, De Paul University, the University of Connecticut and American University, as well as holding distinguished research chairs in the Netherlands, Germany and New Zealand. She is the author of *The Cultural Life of Intellectual Properties: Authorship, Appropriation and the Law* (1998) as well as articles in cultural anthropology, legal theory and the globalization of intellectual property. She currently holds a Canada Research Chair in Law, Communication and Culture at York University.

A.W. Eaton is Assistant Professor of Philosophy at the University of Illinois at Chicago. She works on topics in aesthetics, feminism, and value theory.

Ivan Gaskell is at Harvard University where he holds the Margaret S. Winthrop chair in the Fogg Art Museum, and teaches in the history department. He has written, edited or co-edited a dozen books on art and aesthetics.

Susan Haley holds a doctorate in philosophy but has been a full time writer for 20 years. She is the author of seven novels, including *The Complaints Department* (2000) and *The Murder of Medicine Bear* (2003), which draw on her experience of life in mainly Aboriginal communities. She is presently at work on an eighth novel.

James (Sa'ke'j) Youngblood Henderson holds a J.D. from the Harvard Law School. He is the author or co-author of eleven books and is currently the Research Director of the Native Law Centre of Canada at the University of Saskatchewan. He is a tribal citizen of the Chickasaw Nation.

Travis Kroeker holds a doctorate from the University of Chicago. He is the author of two books and many articles on religion and ethics. He is Professor of Religious Studies at McMaster University.

Dominic McIver Lopes is Distinguished Professor of Philosophy and an associate dean of arts at the University of British Columbia. His main research interest is the philosophy of art. He is the author of *Understanding Pictures* (1996) and its sequel, *Sight and Sensibility: Evaluating Pictures* (2006). He is also co-editor of the *Routledge Companion to Aesthetics* and several specialized collections in aesthetics. His most recent work focuses on new art media, especially interactive media, and theories of art, taking into account cross-cultural perspectives.

George P. Nicholas is a professor of archaeology at Simon Fraser University, Burnaby, British Columbia, and director of the international research initiative 'Intellectual Property Issues in Cultural Heritage: Theory, Practice, Policy'. He was founding director of Simon Fraser University's Indigenous Archaeology Program in Kamloops, BC (1991–2005). Nicholas' research focuses on Indigenous peoples and archaeology, intellectual property issues relating to archaeology, the archaeology and human ecology of wetlands, and archaeological theory, all of which he has published widely on. He is series co-editor of the World Archaeological Congress' *Research Handbooks in Archaeology*.

Daryl Pullman is Associate Professor of Medical Ethics at Memorial University in St. John's, Newfoundland. He has published widely in legal, medical and philosophical journals.

Geoffrey Scarre is Professor of Philosophy at the University of Durham, UK. In recent years he has taught and published mainly in the areas of moral theory and applied ethics. His latest books are *Death* (Acumen/ McGill-Queens, 2007), *Mill's* On Liberty: *A Reader's Guide* (Continuum, 2007) and the edited collection (with Chris Scarre) *The Ethics of Archaeology* (C.U.P., 2006). His current projects include a book, *On Courage,* to be published by Routledge in 2009.

Maui Solomon is an Aboriginal lawyer in Kawatea Chambers, Wellington, New Zealand. He has worked extensively on bio-piracy and the appropriation of traditional knowledge.

Andrea N. Walsh is a visual anthropologist at the University of Victoria and is of Irish, Scottish, Canadian and Nl'akapamux ancestry. Her main area of interest is twentieth-century and contemporary First Nations visual and material culture. The focus of her research has been on ideas of space and place represented through urban First Nations and Metis artists who are working in the areas of conceptual art, installation, photography, painting and video/film. She also maintains a collaborative community-based research program with the Osoyoos Museum Society (OMS) and the Osoyoos Indian Band (OIB) to research and document a rare collection of Aboriginal children's art from the Inkameep Day School created between 1931 and 1942.

Alison Wylie is Professor of Philosophy at the University of Washington. She is probably the leading authority on the philosophy of archaeology and has written, edited or co-edited five books, including *Thinking from Things* (2002), *Ethics in American Archaeology* (2000) and *Value-Free Science?* (2007).

James O. Young is Professor of Philosophy at the University of Victoria. He has published more than 40 journal articles on the philosophy of language and the philosophy of art and is the author of *Global Anti-realism* (1995) and *Art and Knowledge* (2001) and *Cultural Appropriation and the Arts* (Wiley-Blackwell, 2008).

Preface

The origins of this volume can be traced to the summer of 2002. In July of that year, Conrad Brunk took up the position of professor of philosophy and director of the Centre for Studies in Religion and Society (CSRS) at the University of Victoria. Soon after arriving, he invited the other editor of this volume, James Young, chair of the Department of Philosophy, to have lunch at University Club and discuss possibilities for research collaboration. Conrad was particularly interested in utilizing an interdisciplinary team research model that had produced a number of successful books at his research centre, and wondered if James might have a research topic that would work well using this model. For some time, James had been investigating the ethical and aesthetic issues that arise from the practice of cultural appropriation in the arts. He had become aware that ethical issues arose from cultural appropriation in a variety of other contexts besides the arts. He was also aware that only a large team of specialists from a variety of disciplines could hope to reveal and solve the ethical problems posed by cultural appropriation. At this meeting the editors decided to apply to the Social Sciences and Humanities Research Council of Canada (SSHRC) for support for just such a team of specialists.

The two editors decided to propose a novel modification to the very successful CSRS interdisciplinary team model. In addition to attempting a highly integrated team-authored book, we thought, quite ambitiously, that we could also produce integrated team-authored chapters in the book. We felt that the topic lent itself especially well to this approach, because the various areas in which cultural appropriation takes place have well developed literatures on the issues involved that needed to be taken seriously. This could best be addressed by having persons who *practice* within a particular area work together with a specialist in ethics, so that the ethical discussion was appropriately engaged with the debate and the real issues in the area. This is what we proposed to the SSHRC.

In the spring of 2004 the editors learned that the application for SSHRC funding had been successful, and the first meeting of the research group was held in Victoria in May of 2005. At this four-day meeting the team discussed the objectives and structure of the project and arrived at a 'common mind' on the overall theme and approach to the problems. This meeting was also crucial in establishing a rapport that would enable the authors to work together constructively. This was a challenge because in many cases the members of the research group were previously completely unacquainted. In several cases, members of the same chapter team were unacquainted with each other. The fact that the research group was diverse along a number of dimensions further complicated the process of team building. Members of the group came from a variety of disciplines and five countries: Australia, Canada, New Zealand, the United States and the United Kingdom. An effort was made to ensure that Indigenous people were represented on the research group. (In the end, due to a series of unfortunate health-related events and other causes, Indigenous representation in the group fell short of the editors' goal.) The evolution of a working research group was further complicated by the fact that the team leaders had tried to ensure that a variety of views on cultural appropriation were represented on the research group. The editors wanted the book to construct new conceptual approaches to the ethics of cultural appropriation and felt that a conversation among those who already tended to agree would not accomplish that goal.

Inevitably, given the diversity of the research group, disagreement arose and passions sometimes ran high, but an excellent *esprit de corps* quickly developed, right from the dinner on the first night of the first meeting. By the end of the second meeting (June 2006), where the draft chapters were submitted to critique by the whole team, many members of the group had developed genuine affection for the others in the group. Unexpectedly, the experience of passionate disagreement and coming to terms with it actually strengthened the sense of togetherness. This contributed greatly to the group's lively, collegial and productive discussions. The editors do not hesitate to say that everyone, perhaps most of all themselves, learned a great deal from the group meetings. We hope that something of the flavor of the group's engaged, alert and informed debates is captured in the chapters that follow.

Of course, not everything went according to plan. We have already noted that the contribution of members of Indigenous people was more limited than we had hoped. Cultural appropriation is often most controversial when something is taken from Indigenous people and yet the voices of Indigenous people are often least likely to be heard. These facts made the group leaders particularly concerned to ensure that members of indigenous groups were well represented on the team. This goal was not fully realized. Initially, Suzan Harjo, a Cheyenne and director of the Morning Star Institute, agreed to be one of the authors of the chapter on appropriation of religious beliefs. A death in her family made it impossible for her to participate in the first team meeting and another Indigenous person, Martin Brokenleg, replaced her in the research group. A serious illness made it impossible for him to participate in the team meetings and eventually forced him to withdraw from the project. Terri Janke, an Aboriginal Australian lawyer well known for her work on cultural appropriation, was to have been one of the authors of the chapters on appropriation of artistic content, but other professional commitments made her unable in the end to confirm her participation in the project. Rosemary Coombe, a leading Canadian scholar, fortunately agreed to fill in that role. Sa'ke'j Henderson attended the first meeting of the research group but a medical procedure, scheduled late in the day, prevented him from attending the second meeting. Fortunately, Maui Solomon (a MorIori lawyer working on cultural appropriation issues in New Zealand) joined the research group in time for the second meeting. Andrea Walsh is also a person of partial Indigenous ancestry.

It was possible to have one more contribution to the volume by an Indigenous person. At the second research group meeting, Andrea Walsh raised the question of cover art for this volume and suggested that we consider the work of a Coast Salish artist, lessLIE. The research group viewed several striking images by this exciting young artist and decided to request the use of one of his paintings on the cover of the book. lessLIE agreed, and his artist's statement is also reproduced here. This statement makes clear that the use of the image on the cover is particularly appropriate, involving as it does the appropriation of artistic motifs from Aboriginal cultures other than lessLIE's own.

Although we were keen to ensure that Indigenous people had a voice in this volume, and many of the papers in this volume focus on appropriation from indigenous cultures, cultural appropriation is a much wider phenomenon. Appropriation from ethnic minority cultures (such as African-American culture) and from minority immigrant cultures is also the source of much controversy. Even appropriation by one national state from another can raise ethical questions, even when both are Western countries.

The controversies surrounding the export of antiquities from countries such as Italy and Greece to museums and archives in Britain, the United States and other nations demonstrates this point.

In another respect, the project did not go entirely according to plan. As noted, the plan was to have each type of cultural appropriation addressed by a team consisting of a philosopher and a non-philosopher. In the end, we ended up with two chapters on the appropriation of human remains. This was largely due to the fact that Sa'ke'j Henderson and Geoffrey Scarre had difficulty finding a common language in which to address appropriation of human remains, despite the fact that their views on the appropriation of human remains are substantially similar. Henderson's illness, preventing his participation in the second team meeting, was a critical factor in inhibiting the process that may have fostered greater collaboration at a crucial stage, as it did among several of the other author teams. We do not, however, see the absence of a single chapter on human remains as a failure of the project. Rather, we see the production of two chapters as an alternative, but equally useful, research outcome of the group project, one not foreseen at the outset. In view of the diversity of backgrounds and opinions found on the research group and the novelty of the method we adopted, the only wonder is that this outcome was not more common.

As we have noted, we had a good deal of trouble finding members of the research group who would write the chapter on the appropriation of religious belief. Given the sensitive nature of this topic, we very much wanted an Indigenous person to be involved in the writing of the chapter on this subject. Unfortunately, at no point did we ever have two members working on religious belief present at one of the meetings of the team. Travis Kroeker worked hard on trying to put together a chapter on religious belief, but the absence of a partner who could attend the team meetings and stay with him on the project handicapped his efforts. In the end, the editors decided that the only satisfactory way to deal with the matter was to write an essay on the topic by themselves. We felt that it was important that those who wrote on the topic should have participated in the meetings of the team. We are nevertheless indebted to Travis for his valuable contributions to the research group meetings.

Many people deserve thanks for their assistance in producing this volume. Paul Teel, a doctoral student in philosophy at the University of Victoria, served as the research assistance for the group. At the second meeting of the group, when each team presented its draft chapter, Paul took extensive notes during the presentations and the ensuing discussions. After the meeting, Paul's extensive notes were circulated to all members of the research group. All of the authors found Paul's notes helpful in revising their chapters for publication. Hussein Keshani provided a great deal of assistance in crafting the SSHRC application that made this project possible. Leslie Kenny and the other staff of CSRS were of immense assistance in organizing the team meetings and otherwise running the project. Michael Asch, an anthropologist with extensive experience of working with Indigenous people, attended both meetings of the research group and his knowledge and wisdom were valuable assets upon which we could draw. We thank Jeff Dean, Blackwell's senior acquisitions editor for philosophy, for his support of the project and his patience as we saw it to completion.

Victoria, British Columbia, 2009

Artist Statement

lessLIE

Salmon Vision 2005
17.5″ × 17″

It is a Coast Salish spiRITUAL beLIEf that humans are dependent on animals and forces of nature for spirituality. In the spirit of spindle whorls, two salmon heads as well as a human eye are depicted in this design. The two salmon heads symbolize the spawning stages of a salmon. The salmon is a guardian spirit of a Coast Salish guardian spirit dancer. The vision gifted to the guardian spirit dancer is symbolized by the human eye formed between the two salmon heads.

This design is part of a series of paintings created as a studio component of my Master's degree. Together, this series of paintings are collectively called 'cultural conFUSION'. My 'cultural conFUSION' paintings are an expression of my ambivalence about accepting aesthetic acculturation from northern Northwest Coast art forms. On one hand, my 'cultural conFUSION' paintings are intended to reflect the reality that many contemporary Coast Salish artists are appropriating northern and Wakashan art forms of the Northwest Coast. Some contemporary Coast Salish people are living in cultural conFUSION. Some contemporary Coast Salish people are cultural cons convicted by colonialism, living in a political prison of the constructs of 'Northwest Coast' and 'Indian' culture. Hence the use of red and black, and the 'con' in 'confusion'. On the other hand, these paintings express my hesitant acceptance of influences from northern Northwest Coast art forms on my work as a contemporary Coast Salish artist. Hence the use of red and the peripheral placement of the trigons in the design, and the 'fusion' in 'confusion'.

1

Introduction

Cultural appropriation has been, in recent years, one of the most widely discussed sources of ethical problems. The literature on the subject is huge. Nevertheless, this book is a distinctive contribution to the literature. It is the product of an unusual, perhaps unique, methodology for producing a collection of scholarly papers.

This methodology involved refining a highly successful model developed by the Centre for Studies in Religion and Society (CSRS) at the University of Victoria. The founding director of the Centre, Harold Coward, pioneered a method in which an interdisciplinary research group would be formed for the exploration of an inherently cross-disciplinary issue. The group would have an initial meeting at which a preliminary exploration of the issue would occur. At this first meeting, the various aspects of the issue would be analyzed and the group would attempt to find a common methodology and common mind to address the issue. The members of the group would then go off to conduct further research into their aspect of the issue under discussion. Later, the group would reconvene and members of the group would present the results of their research for discussion and critique by all the members. The final chapters would then be completed and edited for publication as a book. This process has proved very successful and, to date, nearly twenty volumes have been produced under the auspices of CSRS. Each of the volumes has a degree of coherence and a sense of dialogue often lacked by volumes produced by researchers working completely independently. The editors believed that, though the CSRS process had proved successful, it could usefully be adapted for the unique character of this project.

The innovation adopted in this book was to have teams write each of the chapters. A member of each team would be a philosopher, with expertise in ethical theory, and an empirical theorist or practitioner, with knowledge of the on-the-ground realities of cultural appropriation. So, for example, a philosopher and an archaeologist would address the appropriation of archaeological finds. Until this book was produced, artists, literary critics, museum curators, lawyers, advocates of the rights of Indigenous peoples, historians, anthropologists, archaeologists, ethnobotanists, geneticists, and others have grappled with the ethical issues that arise from the practice of cultural appropriation. Remarkably, only a few philosophers, who might be expected to have developed the capacity to deal with normative issues, have addressed questions of cultural appropriation. One goal that the editors set themselves in organizing the research project to which the idea of this book gave rise was to involve philosophers in the ethical debates that cultural appropriation had generated. At the same time, the editors recognized that, while philosophers may have some expertise in addressing normative and conceptual questions, they tend to be less cognizant of the factual complexities in the various contexts of cultural appropriation. Most philosophers know little about the practice of cultural appropriation, the different forms that it takes, the contexts in which it occurs, or its consequences. While the editors could see that philosophers have a role to play in debates surrounding cultural appropriation, they could also see that untutored philosophers would be able to contribute much of value to the discussion.

The editors identified nine areas of cultural appropriation most in need of philosophical scrutiny. The appropriation of archaeological finds has already been mentioned. In addition, research groups were assigned to the study of the appropriation of human remains, genetic material, traditional knowledge, artistic content (stories, songs and so forth), tangible works of art (sculptures and paintings, for example), artistic subject matter (this is sometimes called 'voice appropriation'), and religious beliefs and practices. The final team was to address the role museums play in cultural appropriation.

Although the topics addressed in this book are quite diverse, the authors worked to find elements that are common to the various sorts of cultural appropriation. The most basic commonality is captured in the *Oxford English Dictionary* definition of 'appropriation' as 'the making of a thing private property . . . ; taking as one's own or to one's own use.' What is appropriated differs. This volume includes studies of the appropriation of tangible works of art, subject matters, intellectual property (both scientific and artistic), archaeological finds, genetic material, human remains, religious beliefs and a range of other items. In all cases, something is alleged to be taken and some use is made of it. The other basic commonality is that we are dealing with appropriation from what is asserted as a 'culture'. In all cases, members of one culture are taking something that originates in another cultural context. (Subject matters, the topic of the chapter by Young and Haley, may be an exception to this commonality.)

The decision to describe the appropriation under consideration as *cultural* appropriation is not uncontroversial. The issues addressed in this volume could be framed in a variety of other ways. One could regard the appropriation in question as appropriation from a nation. This could be a nation state, such as Mexico, or a sub-state nation such as the Lakota nation. Alternatively, we could be concerned with appropriation from what is often called an ethnic group (such as African-Americans or the Maori) or from clans (for example, Aboriginal Australian clans, such as the Ganalbingu). For a variety of reasons, we believe that the focus on *cultural* appropriation is the most fruitful. Even in making this choice we recognize that the concept of 'culture' is hotly contested among both social scientists and philosophers.

One might think that the very concept of a 'culture' is dubious and that for this reason one ought not to frame the issues as 'cultural appropriation'. One reason to consider the concept dubious is that it cannot be defined in terms of necessary and sufficient conditions. In other words, we cannot be essentialist about cultures. That said, we believe that there are such things as culture. There is such a thing as, for example, Canadian culture, even if one cannot specify precisely which cultural attributes an individual must possess in order to count as belonging to Canadian culture. We suggest that the concept of a culture is, in Wittgenstein's sense of the term, a 'family resemblance' concept. Wittgenstein's famous example of a family resemblance concept is the concept of a game. A variety of characteristics are associated with games: some have two sides, some are played on a field, some are played on a game board, some employ a ball, some use dice, most have the object of winning, and so on. No game has all of these characteristics, but something counts as a game which has a sufficient number of them. The concept of a culture is similar. Each culture has a number of associated characteristics. Canadian cultural traits, for example, include passion about hockey (ice hockey, of course), commitment to universal health care, suspicion of US foreign policy, having an opinion on federal-provincial politics, and so on. Even if no one has all of these traits, someone who has enough of them participates in Canadian culture.

Although the lines between cultures are not hard and fast, it still makes sense to frame the questions addressed in this book specifically as questions about *cultural* appropriation. No precision is to be gained by framing questions in terms of ethnicity (this is often the practice when dealing with appropriation from African-Americans). Ethnic groups are just as amorphous as cultural groups. Even the concepts of 'nation' and 'clan' have extremely fuzzy borders—causing untold conflict in human history. Membership in such entities often can be precisely determined only by arbitrary and contested legal mechanisms. Still, talk about cultural appropriation is preferable. There can be questions about appropriation from a culture when there is no exact correspondence with any nation. Appropriation from African-American and from Yiddish culture would be examples. Moreover, nothing is really gained by talking about appropriation from nations or clans since these will normally have a corresponding culture, which can be regarded as the entity from which something is appropriated.

Not all of the teams working on this project felt entirely comfortable characterizing their topic as 'cultural appropriation'. In particular, Pullman and Arbour were reluctant to regard the taking of human genetic material as a sort of cultural appropriation. This was due to the fact that they do not regard genetic material as a form of cultural product. Most other members of the research team disagreed with this position. Cultural property need not be limited to artifacts and intellectual property. It seems fairly uncontroversial to say that crop varietals are a cultural product when they are the product of a particular culture's selective breeding or cultivation. Taking such crop varietals can clearly count as a form of cultural appropriation. Similarly, one can regard human characteristics as a sort of cultural product when they have developed in a particular cultural context. That is, even the human genome is, in part at least, a cultural product. There is no question that many people consider their genome to be an essential aspect of their cultural identity (using DNA tests to corroborate or discount cultural membership claims). The taking of genetic material can, for this reason, count as an instance of cultural appropriation.

Not all appropriation from other cultures is morally questionable. Sometimes items are freely transferred from one culture to another. An American tourist who purchases a sculpture from a properly authorized dealer in Australian Aboriginal art has, in a sense, engaged in cultural appropriation, but does nothing objectionable. On the other hand, the seizure of the Benin Bronzes (many still in the British Museum) during the British punitive expedition of 1897 is nearly universally recognized as unethical. We need criteria for distinguishing wrongful from benign appropriation. We suggest that wrongful appropriation causes unjustifiable harm or is a source of 'profound offense', in the sense identified by the philosopher Joel Feinberg.

Two ways in which cultural appropriation can be harmful are easily identified. The first sort of harm is violation of a property right. That is, a culture could have a property right that is violated by an act of appropriation, an act that amounts to theft. Notice that an act of theft counts as an act of cultural appropriation only if something is appropriated that *belongs* to another culture. An individual from one culture can steal something that belongs to a member of another culture without the act counting as an act of cultural appropriation. Suppose that the editors of this volume were to drive across the American border, break into a Seattle mansion, and then hightail it back to Canada with our booty. We would have committed an ordinary act of theft, but not an act of cultural appropriation, despite the fact that we have stolen from members of another culture.

The second sort of harm is an attack on the viability or identity of cultures or their members. Appropriation that undermines a culture in these ways would certainly cause devastating and clearly wrongful harm to members of the culture. If appropriation threatens a culture with assimilation, the same moral issues are raised. Other acts of appropriation potentially leave members of a culture exposed to discrimination, poverty, and lack of opportunity. Again, if acts of cultural appropriation can be shown to be harmful in one of these ways, we have a case for thinking that they are wrong.

Feinberg introduced the concept of profound offense in the context of a theory of jurisprudence, but the concept can be extended to moral reasoning in general. Profound offense is distinct from ordinary offense, such as that caused by an unwashed bus passenger, or a couple who conspicuously engage in sexual intimacies in public. Profound offense strikes at a person's core values and sense of self. It is caused, for example, by the desecration of a religious symbol or by the violation of profound cultural norms, such as those associated with respect for the dead. The Chinese, for example, feel profound offense when Japanese deny or minimize the Rape of Nanjing. One could also feel profound offense if one felt that one or one's culture is not being treated with fairness or with respect. It is common for people to frame their objections to cultural appropriation in terms of offense. For example, a report on appropriation from Australian Aboriginal cultures says that it can be 'inappropriate, derogatory, culturally offensive or out of context'. (Janke 1998: 19) Similarly, the First

Nation Summit in British Columbia objected to certain paintings on the grounds that they are 'highly offensive, demeaning and degrading to First Nations people.' (Archibald *et al.* 2001: 7) We need to be sensitive to this possibility when assessing the morality of acts of cultural appropriation. At least sometimes, there is a *prima facie* reason to believe that profoundly offensive acts are morally wrong.

Just now we mentioned the concept of respect. Some members of the research group believe that the concept of respect is a crucial one in assessing acts of cultural appropriation. On their view, an act of appropriation can be wrong precisely because it fails to indicate due respect for a culture, its beliefs, its values or its members. Certainly, considerations of respect are often crucial. Perhaps, however, the concepts of respect and offense are closely related. To be offensive is to show a lack of respect. Conversely, the showing of proper respect for a culture involves, minimally, avoiding actions that are gratuitously profoundly offensive. There is no doubt that members of many cultures have regarded the appropriation of their cultural products as profoundly offensive.

A basic but often unstated assumption underlies this volume. This is the assumption that there are some fundamental moral values that in some sense transcend, or are shared by, most cultures despite diverse practices and conventions. These shared values make meaningful moral discourse possible. This view is not shared (or at least expressed or assumed) by all the authors of the following chapters. Nevertheless, the approach the editors have taken, and which underlies the objectives of this project, is that the first assumption in working across cultural divides should be the assumption of common ground. Before resorting to the next moral recourse—that of finding accommodation between conflicting value frameworks—the potential common ground should be sought after diligently.

Of course, cultures have a variety of views on what is right and wrong, legal and illegal, that are reflected in their diverse cultural conventions. Indeed, these views, and more frequently, these conventions, often conflict. It is this conflict that makes the appeal to culture-transcendent moral principles so essential. Suppose that, in addressing the moral problems that arise from cultural appropriation, we could appeal to moral views of only one culture or another. If so, there would be no prospect of arriving at a fully consensual or principled resolution to questions about cultural appropriation. Debates about moral questions would be replaced by either negotiations toward some compromise resolution or a brute contest of power.

In either case it is ultimately the balance (more likely the imbalance) of power that determines the outcome. The latter approach was that exhibited by the colonialism that has given rise to so many of the worst examples of cultural misappropriation. The former approach (negotiation) is the one typical of democratic, pluralistic legal systems, but it too is always dogged by questions of power and post-colonial inequalities. The outcomes of such procedures are rarely to the advantage of disadvantaged minority cultures—those most often the subjects of cultural appropriation. We believe that the first objective of an 'ethical' analysis of a problem is to look for ground upon which one can find common values. If the search for such values fails, then negotiation and compromise may be the best next option. But it should never be mistaken for the just, the fair, or the ethical solution. Our search in this book is for the ethical solution to the problems posed by cultural appropriation.

Nevertheless, cultural relativism about morality is fashionable in many circles—both social scientific and philosophical. Here we cannot mount a full-blown case against this view. The editors can only signal their view that belief in culture-transcendent moral values exists and our conviction that this view is actually to the advantage of disadvantaged cultures. This is not to deny that the argument for transcendent values has more often than not been the guise in which the powerful impose their own cultural biases (usually to their own benefit) upon the less powerful, as 'what you ought to accept'. It is in full cognizance of this danger of appeals to 'transcendent' values that we talk in terms of the search for *shared* values. The ethical viewpoint is to be in the position to argue that there are cases where acts of cultural appropriation can be shown to be wrong by standards that the appropriators *ought* to accept, regardless of their firepower or negotiating skills. Of course, the flip side of this argument is that there may be cases of alleged misappropriation that those who view themselves as victims may, on second reflection upon their own basic values, wish to reconsider.

As we have acknowledged, our conviction is not even shared by all members of the research group. In particular, Wylie has expressed skepticism about it. In an essay on ethics and archaeology, she has referred to 'the dream . . . of establishing a bedrock of fundamental [moral] principles.' She then adds that 'this is the dream that fuels religious and moral absolutism . . . convictions of this kind are the cause of considerable harm.' (Wylie 2003: 12) The editors of this volume, at least, do not share the view that belief in fundamental moral principles necessarily entails dangerous absolutism, which we take to be a desire to have others comply with moral views. There is every reason to believe that, whatever moral principles are fundamental, they include the widely shared one that enjoins us to be respectful and tolerant when dealing with people with views that differ from our own. Absolutism, in the sense that we are considering, is not a consequence of any particular meta-ethical views. A desire to have others comply with one's moral principles could just as easily be held by a cultural relativist. Absolutism is the product of a fundamentally unethical stance, if not of a psychological attitude or disorder. All of us need to be aware at all times that our moral beliefs may be mistaken and to be prepared to listen to others as potentially right where one is wrong. Notice, however, that this injunction to be open-minded and aware of one's fallibility is stated in the form of a culture-transcendent moral principle. This is further evidence that we need not fear a meta-ethics committed to culture-transcendent or shared moral principles.

This said, no one can claim to know with certainty all of the shared fundamental moral principles. Even if we knew these principles, we would still need to know how to apply them within widely disparate cultural contexts. If anything is to be learned from this volume it is that the ethical problems to which cultural appropriation gives rise are complex and difficult. Even if one is committed to the idea of culture-transcendent or shared moral principles, one can accept as valuable the suggestion (made by Nicholas and Wylie in their chapter) that archaeologists adopt dialogic methods of negotiation in addressing cultural appropriation. The adoption of similar methods of negotiation between cultures can be recommended in other contexts as well. But to reiterate our previous point: negotiation that is in the service of *ethics* should be a conversation that looks for agreement, not bargaining that looks for acceptable compromise. We think this is likely what Nicholas and Wylie mean. We also think this is the way to understand the concept of the search for 'ethical space' put forward in the chapters by Henderson and by Bannister, Solomon and Brunk.

Certainly, even if culture-transcendent or shared moral principles exist, we must be sensitive to the particularities of cultures. Each culture has its own beliefs and practices that carry with them sensitivities and opportunities for harm and offense. A simple example will illustrate this point. Each year the Zuni culture of the American southwest commissions the sculpting of two war god figurines (*Ahayu:da*) which are thought to guide the people. At the end of the year, the figurines are left in the wild to decay. The Zuni believe that they must be allowed to return to the earth. Anthropologists and collectors appropriated many of these figurines, perhaps thinking that they had been abandoned. In fact, the *Ahayu:da* had not been abandoned and in this case appropriation was theft. Only people who were ignorant of Zuni beliefs could think otherwise. Knowledge of a culture's beliefs and practices will be similarly crucial when assessing other acts of cultural appropriation. This was one of the reasons why the editors, in their initial conception of the project that gave rise to this book, believed that ethical reasoning needs be informed by specialists in various disciplines that deal with cultural appropriation first hand. It was also a reason we tried to have members of Indigenous cultures involved in the project.

Another excellent example of the need to take into account cultural specificity is provided by the Maori concept of *taonga*, or living treasure. Maui Solomon introduced this concept into the discussions of the research group at our second meeting. What may seem a mere artifact to members of a Western culture may be infused with moral significance, even person-hood, from the perspective of Maori culture. Lack of sensitivity to this fact may give rise to unanticipated harm or profound offense.

Moral questions are not the only normative issues raised by cultural appropriation. Aesthetic issues can also arise and these are touched upon in at least four of the essays in this volume. There is the possibility that the cultural appropriation of artistic content (songs, stories, motifs, styles, and so forth) could lead to aesthetic failure. This aesthetic failure could, in turn, lead to moral problems. The appropriation of a style could, for example, lead to a distorted picture of the culture in which the style originates. This could, in turn, lead to harm to the culture or its members. The style could be mistaken, by both members of the culture and outsiders, as an authentic expression of the culture. If this happened, the authentic expression of the culture could become tainted with inauthentic elements. (Other sorts of appropriation, including appropriation of religious belief, give rise to similar concerns about undermining cultures.) Alternatively, the unsuc-cessful appropriation of a style (or another cultural product) could lead non-members of the culture to form a low opinion of the culture. This could, in turn, give rise to harm to members of the culture. When assessing acts of cultural appropriation, one must be sensitive to the possibility of harm that originates in this manner.

We do not suggest that any of the chapters in this book represent the final word on any form of cultural appropriation. We believe, however, that each of the chapters, particularly in conjunction with the others in the volume, makes an important contribution to the understanding of ethical issues that will become only more pressing as time goes by. At very least, this volume has brought to bear on cultural appropriation more of the resources of normative theory than have previously been deployed. We hope that others will follow in our footsteps and combine normative theory and a sound understanding of the facts of cultural appropriation.

References

Archibald, J.-A., Barman, J., Black, B., Lutz, J. and Tsaqwasupp [Art Thompson] (2001). A review of the depiction of Aboriginal peoples in the artworks of the parliament buildings. *Report of the Speaker's Advisory Panel*. Victoria, BC: Legislative Assembly of British Columbia.

Feinberg, J. (1985). *The Moral Limits of the Criminal Law*, Vol. 2., *Offense to Others*. New York and Oxford: Oxford University Press.

Janke, T. (1998). *Our Culture: Our Future: Report on Australian Indigenous Cultural and Intellectual Property Rights*. n.p., Australian Aboriginal and Torres Strait Islander Studies and Aboriginal and Torres Strait Islander Commission.

Wylie, A. (2003). On ethics. In: Zimmerman, L.J., Vitelli, K.D. and Hollowell-Zimmer, J. (eds.) *Ethical Issues in Archaeology*. Walnut Creek, CA: Altamira Press, pp. 3–16.

2

Archaeological Finds: Legacies of Appropriation, Modes of Response

George P. Nicholas and Alison Wylie

In 1999, Zia Pueblo demanded $74 million dollars from the State of New Mexico for the unauthorized use of its zia sun symbol. (AP 1999; Upton 2005) The flag's design was created by Harry Mera, a physician and anthropologist at the Santa Fe Museum of Anthropology, on the basis of a pot on display in the museum that had been made by an anonymous Zia Pueblo potter in the late 1800s. (USDCPTO 1999) The symbol had likely appeared much earlier. The zia sun is also the emblem of Southwest Airlines, and appears on a vast array of merchandise: jewelry, clothing, coffee mugs and Frisbees.

Questions of intellectual rights have been raised about the recently discovered remains of Homo floresiensis, *the diminutive hominid fossils from Indonesia. A claim has been made that the Jakarta Center for Archaeology holds the intellectual property rights not only to the bones themselves, but also to any casts made of them. (Callinan 2005) This has raised questions about who should control the production and dissemination of fossil casts of human ancestors, including those considered part of the shared history of humanity.*

There has been fierce debate and legal action concerning access to, and dissemination of, the results of research on and translation of the Dead Sea Scrolls. (see Liam et al. 2001) Scholars frustrated by the slow pace of publication by the team charged with the task circumvented official policy by obtaining and publishing photographs and other materials, an action that resulted in suits and countersuits. (Carson 1995) In this case, the controversy involves national and international research practices, national politics and religious issues, as well as the question of who has rights to information contained in ancient documents.

Archaeology as a discipline is inherently a practice of cultural appropriation, at least in a significant majority of contexts in which it has become established as a professional research enterprise. Certainly it has often been viewed as a form of scientific colonialism by those Indigenous descendant communities who regard the material record studied by archaeologists as their cultural heritage and who, increasingly, object to its appropriation. This is also the position taken by the governments of a number of comparatively poor nations whose rich cultural patrimony has made them an object of antiquarian fascination and a target for commercial trade in antiquities for centuries, as well as a primary locus for archaeological research under more recent colonial and post-colonial regimes. Furthermore, as the three examples above illustrate, the issues at hand concern not only the appropriation of material artifacts or sites associated with specific (ancient) cultures, but also the question of who should control the information (i.e., the intellectual property) derived from scientific research, ranging from fossil casts of deep antiquity to modern translations of historic documents.

In the last thirty years, the entanglement of archaeology with the politics of cultural appropriation has been sharply contested, both externally by descendant communities reclaiming their heritage and internally as archaeologists come to grips with the implications of these challenges for their conventional forms of practice. Even in contexts where those who do archaeology are, arguably, studying their own heritage, the politics of appropriation figure as the catalyst for intense debate about who 'controls the past': that is, who regulates access to, or the disposition of, the sites, materials and information identified as archaeological; who counts as an expert, whose understanding of the past is authoritative; and whose interests are served by canonical forms of archaeological knowledge. These questions, which are of increasing importance today to the many stakeholders of the past, are the focus of this chapter.

We begin with a brief account of the ways in which archaeologists have conceived their own enterprise and then identify recent challenges to this disciplinary self-understanding that focus attention on issues of cultural appropriation. We are chiefly concerned here with anthropological archaeology rather than archaeology conducted in an art historical or classical tradition. What follows, and what constitutes the core of this chapter, is our working typology of various forms of cultural appropriation that take place in or through this archaeological tradition. As a framework for discussion, we distinguish three intersecting dimensions with respect to which appropriative practice varies:

1) the *objects* of appropriation: what count as archaeological finds?;
2) the *modes* of appropriation: by whom, or by what means, and for what purposes are these diverse objects appropriated?; and
3) the *responses* to appropriation: what are the repercussions of increasingly widespread protests against archaeologically-mediated forms of cultural appropriation?

We identify a number of examples of appropriation in archaeology that illustrate what these cross-cutting distinctions mean in practice and, in connection with the question of repercussions, we distinguish between restrictive and inclusive responses to appropriation, focusing attention on a range of constructive possibilities that archaeologists are currently exploring. We conclude with some forward-looking observations about the ethical challenges archaeologists currently face and the modes of resolution evident in the various forms of reciprocal and collaborative practice that have been taking shape in the last few decades.

Historical Contexts of Cultural Appropriation in Archaeology

Within anthropological archaeology, the rationale for appropriating cultural sites and material has evolved in ethically consequential ways through the last century and a half. Pivotal at each juncture in this history are shifts in the contrasts that archaeologists have drawn between their own emerging traditions of practice and those of a changing cast of non-archaeological stakeholders with interests in archaeological sites and material. (Denning 1999; Wylie 2002, 2005) Initially, the disciplinary, professional identity of archaeology was defined in opposition to nineteenth-century antiquarian interests and to a voracious commercial market for archaeological materials. In recent decades, these foils for disciplinary identity have been augmented by a set of internal contrasts: properly ambitious, scientific archaeology is defined in opposition to a range of 'traditional' forms of (professional) archaeological practice for which the recovery and systematization of archaeological data has become an end in itself. The common denominator here is that the excluded or contested practices are characterized by a preoccupation with the object. What distinguishes archaeology as a discipline—a subfield of anthropology, with an institutional base in museums and universities—is, above all else, a commitment to treat archaeological material as an empirical record of the cultural past.[1] The defining significance of this material, for self-consciously scientific, anthropological archaeologists, lies in its informational content as evidence that bears on historical and anthropological questions about the cultural past, not its aesthetic, commercial or sentimental value. Consider a statement published by the Society for American Archaeology's (SAA) Committee on Conduct and Standards in 1961 that makes this explicit and captures commitments that underpin much contemporary archaeological practice:

> Archaeology, a branch of the science of anthropology, is that area of scholarship concerned with the reconstruction of past human life and culture. Its primary data lie in material objects and their relationships [systematically collected and documented] . . . Value attaches to objects so collected because of their status as documents, and is not intrinsic (Champe *et al.* 1961: 137).

How archaeologists interpret this mandate to use archaeological material as a resource for understanding the cultural past has varied greatly. That said, one persistent theme in the internal debates that have shaped North American archaeology since the late nineteenth century is an insistence that the goal of properly scientific, anthropological archaeology should be to understand not just the specific events and conditions of life that produced the archaeological record, but, through them, the underlying cultural processes that account for cultural diversity, evolution, genesis and collapse. These disciplinary goals received an especially ambitious articulation in the 1960s and 1970s by advocates of the resolutely scientific New Archaeology: archaeological research must be socially relevant, they insisted, and relevance was to be defined in the broadest possible 'processual' terms, as a matter of delivering (in the ideal) universal laws of cultural process. (see O'Brien *et al.* 2005) In principle, scientific knowledge of this scope is a benefit to humanity; it enriches a *common* cultural heritage conceived, in terms characteristic of the Enlightenment, as a body of empirically grounded, rationally credible knowledge that transcends any local, culture-specific (parochial) interests.[2] It is precisely this conception of relevance that has been challenged in the context of public debate about the ethics and politics of cultural appropriation in archaeological contexts.

Informed by this ambitious vision of its scientific mandate, a great many archaeologists have proceeded on the assumption that the primary, indeed the exclusive, obligation governing their research is to maintain the highest standards of scientific practice in the treatment of archaeological finds. Social relevance is defined in disciplinary terms, with reference to a presumed universal interest in scientific understanding of a common human past. David Hurst Thomas, Joe Watkins and others have detailed the history of archaeological practice conducted in this spirit (Thomas 2000; Watkins 2000; also McNiven and Russell 2005), tracing its continuing influence in contemporary practice. Thomas cites a contemporary bio-anthropologist who makes the underlying principles explicit: 'ancient skeletons belong to everyone'; they are 'the remnants of unduplicable evolutionary events which all living and future peoples have the right to know about and understand.' (2000: 209–210) The extension of this principle to all prehistoric and historic remains affirms the conviction that no 'living culture, religion, interest groups, or biological population' (as quoted by Thomas 2000: 209) can justify restricting the research mandate of scientific experts who have the necessary skills and knowledge to make the best use of surviving 'remnants' as evidence.

Such claims have been vigorously challenged by Indigenous and other descendant communities who claim cultural and genetic continuity or association with the material archaeologists treat as evidence. And they have been undermined by fundamental changes in the conditions of archaeological practice that have forced archaeologists to substantially rethink their disciplinary goals and issues of accountability. For present purposes, three dimensions of change have been particularly significant: 1) employment patterns and professionalization; 2) the accelerating destruction of archaeological resources; and 3) moral, legal and political challenges from descendant communities.

Although the specifics vary greatly from one national legislative context to another, there had been an explosive growth of contract archaeology and the culture resource management (CRM) industry beginning in the early 1970s; by the late 1990s, a growing a majority of professional archaeologists were employed by government agencies and in industry under conditions that put tremendous pressure on an unqualified commitment to scientific goals. The ultimate goal in these contexts is to serve a broadly conceived (social, public) interest in expanding our (scientific) understanding of the cultural past, but in practice archaeologists are contractually accountable to a range of stakeholders whose interests are much more local and particular.[3] The tools of archaeological investigation are often applied instrumentally to problems defined by culture resource managers, public interest groups, and legal and political lobbies, rather than to research questions set by the anthropological agenda of academic archaeology. Conflicts among the interests that define professional account-ability, and the need to establish standards to which archaeologists could appeal in negotiating these conflicts (and to which they could be held accountable) were a primary catalyst for the development, in the late 1970s, of the first codes of professional conduct (e.g., by the Society of Profes-sional Archaeologists, now supported by the Register of Professional Archaeologists; SoPA 1991, RPA 2006; see discussion in Wylie 1999, 2005).

A related development in the same period was the articulation, in the mid-1970s, of a 'conservation ethic' for archaeology, a response to wide-spread destruction of archaeological resources that had accelerated at an alarming rate since the 1940s with rapid post-war expansion of land devel-opment and an escalating commercial trade in antiquities.[4] This took the form of an argument that archaeologists should take 'responsibility for the whole resource base', not just the elements relevant to current research problems. (Lipe 1974: 214; see also Lipe 1996) Although this broadens the scope of archaeological accountability, the rationale for advocating conser-vation was often not that archaeological interests should be weighed against other interests in archaeological sites and materials, but rather that con-temporary archaeologists should be prepared to trade off the short-term interests of the research community against longer term interests; they have a responsibility to ensure that future archaeologists will have resources with which to work. A commitment to conservationist principles has since been incorporated into virtually all the evolving statements on ethics endorsed by professional archaeological associations (e.g., Society for American Archaeology 1995/1977, 1996; Archaeological Institute of America 1991; Society for Historical Archaeology 1992; Canadian Archaeological Associa-tion 1997).

By far the most profound challenges archaeologists have faced—the challenges that throw into stark relief the issues of cultural appropriation that concern us here—come from descendant communities, especially Indigenous populations, who have directly challenged the assumptions of privilege that often underpin archaeological research not only when it is animated by scientific goals but also when informed by a commitment to archaeological conservation. This contemporary activism builds on the rich tradition of protest outlined by Thomas (2000), and in a number of contexts it has resulted in new legislation that mandates the repatriation of archaeological material to descendant communities. One prominent but by no means isolated example is the Native American Grave Protection and Repatriation Act (NAGPRA), which was passed into law at a federal level in the United States in 1990. In other contexts Indigenous activists, tribal leaders and traditionalists have used existing historic preservation legislation to assert legal control over archaeological resources on their lands. (Ferguson 1990; Nicholas *et al.* 2007) The national governments of archaeologically rich but economically impoverished countries have tightened their control over access to sites and artifacts, and Indigenous peoples worldwide have become increasingly involved in the process of doing archaeology. (Davidson *et al.* 1995; Nicholas and Andrews 1997a; Swidler *et al.* 1997) The result is a significant broadening of the nature and scope of archaeological accountability for all practitioners, not only for those who are directly employed by tribal groups or public agencies.

As a result of these developments in employment patterns and professionalism, conservation practices and relations with descendant communities, archaeologists have witnessed a profound sea change in the identity and mandate of their discipline. This is reflected in the principles adopted by the Society for American Archaeology in 1996 that make archaeological stewardship the centerpiece of broad guidelines for ethical practice, setting the goals of archaeological science, professional obligations and resource conservation in this overarching framework. (SAA 1996; Lynott and Wylie 2002) It is even more clearly articulated in the codes of conduct established by the World Archaeological Congress (1989) in which accountability to Indigenous peoples takes precedence over any of these other obligations.

Faced with these challenges to long entrenched disciplinary goals, some archaeologists have adopted a stance of intransigent defensiveness (e.g., Clark 1998). But a great many take seriously the need for a fundamental reorientation in the way they do business; they recognize that, at the very least, they must negotiate their interests in the archaeological record with a range of stakeholders and interest groups. (Nicholas and Hollowell 2008) This is reflected in the emergence of a discipline-wide discourse on 'ethics' in which it is recognized that issues of accountability and responsibility are a crucial dimension of archaeological practice, as it has long been understood to be in museology and related fields. While initially motivated by concerns about cultural property—its conservation (as above), its ownership (e.g., Elgin Marbles cases [Meyer 1973; Greenfield 1989; Messenger 1999]), the commercial trade in antiquities (see discussion by Vitelli and other contributors to Green 1984; Wylie 1995, 1996) and its management (in connection with CRM and contract archaeology, described above)—it soon broadened into the realm of social responsibility and practice (e.g., Pluciennik 2001; Vitelli and Colwell-Chanthaphonh 2006). Archaeological ethics now constitute a rapidly expanding subfield reflected in publications and conference programs; a growing number of introductory archaeological textbooks that incorporate sections on ethics; an annual 'Ethics Bowl' sponsored by the Society for American Archaeology (Cowell-Chanthaphonh *et al.* 2008), and a set of guidelines for undergraduate training in archaeology generated by a committee of the SAA that takes, as its core, the requirements of archaeological stewardship. (Davis *et al.* 1999)

There is reason for concern, however, that this focus on ethics simply formalizes standards of practice that leave entrenched disciplinary values unchanged. The ideals of stewardship central to the recently adopted SAA Principles have been a primary target of such critiques (e.g., Zimmerman 1995; Pyburn and Wilk 1995; see discussion in Wylie 2005), which throw into sharp relief all the ways in which archaeological claims to stewardship can serve simply to reassert traditional privileges of access and control. When archaeological stewards fail to seek input from tribes—when stewardship is asserted unilaterally, rather than on a joint or collaborative model—it perpetuates the power imbalances that underpin, and are embodied in, the forms of cultural appropriation for which archaeologists are now called to account. In response to these challenges (many of which predate the SAA principles of stewardship), a growing constituency of archaeologists world-wide has taken a more proactive approach, exploring the possibilities for a more equitable and relevant archaeology. The advocates of 'critical archaeology', and of socially responsible archaeology more generally, have committed themselves to using archaeology as a means to achieve social change, with varying degrees of emphasis on transforming archaeology in the process (e.g., Leone *et al.* 1987; Schmidt and Patterson 1996; McGuire and Reckner 2003; Pyburn 2003).

Some of the most creative of these initiatives are predicated on a commitment to involve Indigenous peoples directly in the practice of archaeology, a process that often significantly reframes and enriches archaeological practice.[5] Descendant Indigenous communities often raise questions that archaeologists had never addressed, and their traditional knowledge is vital for understanding the material traces of antecedent land-use patterns, resource-harvesting practices, and a range of other more social aspects of past lifeways that may be found in the archaeological record; recent discussion of the relevance of oral history to archaeological practice is one especially fruitful area in which this cross-fertilization is evident (e.g., Echo-Hawk 1993, 1997, 2000; but see Mason 2006). Members of these communities are often the only people who have the expertise to recognize the non-scientific significance of sites subject to cultural management (e.g., when this depends on an appreciation of values associated with a specific cultural worldview and historical events). Where archaeologists have embraced ideals of collaborative practice, the result has been a long overdue broadening of discourse, and the emergence of an archaeology that is not only more ethically responsible, but also more theoretically robust, informed by critical self-consciousness of the ways in which it has been constituted in and through practices of cultural appropriation (e.g., Dowdall and Parrish 2002; Smith and Wobst 2005; Atalay 2006; Colwell-Chanthaphonh and Ferguson 2008).[6]

A Typology of Cultural Appropriation in Archaeology

The appropriation of archaeological finds is both widespread and long-lived, as is evident in the examples noted so far. To clarify the issues at hand, and to better define some of the social benefits and costs that attach to them, we offer a working typology of the forms of cultural appropriation in which archaeologists are directly or indirectly implicated. The cross-cutting dimensions of difference in our tripartite scheme are, as indicated above, (1) the objects of appropriation, (2) the agents and means by which appropriation is accomplished, and (3) responses to appropriation.

Objects of appropriation

Archaeological sites and artifacts have long captured the public's interest (see Lowenthal 1985), satisfying not only its curiosity about past peoples and lifestyles, but also serving as a touchstone to the past. Archaeological materials are sought after as an expression of antiquity and the culturally exotic: some people collect artifacts, often derived from the cultural past of others, in order to hold something that is hundreds or thousands of years old; others value them as commodities, pursuing a speculative commercial interest that drives the international trade in antiquities;[7] and others make use of archaeological sites and materials instrumentally, to justify both territorial expansion and cultural exclusion.

As already noted, archaeologists have long deplored, and have defined themselves professionally in opposition to, forms of appropriation motivated by commercial, aesthetic and political interests; their own interests are identified with a disciplinary commitment to advance the goals of scientific, anthropological knowledge. But even if these distinctions can be sustained—and the development of contract archaeology and culture resource management, as well as internal critique of assumptions of value/ interest neutrality, has put them under intense pressure—archaeological practice is often indirectly implicated in all these other forms of cultural appropriation. At the very least, archaeological research is crucial in establishing the age and cultural affiliation, and therefore the commercial value, of the antiquities traded on both local and international markets.[8] And it is often a key source of information about cultural traditions that is quickly taken up in a range of forms of secondary cultural appropriation in commercial settings and the public domain.

It is thus not surprising that what is at issue in archaeological debates about cultural appropriation varies widely. Tangible archaeological objects—artifacts, sites and human remains, among other materials—are the most obvious target of appropriation in Western society. But it is not just the objects themselves that are appropriated; archaeologically derived images and symbols have a remarkably active life in advertising. Upper Paleolithic art is used to sell house paint; the *moai* (giant heads) of Easter Island are used to sell cold remedies and tissue dispensers; the South African and Macedonian flags incorporate images drawn from ancient materials; and rock art images from around the world appear on t-shirts, jewelry, pot-holders, and refrigerator magnets. In the Canadian Arctic, images of *inukshuk* (traditional standing stone arrangements that date to antiquity) have been used in over 100 advertisements to sell everything from real estate to erectile dysfunction drugs; a stylized version has recently been chosen by the International Olympic Committee as the symbol for the 2010 Olympics in Vancouver, British Columbia.[9]

Even when it is the original objects and archaeological sites that are at issue, it is important to recognize that their cultural significance often is not manifest in their material form. This is evident in the case of sacred sites and landscapes such as Uluru (Ayers Rock) in Australia; the images of such sites appear on tea towels and they have become a destination for cultural tourism and New Age pilgrimages. Where archaeological significance is concerned, the *intangible* products of archaeological research are often as significant as the material itself, and can be as widely distributed and effectively commodified as literal finds in the context of archaeotourism, education and museum displays. Such intangibles include empirical data recovered through archaeological fieldwork, as well as the interpretive and explanatory claims that archaeologists and others base on this material; they range from bioarchaeological and ethnobotanical data, to culturally-specific forms of technical, agricultural and ecological knowledge, to symbolic vocabulary and artistic imagery. Given the precedents set by genetic and ethnobotanical research, where patents and other legal protections have been sought and granted (as discussed by other contributors to this volume), it seems likely that archaeologically derived information will play a role in generating potentially patentable results (Upano 2004), which raises a number of perplexing questions.[10] For example, archaeological resources might be crucial for identifying communities and tracing lineages, in the way that archival, historical research has proven to be in some recent epidemiological studies.[11] One such study has identified a mutated gene (Delta 32) in the descendants of medieval-era bubonic plague survivors; the gateway-blocking features of this gene may have prevented the plague bacterium from entering the host's bloodstream and may be useful in developing new strategies for combating, or preventing, HIV/AIDS. (Galvani and Novembre 2005) When historians or archaeologists play a key role in recovering the human remains or identifying the descendants on whose genetic material the biomedical research is based, what are their responsibilities and rights? To what extent should they benefit, and to what extent are they accountable to the descendants of the lineages they study?[12]

Worldwide, the development of virtual museums and other online archives is facilitating the transfer of information and images pertaining to cultural heritage, with clear benefits to both researchers and the general public. This may allow communities to see, for the first time, photographs and even 3-D renderings of ancestral objects now held in repositories in distant parts of the world.[13] At the same time, however, these uses of the internet amplify long-standing concerns raised by descendant communities about the loss of context and the risk that the integrity of their cultural patrimony will be (further) compromised. More generally, the very ease of access and breadth of distribution that makes these media attractive also allows for, even encourages, the appropriation of community-derived information and images, often without community permission. Online repository managers are already dealing with inappropriate re-use of archived material that these technologies and databases make possible (Kilbride 2004).

Finally, there is the appropriation of archaeology itself. This is engagingly exemplified by the work of American artist Mark Dion and his collection, classification and display of objects found on the banks of the Thames, or dredged from the canals in Venice. (Coles and Dion 1999)

Motivations, means and agents of appropriation

Evident in the multiply embedded layers of appropriative practice we noted above are a number of quite different animating interests. For present purposes we distinguish six clusters of motivations: 1) emotional/ sentimental/aesthetic interests; 2) historical/cultural identity; 3) religious/ spiritual connections; 4) commercial interests; 5) political/territorial interests; and 6) scientific/academic interests. Table 2.1 provides a brief description of each, along with examples. Although there is considerable overlap between these categories, the distinctions nonetheless mark consequentially different ways of valuing archaeological material that are enacted by different kinds of agents (individuals, collectivities, institutions), in a variety of ways and with significantly different impact. We suggest these as a framework for discussion because the question of whether particular instances or types of appropriation are pernicious or not, and what forms of response or redress are appropriate, will have to take account of this on-the-ground diversity of motivating interests, targets and modes of appropriation; categorical answers to these normative questions will miss precisely the nuances in which lie the potential for creative response that we explore in the final sections of this paper.

The complexity of interests that animate the appropriation of archaeological material is especially clear in the case of the site of Zimbabwe, located in the former Rhodesia. In 1980, the newly independent country renamed itself after the site, and took as a symbol of cultural and political identity one of the carved soapstone birds that originally graced the site. The political/territorial interests served by this appropriation of an archaeological symbol presuppose its historic/cultural significance, and its effectiveness in marking national identity depends on its power to mobilize emotional/sentimental and perhaps also aesthetic interests. The moral, political valence of this instance of appropriation is constituted along all these dimensions of interest and motivation and each is, itself, a (potential) locus of conflict among stakeholders. Such dynamics are by no means unique or of recent origin; archaeology has long been pressed into service

Table 2.1   Motivations for Appropriation

1. Emotional/Sentimental/Aesthetic Interests

Defining Qualities: an aesthetic appreciation for and/or sense of connection with the past; artifacts and sites serving as a touchstone to the (generic) past; a fascination with the exotic/the Other as intrinsically interesting and as defining one's own identity oppositionally; use of artifacts as cultural capital, an interest in marking social status.

Examples:
- Use of Southwestern *kokopelli* (fluteplayer) images from rock art panels on t-shirts and jewelry
- Tattoos of 'tribal' images, including those derived from archaeological sites (Sloss 2003)

2. Historical/Cultural Identity

Defining Qualities: a sense of connection with a specific past and cultural tradition claimed as one's own (by affiliation and/or appropriation).

Examples:
- Incorporation of the controversial 'Vergina sun' symbol in the flag of Macedonia, which was later modified as a result of political pressure from Greece
- Zimbabwe, Chichen Itza, Gizeh, Stonehenge, Bangladesh, Xian and other heritage sites as centers/symbols of cultural identity

3. Religious/Spiritual Connections

Defining Qualities: an appropriation of ancient material culture, sites or places by contemporary groups for spiritual purposes.

Examples:
- Modern Druid use of Stonehenge and other megalithic sites (Blain and Wallis 2004)
- New Age groups utilizing (and in some cases, reconstructing) prehistoric medicine wheels (circular rock arrangements) that are still sacred to, and utilized by, Native Americans (Brown 2003: 162)
- Sacred Path cards, 'a lavish deck of tarot-style cards that claim to epitomize Native spiritual teaching. Cards include such familiar motifs as Pipe, Sweat Lodge, Vision Quest, Peyote Ceremony, Standing People, Sun Dance, Medicine Wheel, Kokopelli . . .' (Jenkins 2004: 181)

4. Commercial Interests

Defining Qualities: direct, through investment in antiquities and involvement in the antiquities trade; indirect, through the use of archaeologically derived images to sell products.

Examples:
- A 5000-year-old stone carving from Mesopotamia known as the Guennol Lion, sold by Sotheby's for $57.2 million in 2007 (http:// news.bbc.co.uk/2/hi/middle_east/7130337.stm)
- A Mimbres bowl from the American Southwest offered for sale for $22,500 in the 2007 'Heritage for the Holidays' gift catalog (http://www.ha.com/images/holidaycatalog2007.pdf), while a 'superb, massive green stone Teotihuacan mask of pre-columbian Mexico, circa 300 to 600 AD' is listed for $145,000
- A winning bid $216,000 at Christies for a pair of thousand-year-old ivory eye goggles (Hollowell 2007)
- 'Ancient Grains': a breakfast cereal containing spelt, millet, kamut and quinoa grains, featuring a faux-Aztec jade mask on box

5. Political/Territorial Interest

Defining Qualities: historical and archaeological claims used to consolidate nationalist identity and justify claims to territory.

Examples:
- Archaeological sites employed as evidence of tenure by Aboriginal groups in Australia, Canada and elsewhere
- Competing claims to Anasazi sites by Hopi and Navajo interests
- Use of Tomb of China's first emperor at Xian by Chinese government to justify the Cultural Revolution
- The use of archaeological sites by the Nazi regime to justify territorial expansion (Trigger 2006: 240–1; Pringle 2006)

6. Scientific and Academic Interests

Defining Qualities: Claims to priority of access to and control of archaeological material (as a record or data base) and of information derived from it on the basis of expert status and the broad human/ social value of the knowledge served by scientific inquiry.
Examples: (see discussion on modes and agents of appropriation in text).

by national and state interests. Trigger documents the entanglement of archaeology and the political projects of nation building around the world (2006), and Patterson considers the formation of distinct, politically inflected regional research traditions within the United States (1986, 1995).[14]

The examples of commercial appropriation highlighted earlier are similarly complex. The companies that make and distribute products bearing archaeologically derived symbols rarely seem to consider that they are appropriating elements of cultural or spiritual heritage that may have significance well beyond the aesthetic or affective qualities that make them effective marketing devices. Indeed, they systematically elide any distinction between marketing one's own cultural icons and appropriating those of others. Such a broad cross-section of the media-consuming public has seen photographs of the pyramids of Egypt, the stone heads of Easter Island, and Northwest Coast totem poles (repeatedly, in many contexts) that these are now everyday icons, and widely viewed as part of a shared human heritage. Yet many groups, including countries, would argue against this. For example, the Egyptian government is currently developing copyright legislation that would make it illegal to produces copies or images of antiquities and archaeological sites, including the pyramids. (Stanek 2008) This is a response to the widespread marketing, in Egypt and elsewhere, of what is considered Egyptian intellectual property (Figure 2.1).

These forms of commercial appropriation often trade on a complex double gesture. On one hand, as Lowenthal notes, objects of the past may be so seamlessly incorporated into the present that, for example, ancient Egyptian and Greek design elements come to define popular styles in Western architecture. (1985, 84–87) On the other hand, archaeological icons are often compelling precisely because they are firmly located in 'the past'; their interest depends on their disconnection from anything that is familiar in present contexts, on their location in the past conceived as a 'foreign country' (from Lowenthal's title, 1985). In this case, the flattened landscape of temporal distance undercuts any appreciation that these icons differ greatly in the degree to which they are embedded in, or have culture- and heritage-specific significance for, living descendent cultures. Under these conditions, commercial interests are often just as voracious in appropriating the heritage of the powerful as of the marginal; not only do Indigenous rock art images grace t-shirts, and Hawaiian *tiki* gods and upper Paleolithic Venus figures appear as key chain fobs, but one can purchase scarves with images derived from the Dead Sea Scrolls or a sample of

Figure 2.1 Wares for sale, Giza Pyramid Complex, 2008 (photo: G. Nicholas).

medicinal Moor Mud,[15] accompanied by a testimonial photograph of Denmark's remarkably well-preserved Neolithic-age Tollund Man. In addition, there is also a market for artifacts and replicas from American Civil War battlefields and even the *RMS Titanic* passenger liner, which sank in 1912.

The scientific, academic appropriation of archaeological material incorporates several other dimensions of complexity in the agency and mode of appropriation. Archaeological appropriation in the name of science can take place at a number of different junctures in the research process: in the design of a research project; in drafting protocols and seeking permissions; in the actual conduct of the research, for example, in the extent to which archaeologists employ and/or train members of descendant communities, or take local knowledge seriously; in the communication of results; and in the distribution of any financial, social or intellectual benefits generated by archaeological research. In addition, these appropriations take place at a number of different loci, mediated by a range of institutions, and the results are disseminated not only by archaeologists themselves, through scholarly or professional publication, but by museums, government agencies, community groups and popular media. Although scholarly research holds special authority and still dominates professional journals it is, by virtually any measure, a minority form of archaeological practice as assessed, for example, by funding, personnel, number of projects, and volume of reporting. Most archaeological research is undertaken on contract, in the context of environmental impact assessments or as required for compliance with state and federal heritage legislation. It is also a component of educational and public outreach programs (e.g., in field schools and through networks of avocational projects), and it is developed in conjunction with community projects, most visibly as the basis for National Register and World Heritage nominations, or as a component of land management or site development, for example, as a publicly sponsored or commercial undertaking intended to foster tourism (e.g., Johnston 2006).

As this diversity of sites and forms of appropriative practice suggests, although archaeologists play a significant role in putting archaeological material into circulation and in articulating narratives of its significance, by no means are they solely responsible for its appropriation; indeed, archaeologists have far less control over the patterns of appropriation we have described than they commonly assume. (Hollowell and Nicholas, 2007) Avocational networks, the looters, dealers and collectors involved in the commercial trade in antiquities, a range of public institutions (museums, educational institutions), entrepreneurs and enterprising communities are all key players. Local communities, both of European and Indigenous descent, enlist archaeology in the development of cultural heritage and cultural tourism programs that publicly venerate particular periods or dimensions of their history (e.g., the Gold Rush). Trouillot says of history that it is produced at innumerable sites, relatively few of them controlled by 'the guild'. (1995: 8) He refers here to professional historians; we would expand his account to include archaeologists.

Nonetheless, in their combined roles as scientists and self-identified stewards of the past, archaeologists have long enjoyed considerable privilege of access and authority in determining how archaeological materials should be used, by whom, and for what purposes. The primary value assigned archaeological material as evidence underwrites scientifically driven protocols of cataloging, storage and analysis (including destructive analysis), and mandates controlled access for restudy by peers, often to the explicit exclusion of non-archaeologists, whatever their personal or cultural connections to the material. Internally defined research conventions—governing artifact illustration, the form and content of descriptive summaries, interpretive narratives and explanatory theorizing—determine how the results of archaeological inquiry will be presented in professional books and journal articles, 'plain language' reports and popular media.[16] This role as a primary (expert) consumer of archaeological resources has fostered in professional archaeologists and physical anthropologists a proprietary interest in archaeological finds and a presumption that this interest takes precedence over those of descendant communities regardless of their relationship to the creators of these finds. Indeed, when archaeologists have been obliged to seek permission to publish photographs of artifacts, it has typically been from the museums that today 'own' those items—contact with those whose ancestral property is being publicized has generally been considered neither necessary nor advisable. It is these traditions of practice and their justifying interests that have been challenged, with increasing insistence and success, by those for whom archaeological material (in the broad sense discussed earlier) has significance as a component of their (living) cultural heritage.

The effects of and responses to appropriation

The responses of the various parties affected by appropriation—the third dimension of this typology—vary enormously depending on context and as a function of the power dynamics and histories that structure relationships between stakeholders. Although everyone has a stake in the archaeological record, and everyone's past has been appropriated in some manner or another (Lowenthal 1985; Ginsberg 2004), archaeologically based practices of appropriation have had a disproportionate impact on Indigenous peoples. There are many reasons for this. The extent to which the cultural and intellectual property of Indigenous North Americans has been the target of appropriation by others is well-documented. (Brown 2003; Nicholas and Bannister 2004; Thomas 2000) Examples include attempts to copy aspects of Native American architecture and lifestyle (e.g., the German Indian hobbyists, the Karl May festival, the early twentieth-century Native American impostor Grey Owl and New Age appropriations of sacred sites); the passion for collecting, which has fueled traditions of appropriation ranging from apparently appreciative aesthetic and cultural connoisseurship to the collection of artifacts and human remains as trophies of conquest; and the legitimation of appropriation by scientific colonialism in the interest of salvaging cultures presumed to be on the brink of extinction. Indigenous communities have often had little say over, and few resources to counter, the determined use of their cultural and intellectual property by others in ways that they consider inappropriate or sacrilegious.

It is important to put these claims about appropriation in historical context and recognize the impact of shifting power dynamics (as Coleman and Coombe do in their contribution to this volume). In the late nineteenth and early twentieth centuries, many Native people willingly sold totem poles, masks and regalia to outsiders. (Cole 1985) Later generations have since called for the return of these items, sometimes contending that they were sold under duress; the conditions of social disruption and economic hardship caused by colonial incursions made the trade in cultural material a necessity for many. There were also numerous instances of genuine theft (of artifacts, grave goods, burials) acknowledged as such by anthropologists themselves in their field notes; for example, although Franz Boas and Harlan Smith did pay for many of the items they collected in British Columbia, they also knowingly took items without permission. (Carlson 2005) The loss of cultural heritage in this way, under these conditions, is one aspect of a colonizing process that targeted social identity and cultural integrity as surely as it did physical survival and material well-being. One legacy of this process is the presumption that the rights and wrongs of cultural appropriation can (only) be assessed in terms of categorical principles that obscure not only power inequities but also the nuances of cultural difference. A particularly salient difference is that, in the worldview of many Indigenous peoples, there is not the same kind of separation of past from present as is typical of a Western worldview; 'ancient' artifacts, human remains and culturally significant places retain their currency, their special, spiritual qualities. In short, cultural appropriation is not just a matter of the alienation of property.

Given this contextualization of archaeological practice, we identify two different types of response to appropriation: *restrictive responses*, which make use of various (legal, social, political) mechanisms for controlling or restricting access to archaeological materials and information; and a range of more *inclusive responses*, which include various forms and degrees of consultation, reciprocation and collaborative practice.

Restrictive Responses   One response to contested practices of appropriation that is already well established in our socio-legal systems are various options for restricting access to, or use of, valuable objects and ideas; this is something we deal with daily in the form of trademarks, copyrights and fair-use practices.[17] Not surprisingly, given the traditions of practice described above, there continues to be stiff resistance among academics to any proposal that their access to, or control over, scientifically valuable material and information might be restricted. But such restrictions are increasingly a fact of life. Indeed, although calls for revising scientific or academic practice are often decried as politically motivated—a matter of misconceived political correctness—many archaeologists believe that the restoration to Indigenous peoples of control over their own heritage is an important step in decolonizing the discipline (see discussions in Atalay 2006; Smith and Wobst 2005).

Under the rubric of repatriation laws in various countries, both settler communities and Indigenous groups have sought the return of artifacts, historic photographs and ethnographic information, as well as human remains that were in the public domain but largely accessible only to professional archaeologists and museum personnel. In a number of contexts in the US and Canada, Indigenous groups like the Navajo and the Shuswap are now responsible for and, increasingly, direct any archaeological work undertaken in their territories. They have developed protocols that include archaeological permitting systems, as well as provisions for the ownership of excavated materials and notes, and sometimes they restrict what researchers may or may not publish without prior permission. Even when archaeological sites and materials remain in the public domain (in museums, on public land), descendant communities and organizations may exercise control over access and disposition; sacred sites and artifacts may be strictly off limits, or may require archaeologists to get permission from all interested descendant communities for specific forms of access or use. One example that illustrates what this can involve, although it does not concern archaeological material, is the case of a colleague who was informed that, if he was to view photographs of the Arapaho, Cheyenne and Blackfoot shields held by a Midwestern museum, he would have to get letters of permission from each of the tribes. As suggested earlier, electronic media exacerbate these problems; managers of the online archive of data from the Spitalfields Project in England (photographs, field notes, recording sheets) face particular challenges in obtaining permissions from the multiple parties involved, including all research team members. (Kilbride 2004) Additional examples are provided in Table 2.2.

Perhaps the best known and most successful example of a restrictive response to the appropriation of Native American heritage is the NAGPRA legislation mentioned earlier. The repercussions of this act were immediate and widespread; it has changed in significant ways the process of archaeological research in North America. By law, all human remains and any associated grave goods that can be linked to contemporary federally recognized tribes had to be returned to them. Although comparable federal legislation has not been passed in Canada and Australia, state and provincial policies as well as political pressure and goodwill, have proven to be effective mechanisms in enabling Indigenous groups to exercise control over their ancestors' remains and other aspects of the(ir) archaeological record. Questions about intellectual property are also receiving greater scrutiny in contexts where descendant communities are seeking access to and control over their cultural heritage (e.g., Brown 1998; Nicholas and Bannister 2004; Nicholas and Hollowell 2004).[18] In short, restrictive responses often play an important role in redressing entrenched practices of cultural appropriation when descendant communities and other stakeholders challenge presumptions about who owns, controls and profits from the archaeological record.

Inclusive responses   While restrictive strategies for responding to appropriation have dominated internal debate and public attention, in the last several decades a growing number of archaeologists have responded to critiques of scientific colonialism by developing more inclusive working relationships with descendant communities. Most broadly stated, their aim

Table 2.2   Additional Examples of Restrictive Responses

- In British Columbia, the Nanaimo First Nation successfully reg-istered with the Canadian Intellectual Property Office ten ancient petroglyphs as 'official marks' to prevent them from being copied and reproduced by anyone for any purpose, arguing the images are sacred and copies for any reason are sacrilegious. (AP 2000)
- In Hawaii, the Bishop Museum has restricted access to photo-graphs of human remains and locations of burial caves and other sacred sites at the request of a Native Hawaiian organization.
- A mural of images from Pottery Mound ruin commissioned for the new archaeology building at the University of New Mexico was cancelled in deference to objections raised by Acoma Pueblo. Pottery Mound is an 800-year-old pueblo site excavated in the 1950s and 1960s. The Acoma acknowledge admit that their ances-tors had nothing to do with the artwork at the site. (Duin 2003)
- A book on British Columbia rock art (Nankivell and Wyse 2003), which included GPS locations (as well as information from the BC Archaeology Branch) raised the ire of some First Nations. A provincial agency later purchased the publisher's remaining stock and gave it to the Upper Similkameen Indian Band, which had objected to the volume.
- Some private companies maintain proprietary claims to all archaeological data and reports produced by projects they have funded; archaeologists working for them must request permission to publish research results or to speak of them at professional conferences.
- Under its Territorial Heritage Conservation Law, the Kamloops Indian Band, British Columbia, states that 'All data, maps, jour-nals and photographs and other material generated through or found as the result of [studies conducted under Band permit] are the exclusive property of the Band.' (Kamloops Indian Band 1998)

has been to make archaeology more responsible to and relevant for descendant communities. At the same time, as Ferguson notes, 'Native Americans have called for the development of a reciprocal archaeology that includes more types of information in the study of their past and that has more outcomes that address their contemporary needs [including] employment, resource management, land claims, social issues, education, and ecotourism.' (2003: 137, fig. 12.2)

These initiatives take various forms and are, to different degrees, transforming archaeological practice. (Davidson *et al.* 1995; Nicholas and Andrews 1997a; Swidler *et al.* 1997; Dongoske *et al.* 2000; Colwell-Chanthaphonh and Ferguson 2004; Silliman 2008) At a minimum, the commitment to a more responsive and responsible archaeology requires consultation with descendant communities, undertaken with the aim of ensuring that archaeological research is conducted in such a way that it respects their interests and sensibilities. On this model, archaeologists retain control over the research agenda but, as now required in many jurisdictions, they actively inform those affected by their work and negotiate terms of access and often consent. These are the baseline requirements set out by the first two 'rules to abide by' in the World Archaeological Congress First Code of Conduct (1989).

Sometimes these processes of consultation result in restrictive demands, especially in the more problematic areas of stewardship and curation. In the case of the Zuni war god effigies, the *Ahayu:da*, Zuni tradition requires that repatriated effigies be left out in the elements and allowed to disintegrate. This is not a matter of disregard or discard, as Ladd (2001) argues,[19] but of according proper treatment to sacred things and places, a practice that raises awareness of their continuing sacred quality. In another case, Janet Spector describes a request from the Minnesota Indian Affairs Council that a colleague, working on a project she was directing, not excavate a section of a contact period site that might have been a sacred dance floor:

> Although our Dakota colleagues had not done so when we worked together at Little Rapids, some council members strongly objected to any excavation there. To them, a dance area—even a suspected one—was sacred and, like a burial place, should not be disturbed. Respecting their views, Randy did not dig further in the enclosure or embankment. . . . Do I wish we might have had a chance to follow these tantalizing leads? Yes. Would I knowingly dig in sacred areas? No. (Spector 1993: 121, 122)[20]

Spector makes it clear, throughout her account of work at Little Rapids, that foregoing the opportunity to pursue this particular line of inquiry was vastly outweighed by innumerable ways in which her ongoing consultation with the Dakota Sioux enriched this project.

Sometimes creative solutions arise from consultations that recognize and accommodate what are otherwise dissonant interests. One example is the disposition of the remains of 'Mungo Lady', a skeleton dating to roughly 25,000 years ago that was excavated in south-central Australia:

> When the remains were returned to Aboriginal custodianship at the place where she was excavated, and placed in a locked vault, one of the tribal elders said to archaeologist Alan Thorne that 'they wanted a new start, and that there were to be two keys to the vault, an Aboriginal one and one for scientists; so their leader kept one key and I was given the other in what was a very moving and dignified ceremony.' (Alan Thorne, pers. comm., 1996; Nicholas and Andrews 1997b: 9)

In another Australian example, Claire Smith describes a negotiated agreement with the Barunga people that accorded them 'the right to censor any aspect of my research that they find distressing or offensive,' while retaining control over publication of the research project as a whole and the intellectual property arising from the research. (1996: 96)

As these cases suggest, the minimal requirement of consultation often gives rise to a more substantial, reciprocal engagement between archaeologists and descendant communities. Increasingly, archaeological research is framed by a commitment to return to specific descendant communities— not only to the discipline, to an amorphous 'public' or to society/humanity as a whole—various economic, technical, legal, social or intellectual benefits that may flow from archaeological practice. This requires, minimally, that archaeologists undertake public education and outreach; that they develop plain language reports and otherwise ensure that descendant communities are apprised of the results of their research; and that they employ or otherwise involve members of local communities in various aspects of archaeological research. As documented in many of the *SAA Newsletter*'s 'Working Together' columns,[21] sometimes this means addressing archaeological questions that matter to the descendant community but are not central to the archaeological research agenda (see Nicholas *et al.* 2008). Often it is a matter of involving members of local and descendant communities directly in archaeological projects. Yellowhorn urges, in this connection, a practice of training, not just employing, members of descendant and local communities in the full range of skills required to do archaeology effectively. (Yellowhorn 2000a, 2000b) He describes what this capacity building requires in connection with the structure of archaeological labor, urging initiatives that disrupt conventional patterns of stratification in archaeological work that keep non-archaeologists on the margins. Sometimes the demands of reciprocity require archaeologists to take on quite different projects than they would normally consider, for example, the development of community-based heritage programs and cultural centers, archaeotourism initiatives and other economic alternatives.[22]

Beyond reciprocity are forms of collaborative practice that involve descendant communities in the intellectual work of archaeology, in its design as well as its conduct. Collaboration in this spirit means more than just negotiated consent or reciprocation, 'it also entails mutual respect, meaningful dialogue, a long-term commitment of time, and expanding "research" to embrace processes and objectives that may not be perceived as conducive to the production and dissemination of scientific knowledge'. (Nicholas *et al.* 2008: 291) To achieve this, archaeologists must be willing to recognize that traditionally their discipline and their practices are structured by significant power imbalances; making archaeology more equitable requires according others control over the research process, setting its agenda and shaping both the process and the products of archaeological inquiry. Indigenous archaeology, as it has taken shape in a few key projects over the last few decades, is collaborative research in its most fully developed form. One important example is T. J. Ferguson's twenty-five-year collaboration with Pueblo, Apache and O'odham tribes in Arizona on projects that involve tribal members not only in the doing of archaeology, as guides and field hands, but also in making decisions where sensitive information and intellectual property rights are paramount concerns (e.g., Ferguson 2003).

Another example is the set of protocols developed for treatment of Kwäday Dän Ts'inchi ('Long-Ago Person Found'), a 550-year-old glacier body discovered by hunters in northern British Columbia, in the traditional territory of the Champagne and Aishihik First Nations (CAFN). (Beattie *et al.* 2000) The First Nations wanted something positive to come out of what was clearly an ancient tragedy and chose to collaborate with provincial authorities as full and equal partners (BC Archaeology Branch and Royal British Columbia Museum); they were centrally concerned to ensure that local Indigenous values were respected in treatment of the deceased. Both parties (the province and the First Nations) reviewed and approved all research related to the human remains, with the province hosting and administering the agreed upon research. The First Nations took the lead on cultural ceremonies in consultation with members of neighboring First Nations, and oversaw studies related to many of the artifacts/belongings associated with Kwäday Dän Ts'inchi. (Sheila Greer, pers. comm. 2005) They also initiated a community DNA study (still in progress) to see if living relatives of the deceased could be identified: seventeen were identified, fifteen of whom are members of the Wolf Clan. (Langdon 2008) In addition to the Champagne and Aishihik people, who are Dene (or Athapaskans), the neighboring Tlingit and Southern Tutchone also have an interest in Kwäday Dän Ts'inchi; there has long been extensive interaction and intermarriage between these First Nations. Notwithstanding these protocols and consultation, in October 2005, CAFN representatives were surprised to learn that a reproduction of the hat found with Kwäday Dän Ts'inchi was being offered for sale in a fund-raising auction for a non-profit foundation that promotes the work of Aboriginal artist Bill Reid; it had been made by an Indigenous weaver in the Tlingit style, like the original. The Foundation removed all mention of Kwäday Dän Ts'inchi from the catalog description when the Champagne and Aishihik raised their concerns, but this example shows how complex collaborative practice can be where issues of control over cultural patrimony, and cultural and intellectual property rights, are concerned. Additional examples of inclusive responses are provided in Table 2.3.

Modes of Resolution

Archaeologists are deeply implicated in practices of cultural appropriation that raise challenging questions about the ownership of, access to, and appropriate use of cultural and intellectual property. Conflicts over these issues are an unavoidable feature of the archaeological landscape and, as we have indicated, they are by no means limited to cases of direct involvement or control by archaeologists. As complex and intractable as they may seem, however, we argue that there is much that can be done by archaeologists, anthropologists and others who work in the realm of cultural heritage to promote ethical and equitable forms of practice, especially when it comes to working with descendant communities and their cultural patrimony. Here and elsewhere, promoting inclusive over restrictive responses has a great deal to offer, redressing historic power imbalances and resolving a variety of intellectual and cultural property issues. It is to be hoped that, if archaeologists can establish consultative, reciprocal and collaborative

Table 2.3 Additional Examples of Inclusive Responses

- Based at the University of British Columbia, the Reciprocal Research Network is an initiative linking UBC's Museum of Anthropology with Aboriginal communities and both national and international museums. Developed in conjunction with the Musqueam Indian Band, Sto:lo Nation and U'mista Cultural Society, it is designed to support collaborative research through a virtual museum-type platform (http://www.moa.ubc.ca/RRN/about_overview.html).
- Based on her research on Inca textiles from archaeological sites in Peru, archaeozoologist Jane Wheeler has established a DNA bank to restore a genetic line of alpaca bred centuries ago for its exceptionally fine wool, far superior to what local weavers use today.
- An example of progressive thinking on intellectual property issues is Claire Smith's arrangement with the Barrunga Community (South Australia). She has agreed to have any aspect of her research subject to vetting, to pay them for the right to publish photographs of their land and to promote the idea of turning over book royalties. (Smith 2004)
- Cases of repatriation where archaeologists and museum personnel support Aboriginal Australian communities in developing their own heritage policies and repositories.
- Various Aboriginal communities in British Columbia are cooperating with a research team led by archaeologist Jerome Cybulski, which is conducting a systematic study—including aDNA and radiocarbon dating—of pre-contact human skeletal remains.

forms of practice as a disciplinary standard, this will have a 'trickle up' effect in the public domain and market place where so much second-order appropriation of archaeological finds occurs.

Reflecting on the complexity of the issues archaeologists confront, we conclude that there will be no widely generalizable set of rules for developing meaningful, productive and effective collaborations: these are 'generally difficult, messy, and both time- and resource-intensive . . . often fragile . . . [and require] deliberate nurturing and a shared vision of the long-term benefits to be gained by those confronted with the day-to-day struggles of partnership'. (Nicholas *et al.*, 2007) So we recommend a strategy of working from examples of best practice, assembling a broad cross-section of promising initiatives, learning in detail both their successes and their pitfalls, and drawing from them recommendations that might fruitfully be extended to other contexts. At the same time, there are a number of ground-tested models of reciprocal and/or collaborative practice, emanating both from within and from outside archaeology, that offer elements of a promising alternative to the forms of appropriative practice that have so frequently disempowered and alienated descendant communities whose cultural heritage has been studied by archaeologists.[23] We identify four models that have influenced archaeological practice, and that make explicit orienting principles that are emerging in the consultative, reciprocal and collaborative examples described above: dialogic; alternative dispute resolution; participatory and community action research; and virtue ethics. The most useful of these focus attention on the power inequities that structure appropriation; in this sense they are examples of decolonizing methodologies. (Smith 1999) The key elements of these models are central to rationale for a new WAC 'General Code of Ethics' that is currently under discussion (Ulm and Hodder 2007); the orienting principle is a commitment to social justice that requires not just taking account of global inequalities but seeking to redress them.

Dialogic models   One example of a dialogic model that has received some attention in archaeology is Tully's account of non-modern forms of constitutional negotiation. (1995; Wylie 2005) These are processes of dispute resolution that make cultural difference the basis for negotiation, rather than requiring the interested parties to transcend their cultural particularities and engage on the presumptively neutral terrain of universal reason. As Tully describes these forms of negotiation, their success depends on two preliminary stages of engagement—mutual recognition and claims of continuity (1995: 116–124)—the purpose of which is to draw each party to an understanding of the world view and interests that inform the claims articulated by others. Here the groundwork is laid for working out an accommodation that will be acceptable to all parties in a final third stage of the process. Wood and Powell (1993) promote such practice in archaeological contexts, and also a commitment to respectful engagement across diff?r?nce—to a consultative approach that does not presuppose a ground of sha?ed, universal principles but is, rather, a matter of learning what may be very different norms and conventions—is evident in many of the most successful examples of archaeology undertaken in the mode of 'working together'.

Tully's model offers a useful general framework for consultation in this spirit; it makes principles of recognition and reciprocity the foundation for any engagement between archaeologists and descendant communities or other interested parties. But it provides little in the way of guidelines for dealing with crucial disparities in power among stakeholders. Much depends on who is identified as a party to the negotiation and what specific negotiative procedures are adopted; unless guidelines for settling these issues are more closely specified, the process outlined by Tully runs the risk of reinforcing a tendency to pay lip service to the need for more equitable practice without relinquishing control or moving beyond the 'management of' diverse interests. Dialogic models leave crucial power structures unchallenged.

Alternative Dispute Resolution practices (ADR)   Broadly construed, alternative dispute resolution encompasses any means of settling conflict out of court; it includes various forms of arbitration and mediation, ranging from highly structured, quasi-legal third-party arbitration to informal strategies for bringing parties together to work out a settlement. An important dimension of much ADR practice is a commitment to cultivate an awareness of the broader contexts of cultural difference and power relations that underpin specific points of conflict and that structure communication about them. ADR practices that are designed to facilitate negotiation and conflict resolution across cultural difference offer promising guidelines for specifying the claims of continuity and interest central to dialogic models (e.g., Coombe and Herman 2001). They are especially relevant when competing interests in the archaeological record arise from underlying value conflicts. These include not only disputes that reflect fundamentally different Western and non-Western approaches to valuing the material dimensions of cultural heritage, but also conflicts that arise within a broadly Western context, for example, between those who advocate free access to and wide distribution of knowledge (based on libertarian ideals) and those who argue that descendant communities should be recognized to have special interests in, and be accorded control over, archaeological 'finds' and the results of archaeological inquiry (based on liberal ideals).

Such conflicts have been especially sharply drawn in connection with demands for control over sacred sites and human remains, claims for recognition (and compensation) by researchers who play a role in identifying and extracting cell lines from ancient DNA, and disputes about who should control, and benefit from, the development of archaeotourism. In these cases there is an acute need for negotiative processes that not only take into account the context of competing interests (their historical and cultural particularity), but that provide a framework for addressing the structural inequities that entrench counterproductive patterns of interaction and give rise to cultural appropriation in a negative sense. Some forms of ADR may be especially useful in this connection: for example, those based on models of consensual and collaborative dispute resolution (Isenhard and Spangle 2000), peace building, conflict transformation and reconciliation. (Abu-Nimer 2001; Reychler and Paffenholz 2001), and transformative mediation. (Folger and Bush 1996)

Participatory Action Research (PAR) and Community-Based Participatory Research (CBPR)   Another external source of inspiration for reciprocal and collaborative practice in archaeology is to be found in the well established traditions of participatory research that have flourished in fields as diverse as urban sociology and community forestry, literacy training and economic development, natural resource management and community health. In recent histories and typologies of PAR and CBPR, a number of forms of practice are identified that closely parallel those emerging in archaeology (e.g., see also Whyte 1991; Petras and Porpora 1993; Castellanet and Jordan 2002: Part I; Minkler and Wallerstein 2003). Current debate about the promise of participatory practice and its now well-rehearsed pitfalls suggest some useful guidelines for building creative, sustainable collaborations. (Hickey and Mohan 2004; Kesby 2005)

Powerful critiques of the ways in which participatory approaches had become a 'tyranny', and had served to deepen patterns of dependence and exploitation in many development contexts (Cooke and Kothari 2001), have directed attention to precisely the issues of reciprocity and power imbalances that are pressing in archaeological contexts. In response to these concerns, Hickey and Mohan offer a useful analysis of several different continua of power that must be addressed if all parties are to participate effectively, as well as strategies for assessing the 'transformative potential' of power relations indexed to particular places and levels of engagement (2004: 34–6). The protocols for medical and social research that have been cooperatively developed with First Nations in western Canada are rich examples of CBPR modes of practice that embody the potential of such approaches (e.g., Ryan and Robinson 1992; Menzies 2004; Bell and Napoleon 2008). A First Nations health initiative organized around the principles of Ownership, Control, Access, and Possession, the OCAP model, illustrates the potential for community-based collaboration that directly involves affected communities in data collection and interpretation. (Scranch 2004)

Virtue ethics As proposed for archaeological contexts by Colwell-Chanthaphonh and Ferguson (2004), virtue ethics offers a framework for collaborative practice that shifts the focus of the negotiative process from a preoccupation with rules and mechanisms for adjudicating conflict to the cultivation of virtues that foster a capacity for responsive, respectful engagement across difference. In describing their projects in the American Southwest, they emphasize the importance of understanding 'the historical and socio-political context in which collaboration takes place' (2004: 9) and they characterize this not as a preliminary stage in negotiation (a matter of establishing recognition and claims of continuity), but as an ongoing, fluid process in which the goals of the project evolve, and the participants themselves are transformed. Crucial to this process is a commitment to ensure that all participants have 'some measure of power' (2004: 11) and that all are actively involved as partners in a shared undertaking.

To bring these ideals into practice, Colwell-Chanthaphonh and Ferguson argue, good intentions and guidelines for right action are not enough; what matters is a commitment to tune one's moral sensibilities so that, in the ongoing process of negotiating a working relationship with community partners, archaeologists' conduct embodies the kinds of virtues that will sustain trust and dialogue. They compare the sorts of virtues endorsed by ethicists who draw inspiration from Aristotelian virtue theory with those endorsed by the Native American advisors with whom they work. At the points of overlap they identify such virtues as awareness, openness, and respect—also humility, honesty, generosity, patience, a willingness to learn—as the foundation for a research ethic that is rooted, not in narrow maxims and guidelines, but in forms of 'habituated action' that are responsive to specific contexts of engagement and 'grounded within the framework of these virtues.' (2004: 21) The virtue ethics approach outlined by Colwell-Chanthaphonh and Ferguson suggests a way forward, not just in negotiating specific collaborative partnerships, but in articulating an overarching research ethic for archaeology.

Conclusions

The appropriation and commodification of cultural and intellectual property derived from the archaeological record is a matter of growing concern for archaeologists, descendant communities and other stakeholders. For archaeologists, the focal issues are access to knowledge, knowledge transfer, restrictions of the scope of inquiry and sometimes censorship of its results. For Indigenous peoples and members of other descendant communities, the context for negotiation of these issues is a history of disenfranchisement as colonized peoples, one particularly painful aspect of which has been the loss of access to, and control over, their own heritage. Ultimately what is at stake, most simply put, is the question of who owns and controls the products of archaeology: the individuals who make the discoveries or the descendants of those who created the archaeological record in the first place. More fundamentally, what is at issue are the very conceptions of ownership that underpin claims of continuity and demands for recognition on all sides.

When the Native American Graves Protection and Repatriation Act was enacted in 1990, many archaeologists believed that the discipline of archaeology, as they knew it, was coming to an end. This clearly did not happen. Instead, what has emerged in many quarters is increased dialogue, more sustained and creative forms of collaboration between archaeologists and Indigenous peoples, and new ways of thinking about and doing archaeology that are predicated on a commitment to counter the legacy of cultural appropriation (Spector 1993; Watkins 2000; Nicholas 2008).[24] The conditions of archaeological practice have changed profoundly in recent decades, and will continue to change; it behooves archaeologists to respond proactively rather than reactively to the challenges they face, especially given the growing roster of examples that illustrate what is to be gained by embracing collaborative forms of practice.

We recommend a procedural approach to mitigating and resolving conflicts over cultural appropriation, and we see great potential for this in the consultative, reciprocal, and collaborative forms of practice that are currently taking shape. This approach requires that negotiations be local and creative—there will be no fixed set of rules governing practice— although the models for such practice that we have considered suggest three broad guidelines:

1) protocols for proceeding must be clear and must be negotiated at the outset, whether the response to demands for accountability is restrictive or inclusive, consultative, reciprocal or collaborative;
2) trust is the crucial foundation for a good working relationship;
3) building trust, and designing effective protocols based on trust, requires a commitment to long-term involvement, reciprocity, and the cultivation of virtues that habituate integrity and trustworthy action.

Notes

1 Some Indigenous peoples do not recognize an 'archaeological record'. As noted for the Hul'qumi'num of British Columbia, 'Archaeological sites are perceived not as abstract scientific resources, but as the "cemeteries" of family Ancestors. This entails a much different type of archaeological ethos, one that views artifacts and sites as entities that bridge past and present on a timeless cultural landscape'. (Nicholas 2006: 363; see McLay *et al.* 2008)

2. Ironically, this focus on the interests of humanity figures in non-universalizing research programs ranging from the historical particularism of Franz Boas, the founding father of contemporary anthropology, to some of the counter-universalistic positions advocated by postprocessual archaeologists.

3 See, for example, the number of dimensions of accountability identified in the 'Code of Conduct' endorsed by the Register of Professional Archaeologists (RPA 2006). These include responsibilities to clients and employers, employees and students, descendant communities and the public at large, as well as the field of archaeology and its scientific goals. These areas of accountability are often hierarchically ranked, as a consequence of legal obligations that give priority to the responsibilities of consulting archaeologists to their clients, or as a function of disciplinary commitments in the case of the principles of the professional organization.

4 For example, Stilles (2002: 77) reports that illegal sales of antiquities rank third in the world's black market (with sales estimated between two and six billion dollars each year), surpassed only by the drugs and arms trade.

5 This potential for transforming archaeological practice in fruitful ways is described, for example, in contributions to the 'Working Together' column in the the *SAA Newsletter*, now available in an edited volume *Working Together* (Dongoske *et al.* 2000). Other key examples are to be found in Atalay 2006;

Dowdall and Parrish 2002; Colwell-Chanthaphonh and Ferguson 2005; Kerber 2006; Silliman 2008.

6   Although these approaches—the concern with ethical practice, and collaborative initiatives—have independent trajectories of development (in the sense that their motivations are distinct and each is associated with a distinct literature), there are important points of convergence between them as in the work undertaken by T. J. Ferguson and Roger Anyon with the Zuni in the early 1970s. This represents one of the earliest expressions of what would later become known as Indigenous archaeology (see Nicholas and Hollowell, 2008). A parallel set of initiatives is also evident in Isabel McBryde's provocative edited volume *Who Owns the Past?* (1985), which drew attention to issues of cultural appropriation and control of cultural heritage in Australia.

7   Pendergast distinguishes between several kinds of commercial interest, contrasting collectors with 'acquisitors'. (1991)

8   Vitelli (1984) details the dynamics by which archaeological research can catalyze a destructive market for antiquities in connection with the case of Ban Chiang ceramics; a number of other examples are described in Vitelli (1996) and Harringon (1991). See also Gill and Chippindale (1993) who offer an analysis of ways in which such entanglement with the antiquities trade can profoundly compromise scholarly research, in the much discussed case of Cycladic figurines.

9   Additional examples can be found in Brown (2003), Johnson (1996), Layton and Wallace (2006), Nicholas and Bannister (2004) and Nicholas and Hollowell (2004).

10 Given the rapid pace of technological developments in genetics, we believe that this will lead to profound changes in the methods used by archaeologists (Nicholas 2005). In Florida, the Yukon Territory, and the Italian Alps, the recovery of preserved human tissue from wetland or glacial archaeological contexts has led to the recovery of early human genetic material. If ancient human DNA begins to play a critical role in future medical treatments for diseases, or in other forms of research that promise social or economic benefit, there are many important issues to resolve involving cultural heritage and intellectual property rights, especially given that human genetic material is patentable in many countries. (Nicholas and Bannister 2004)

11 Related to this are such controversial initiatives as the National Geographic's and IBM's co-sponsored Genographic Project (URL: www.genographic.com), and its short-lived predecessor, the Human Genome Diversity Project, in which the studies of DNA from contemporary populations is being used to reconstruct past population movements. For reviews of aspects of such projects, see Reardon 2005, and Hollowell and Nicholas, forthcoming.

12 This question is currently playing out at a national level in Iceland. (Rose 2003, and others)

13   Existing technologies now make it possible to digitally scan objects, and then use the data to reconstitute physical copies, identical to the original, by use of a 3-D printer that solidifies liquid polymers. The scanned data can be stored, transferred electronically or otherwise manipulated. The Arius 3D laser-scanning system (URL: http://www.arius3d.com/) is in use by the Canadian Museum of Nature and the Royal Ontario Museum, among others, and has been applied to a wide array of artifacts, as well as human and hominid skeletal remains.

14   For one especially trenchant contemporary example, consider Mao's statement that 'the past must serve the present'. Near the end of the Cultural Revolution, the Gang of Four enacted this principle in a political campaign in which, Stilles (2002: 52) argues, 'the discovery of the terracotta warriors [at Xian] was used explicitly in [a] struggle against [former Prime Minister] Lin Biao and against the neo-Confucianism of the part bureaucracy'.

15   For the Dead Sea Scroll scarves see: www.ancientties.com/catalog/dead_sea_scroll_13x60_silk3731843.htm. And for Moor Mud: www.torfspa.com/about_moor.html.

16   Notoriously, these requirements of publication have all too often been honored in the breach, even though they are often invoked in defense of professional privileges of access and control. (Fagan 1993)

17   See Drahos and Braithwaite (2003) for a comprehensive and scathingly critical appraisal of such responses in connection with intellectual property.

18   A major research initiative is the global, multi-sectoral project 'Intellectual Property Issues in Cultural Heritage: Theory, Practice, Policy, Ethics' [URL: http://www.sfu.ca/ipinch] which is funded by the Social Sciences and Humanities Research Council (Canada).

19   'When a new image of the *Ahayu:da* is installed in a shrine, the "old" one is removed to "the pile", which is where all the previous gods have been lain. This act of removal specifically does not have the same connotations as 'throwing away' or "discarding". The image of the god that has been replaced must remain at the site to which it was removed and be allowed to disintegrate there.' (Ladd 2001: 107, emphasis in original).

20   The rest of this passage reads: 'This episode of the Little Rapids drama was a humbling reminder of the ethical dilemmas of practicing archaeology. None of us intended to be disrespectful or insensitive in pursuing our hunch that members of the Little Rapids community might have danced within the enclosure. In fact, we will never know for certain that this feature of the landscape or the pieces of necklace found nearby were associated with the medicine dance. Still, the archaeological clues, combined with Eastman's illustrations and Ponds's and Skinners accounts, elicited images of life at Little Rapids that we would have missed otherwise.' (Spector 1993: 122).

21   A selection of these were published as an edited volume by Dongoske *et al.* (2000).

22 For example, the El Pilar/BRASS initiative undertaken by Anabel Ford (http://www.marc.ucsb.edu/elpilar/) and the collaboration Walter Alva has undertaken with Peruvian villagers living at the site of the Sipan tombs. (Alva and Donnan 1994)

23 Nicholas and Hollowell (2008: 67–73) identify six approaches that promote ethical practice which complement and extend, in various ways, the four models we discuss here: 1) community archaeology; 2) participatory archaeology; 3) Indigenous archaeologies; 4) feminist epistemology; 5) Marxist archaeology; and 6) virtue ethics.

24 These changes are by no means solely the result of NAGPRA, rather, they reflect the impact of sociopolitical developments that are fundamentally changing the conditions of cultural and political engagement for Indigenous and other formerly colonized peoples in many parts of the world.

Acknowledgments

We are grateful to Conrad Brunk and James Young for their invitation to participate in this project, and to Kelly Bannister, Sheila Greer and Julie Hollowell for information and advice they provided along the way.

References

Abu-Nimer, M. (2001). *Reconciliation, Justice, and Coexistence: Theory and Practice*. Lexington Books, Boulder CO.

Alva, W. and Donnan, C. B. (1994). *Royal Tombs of Sipan*. Fowler Museum of Cultural History Publications, Los Angeles.

Archaeological Institute of America (AIA) (1991). Code of ethics. *American Journal of Archaeology* **95**, 285.

Associated Press (AP) (2000). Indian Band Applies for Trademark on Ancient Petroglyph. February 16.

Atalay, S. (ed.) (2006). Decolonizing archaeology. Special issue, *American Indian Quarterly* **30**(1), 350–80.

Beattie, O., Apland, B., Blake, E.W. *et al.* (2000). The Kwäday Dän Ts'inchi discovery from a glacier in British Columbia. *Canadian Journal of Archaeology* **24**(1), 129–48.

Bell, C., and Napoleon, V. (2008). Introduction, methodology and thematic overview. In: Bell, C. and Napoleon V. (eds.) *First Nations Cultural Heritage and Law: Case Studies, Voices and Perspectives*. UBC Press, Vancouver, pp. 1–32.

Blain, J., and Wallis, R. J. (2004). Sacred sites, contested rites/rights. *Journal of Material Culture* **9**(3), 237–61.

Brown, M. (1998). Can culture be copyrighted? *Current Anthropology* **39**(2), 193–222.

Brown, M. (2003). *Who Owns Native Culture?* Harvard University Press, Cambridge, MA.

Callinan, R. (2005). Small bones, big feud. *Time*, March 14, 2005.

Canadian Archaeological Association (CAA) (1997). Statement of principles for ethical conduct pertaining to Aboriginal peoples. *Canadian Journal of Archaeology* **21**, 5–6.

Carlson, C. C. (2005). Letters from the field: Reflections on 19th-century archaeology of Harlan I. Smith in the southern interior of British Columbia, Canada. In: Smith, C. and Wobst, H. M. (eds.) *Indigenous Peoples and Archaeology: The Politics of Practice*. Routledge, London, pp. 134–69.

Carson, C. A. (1995). Raiders of the lost scrolls: The right of scholarly access to the content of historical documents. *Michigan Journal of International Law* **16**(2), 300–48.

Castellanet, C., and Jordan, C. F. (2002). *Participatory Action Research in Natural Resource Management*. Taylor and Francis, New York.

Champe, J. L., Byers, D. S., Evans, C. *et al.* (1961). Four statements for archaeology. *American Antiquity* **27**, 137–9.

Clark, G. A. (1998). NAGPRA: The conflict between science and religion, and political consequences. *Society for American Archaeology Bulletin* **16.5, 22**, 24–5.

Cole, D. (1985). *Captured Heritage: The Scramble for Northwest Coast Artifacts*. Douglas and McIntyre, Vancouver.

Coles, A., and Dion, M. (eds.) (1999). *Mark Dion: Archaeology*. Black Dog Publishing Ltd., London.

Colwell-Chanthaphonh, C., and Ferguson, T. J. (2004). Virtue ethics and the practice of history: Native Americans and archaeologists along the San Pedro Valley of Arizona. *Journal of Social Archaeology* **4**(1), 5–27.

Colwell-Chanthaphonh, C., and Ferguson, T. J. (eds.) (2008) *The Collaborative Continuum: Archaeological Engagements with Descendant Communities*. AltaMira Press, Lanham MD.

Colwell-Chanthaphonh, C., Hollowell, J., and McGill, D. (2008). *Ethics In Action: Case Studies in Archaeological Dilemmas*. SAA Press, Washington, DC.

Cooke, B. and Kothari, U. (eds.) (2001). *Participation: The New Tyranny?* Zed Books, London.

Coombe, R. J., and Herman, A. (2001). Culture wars on the net: Intellectual property and corporate property in digital environments. *The South Atlantic Quarterly* **100**(4), 919–47.

Davidson, I., Lovell-Jones, C. and Bancroft, R. (eds.) (1995). *Archaeologists and Aborigines Working Together*. University of New England Press, Armidale.

Davis, H. A., Altschul, J. H., Bense, J. *et al.* (1999). Teaching archaeology in the 21st century. *Society for American Archaeology Bulletin* **17**(2), 18–22.

Denning K. (1999). On Archaeology and Alterity. PhD dissertation. Conferred September 1999. Department of Archaeology and Prehistory, University of Sheffield.

Dongoske, K. E., Aldenderfer, M., and Doehner, K. (eds.) (2000). *Working Together: Native Americans and Archaeologists.* Society for American Archaeology, Washington DC.

Dowdall, K., and Parrish, O. (2002). A meaningful disturbance of the earth. *Journal of Social Archaeology* **3**(1): 99–13.

Drahos, J., and Braithwaite, J. (2003). *Information Feudalism: Who Owns the Knowledge Economy.* Oxford University Press, Oxford.

Duin, J. (2003). Tribes veto Southwest mural. *Washington Times,* Feb. 18. http://www.nathpo.org/News/NAGPRA/News-NAGPRA29.htm.

Echo-Hawk, R. C. (1993). Working together—Exploring ancient worlds. *Society for American Archaeology Bulletin* **11**, 5–6.

Echo-Hawk, R. C. (1997). Forging a new ancient history for Native America. In: Swidler, N., Dongoske, K. E., Anyon, R., and Downer, A. S. (eds.) *Native Americans and Archaeologists: Stepping Stones to Common Ground.* AltaMira Press, Walnut Creek CA, pp. 88–102.

Echo-Hawk, R. C. (2000). Ancient history in the new world: Integrating oral traditions and the archaeological record in deep time. *American Antiquity* **65**(2), 267–90.

Fagan, B. (1993). The arrogant archaeologist. *Archaeology* **46**, 14–16.

Ferguson, T. J. (1990). NHPA: Changing the role of native americans in the archaeological study of the past. *Society for American Archaeology Bulletin* **17**(1), 33–7.

Ferguson, T. J. (2003). Archaeological anthropology conducted by Indian tribes: Traditional cultural properties and cultural affiliation. In: Gillespie, S. D. and Nichols, D. (eds.), *Archaeology is Anthropology.* Archaeological Papers of the American Anthropological Association No. 13. American Anthropological Association, Washington, DC, pp. 137–44.

Folger, J. P., and Bush, R. A. B. (1996). Transformative mediation the third-party intervention: Ten hallmarks of a transformative approach to practice. *Mediation Quarterly* **13**(4), 263–78.

Galvani, A. P., and Novembre, J. (2005). The evolutionary history of the CCR5-Δ32 HIV-resistance mutation. *Microbes and Infection* **7**, 302–9.

Gill, D. W. J., and Chippindale, C. (1993). Material and intellectual consequences of esteem for Cycladic figures. *American Journal of Archaeology* **97**(4), 601–60.

Ginsberg, R. (2004). *The Aesthetics of Ruins.* Rodopi, New York.

Green, E. L. (ed.) (1984). *Ethics and Values in Archaeology.* Free Press, New York.

Greenfield, J. (1989). *The Return of Cultural Treasures*. Cambridge University Press, Cambridge.

Harrington, S. P. M. (1991). The looting of Arkansas. *Archaeology* **44**, 22–31.

Hickey, S. and Mohan, G. (2004). *Participation: From Tyranny to Transformation?* Zed Books, London.

Hollowell, J. J. (2007). Ancient ivories from the Bering Strait: Lessons from a legal market in antiquities. *Athena Review* **4**(3), 46–54.

Hollowell, J. J., and Nicholas, G. P. (2007). Archaeological capital as cultural knowledge. Paper presented at the Society for American Archaeology conference, Austin, Texas. (ms. in possession of the authors).

Hollowell, J. J., and Nicholas, G. P. (forthcoming). Decoding implications of the genographic project for cultural heritage studies. Submitted to the *International Journal of Cultural Property*.

Isenhard, M. W., and Spangle, M. (2000). *Collaborative Approaches to Resolving Conflicts*. Sage Publications, Thousand Oaks CA.

Jenkins, P. (2004). *Dream Catchers: How Mainstream America Discovered Native Spirituality*. Oxford University Press, New York.

Johnson, V. (1996). *Copyrites: Aboriginal Art in the Age of Reproductive Technologies. Catalogue for a Touring Exhibition*. National Indigenous Arts Advocacy Association and Macquarie University, Sydney AUS.

Johnston, A. M. (2006). *Is the Sacred for Sale? Tourism and Indigenous Peoples*. Earthscan, London.

Kamloops Indian Band (KIB) (1998). Territorial Heritage Conservation Law. Kamloops Indian Band, Kamloops, BC.

Kerber, J. E. (2006). *Cross-Cultural Collaboration: Native Peoples and Archaeology in the Northeastern United States*. University of Nebraska Press, Lincoln.

Kesby, M. (2005). Retheorizing empowerment-through-participation as a performance in space: Beyond tyranny. *Signs* **30**(4), 2037–65.

Kilbride, W. (2004). Copyright and intellectual property rights: A case study from the web face. Arts and Humanities Data Service. http://ahds.ac.uk/creating/case-studies/protecting-rights/

Ladd, E. J. (2001). A Zuni perspective on repatriation. In: Bray, T. (ed.) *The Future of the Past: Native Americans, Archaeologists, and Repatriation*. Garland Press, NY, pp. 107–137.

Langdon, M. (2008). Scientists link 17 living people to an Aboriginal man found in glacier. *Globe and Mail* (April 28).

Layton, R., and Wallace, G. (2006). Is culture a commodity? In: Scarre, C., and Scarre, G. (eds.) *The Ethics of Archaeology: Philosophical Perspectives on Archaeological Perspectives*. Cambridge University Press, Cambridge, pp. 46–68.

Leone, M.P., Potter, P.B. Jr., and Shakel, P. A. (1987). Toward a critical archaeology. *Current Anthropology* **28**(3), 283–302.

Liam, T., Carmichael, C., and MacQueen, H. (eds.) (2001). *On Scrolls, Artifacts and Intellectual Property.* Continuum, Sheffield.

Lipe, W. D. (1974). A conservation model for American archaeology. *The Kiva* **39**, 213–45.

Lipe, W. D. (1996). In defense of digging: Archaeological preservation as a means, not an end. *CRM* **19**(7), 23–7.

Lowenthal, D. (1985). *The Past is a Foreign Country.* Cambridge University Press, Cambridge.

Lynott, M. J., and Wylie, A. (eds.) (2002). *Ethics in American Archaeology,* 2nd Revised Edition. Society for American Archaeology, Washington DC.

McBryde, I. (ed.) (1985). *Who Owns the Past?: Papers from the Annual Symposium of the Australian Academy of the Humanities.* Oxford University Press, Melbourne.

McGuire, R. H., and Reckner, P. (2003). Building a working class archaeology: The Colorado Coal Field War project. *Industrial Archaeology Review* **25**(2), 83–95.

McLay, E., Bannister, K., Joe, L., Thom, B. and Nicholas, G. (2008). A'lhut tu tet Sul'hweentst 'respecting the ancestors': Understanding Hul'qumi'num heritage laws and concerns for protection of archaeological heritage. In: Bell, C. and Napoleon, V. (eds.) *First Nations Cultural Heritage and Law: Case Studies Voices, and Perspectives.* UBC Press, Vancouver, pp. 150–202.

McNiven, I. J., and Russell, L. (2005). *Appropriated Pasts: Indigenous Peoples and the Colonial Culture of Archaeology.* AltaMira Press, Lanham MD.

Mason, R. J. (2006). *Inconstant Companions: Archaeology and North American Indian Oral Traditions.* University of Alabama, Tuscaloosa.

Menzies, C. R. (2004). Putting words into action: Negotiating collaborative research in Gitxala. *Canadian Journal of Native Education* **28**(1+2), 15–32.

Messenger, P. (1999). *The Ethics of Collecting Cultural Property.* University of New Mexico Press, Albuquerque NM.

Meyer, K. (1973). *Our Plundered Past: The Story of Illegal International Traffic in Works of Art.* Atheneum, New York NY.

Minkler, M., and Wallerstein, N. (eds.) (2003). *Community Based Participatory Research for Health.* Jossey-Bass, San Francisco.

Nankivell, S., and Wyse, D. (2003). *Exploring BC's Pictographs: A Guide to Native Rock Art in the British Columbia Interior.* Mussio Ventures, Ltd., New Westminster, BC.

Nicholas, G. P. (2005) On mtDNA and archaeological ethics. *Canadian Journal of Archaeology* **29**(2), iii–vi.

Nicholas, G. P. (2006). Decolonizing the archaeological landscape: The practice and politics of archaeology in British Columbia. In: Atalay, S. (ed.) Special Issue on Decolonizing Archaeology. *American Indian Quarterly* **30**(1), 350–380.

Nicholas, G. P. (2008). Policies and protocols for archaeological sites and associated cultural and intellectual property. In: *Protection of First Nations Cultural Heritage: Laws, Policy, and Reform*, edited by C. Bell and Robert Paterson. UBC Press, Vancouver.

Nicholas, G. P., and Andrews, T. D. (eds.) (1997a). *At a Crossroads: Archaeologists and First Peoples in Canada*. Archaeology Press, Simon Fraser University, Burnaby BC.

Nicholas, G. P., and Andrews, T. D. (1997b). Indigenous archaeology in the postmodern world. In: Nicholas, G. P., and Andrews, T. D. (eds.) *At a Crossroads: Archaeology and First Peoples in Canada*. Archaeology Press, Simon Fraser University, Burnaby BC, pp. 1–18.

Nicholas, G. P., and Bannister, K. P. (2004). 'Copyrighting the past?': Emerging intellectual property rights issues in archaeology. *Current Anthropology* **45**(3), 327–50.

Nicholas, G. P., and Hollowell, J. J. (2008). Ethical challenges to a postcolonial archaeology. In: Hamilakas, Y. and Duke, P. (eds.) *Archaeology and Capitalism: From Ethics to Politics*. Left Coast Press, Walnut Creek, CA, pp. 59–82.

Nicholas, G. P., and Hollowell, J. J. (2004). Intellectual property rights in archaeology? *Anthropology News* **45**(4), 6, 8.

Nicholas, G. P., Welch, J. R., and Yellowhorn, E. C. (2008). Collaborative encounters. In: Colwell-Chathaphonh, C. and Ferguson, T. J. (eds.) *The Collaborative Continuum: Archaeological Engagements with Descendant Communities*. AltaMira Press, Walnut Creek CA, 273–98.

O'Brien, M. J., Lyman, R. L., and Schiffer, M. B. (2005). *Archaeology as a Process: Processualism and its Progeny*. University of Utah Press, Salt Lake City.

Patterson, T. C. (1986). The last sixty years: Toward a social history of Americanist archaeology in the United States. *American Anthropologist* **88**, 7–22.

Patterson, T. C. (1995). *Toward a Social History of Archaeology in the United States*. Harcourt Brace, Orlando.

Pendergast, D. M. (1991). And the loot goes on: Winning some battles, but not the war. *Journal of Field Archaeology* **18**, 89–95.

Petras, E. M., and Porpora, D. V. (1993). Participatory research: Three models and an analysis. *American Sociologist* **23**(1), 107–26.

Pluciennik, M. (ed.) (2001). *The Responsibilities of Archaeologists: Archaeology and Ethics, Archaeopress*, Oxford. Lampeter Workshop in Archaeology **4**, BAR S981.

Pringle, H. (2006). *The Master Plan: Himmler's Scientists and the Holocaust*. Hyperion, New York, p. 54.

Pyburn, A. (2003). Archaeology for a new millennium: The rules of engagement. In: Derry, L. and Malloy, M. (eds.) *Archaeologists and Local Communities: Partners in Exploring the Past*. Society for American Archaeology, Washington, DC.

Pyburn, K. A., and Wilk, R. R. (1995). Responsible archaeology is applied anthropology. In: Lynott, M. P. and Wylie, A. (eds.) *Ethics in American Archaeology:*

Challenges for the 1990s. Society for American Archaeology, Washington D.C., pp. 78–83.

Reardon, J. (2005). *Race to the Finish: Identity and Governance in an Age of Genomics.* Princeton University Press, Princeton, NJ.

Register of Professional Archaeologists (2006). Code of Conduct and Standards of Research Performance. URL: http://www.rpanet.org/

Reychler, L., and Paffenholz, T. (eds.) (2001). *Peacebuilding: A Field Guide.* Lynne Rienner Publishers, Boulder CO.

Rose, H. (2003). The commodification of virtual reality: The Icelandic health sector database. In: Goodman, A. H., Heath, D., and Lindee, M. S. (eds.) *Genetic Nature/Culture: Anthropology and Science Beyond the Two-Culture Debate.* University of California Press, Berkeley, pp. 77–92.

Ryan, J., and Robinson, M. P. (1992). *Participatory Action Research: An Examination of Two Northern Case Studies.* Arctic Institute of America, Edmonton.

Schmidt, P., and Patterson, T. C. (eds) (1996). *Making Alternative Histories: The Practice of Archaeology and History in Non-Western Settings.* School of American Research Press, Santa Fe.

Scranch, B. (2004). Ownership, control, access, and possession (OCAP) or self-determination applied to research: A critical analysis of contemporary First Nations research and some options for First Nations Communities. *Journal of Aboriginal Health* **1**(1), 80–95.

Silliman, S. (ed.) (2008). *Indigenous Archaeology at the Trowel's Edge: Teaching and Learning in Indigenous Archaeology.* University of Arizona Press, Tuscon.

Sloss, A. (2003). *Tribal Tattoos.* Carlton Books, London.

Smith, C. (1996). *Situating Style: An Ethnoarchaeological Study of Social and Material Context in an Australian Aboriginal Artistic System.* Ph.D. Dissertation, University of New England, Armidale.

Smith, C. (2004). On intellectual property rights and archaeology: Reply to Nicholas and Bannister. *Current Anthropology* **45**(4), 527–528.

Smith, C. and Wobst, H. M. (eds.) (2005). *Indigenous Peoples and Archaeology: The Politics of Practice.* Routledge, London.

Smith, L. T. (1999). *Decolonizing Methodologies: Research and Indigenous Peoples.* Zed Books, London.

Society for American Archaeology (SAA) (1995 [1977]). By-Laws. In: *Archaeologists of The Americas: 1995 Membership Directory.* Society for American Archaeology, Washington DC, pp. 17–25.

Society for American Archaeology (SAA) (1996). Principles of archaeological ethics. *American Antiquity* 61, 451–452.

Society for Historical Archaeology (SHA) (1992). Ethical positions. Article IV, Constitution and bylaws of the Society for Historical Archaeology. *Society for Historical Archaeology Newsletter* **25**, 32–6.

Society of Professional Archaeologists (SoPA) (1991). Code of ethics. In: *Guide to the Society of Professional Archaeologists.* Society of Professional Archaeologists, pp. 7–11.

Spector, J. D. (1993). *What This Awl Means: Feminist Archaeology at a Wahpeton Dakota Village.* Minnesota Historical Society Press, St. Paul.

Stanek, S. (2008). Can Egypt copyright the pyramids? *National Geographic News.* URL: http://news.nationalgeographic.com/news/2008/01/080115-egypt-copyright.htm.

Stilles, A. (2002). *The Future of the Past.* Farrar, Straus and Giroux, New York.

Swidler, N., Dongoske, K. E., Anyon, R., and Downer, A. (eds.) (1997) *Native Americans and Archaeologists: Stepping Stones to Common Ground.* AltaMira, Walnut Creek, CA.

Thomas, D. H. (2000). *Skull Wars: Kennewick Man, Archaeology, and the Battle for Native American Identity.* Basic Books, New York.

Trigger, B. G. (2006). *A History of Archaeological Thought* 2nd ed. Cambridge University Press, Cambridge.

Trouillot, M.-R. (1995). *Silencing the Past: Power and the Production of History.* Beacon, Boston.

Tully, J. (1995). *Strange Multiplicity: Constitutionalism in an Age of Diversity.* Cambridge: Cambridge University Press.

Ulm, S., and Hodder, I. (2007) Rationale for a General Code of Ethics: WAC Ethics. Available at: http://humanitieslab.stanford.edu/WACEthics/36

Upano, A. (2004). DC team gets to the root of the problem. *Legal Times* 27(2).

United States Department of Commerce, Patent and Trademark Office (USDCPTO). (1999) Public Hearing Regarding Issues Surrounding Trademark Protection for the Official Insignia of Federally- and/or State-Recognized Native American Tribes. URL: http://www.uspto.gov/go/com/hearings/natinsig/nahear3.htm

Upton, R. (2005). Zia Pueblo receiving money for use of sun symbol. National Association of Tribal and Heritage Protection Officers. URL: www.nathpo.org/News/Legal/News-Legal_Issues27.html

Vitelli, K. D. (1984). The international traffic in antiquities: Archaeological ethics and the archaeologist's responsibility. In: Green, E. L. (ed.) *Ethics and Values in Archaeology.* Free Press, New York, pp. 143–55.

Vitelli, K. D. 1996 (ed.). *Archaeological Ethics.* AltaMira Press, Walnut Creek CA.

Vitelli, K. D., and Colwell-Chanthaphonh, C. (eds.) (2006). *Archaeological Ethics,* 2nd ed. AltaMira Press, Lanham MD.

Watkins, J. (2000). *Indigenous Archaeology: American Indian Values and Scientific Practice.* AltaMira Press, Walnut Creek CA.

Whyte, W. F. (ed.) (1991). *Participatory Action Research.* Sage Publications, Newbury Park CA.

Wood, J., and Powell, S. (1993). An ethos for archaeological practice. *Human Organization* **52**(4), 405–13.

World Archaeological Congress (1989). Rules to adhere to: WAC first code of conduct. URL: http://worldarchaeologicalcongress.org/site/about_ethi.php.

Wylie, A. (1995). Archaeology and the antiquities market: The use of 'looted' data. In: Lynott, M. J. and Wylie, A. (eds.) *Ethics in American Archaeology: Challenges for the 1990s.* Society for American Archaeology, Washington DC, pp. 17–21.

Wylie, A. (1996). Ethical dilemmas in archaeological practice: Looting, repatriation, stewardship, and the (trans)formation of disciplinary identity. *Perspectives on Science* **4.2**, 154–194.

Wylie, A. (1999). Science, conservation, and stewardship: Evolving codes of conduct in archaeology. *Science and Engineering Ethics* **5**(3), 319–336.

Wylie, A. (2002). *Thinking From Things: Essays in the Philosophy of Archaeology.* University of California Press, Berkeley.

Wylie, A. (2005). The promise and perils of an ethic of stewardship. In Meskell, L. and Pells, P. (eds.) *Embedding Ethics.* Berg Press, London, pp. 47–68.

Yellowhorn, E. (2000a). Strangely estranged: Native studies and the problem of science. *Native Studies Review* **13**(1), 71–96.

Yellowhorn, E. (2000b). Indians, archaeology and the changing world. In: Lynott, M. J. and Wylie, A. (eds.) *Ethics in American Archaeology: Challenges for the 1990s.* Society for American Archaeology, Washington DC, pp. 126–37.

Zimmerman, L. J. (1995). Regaining our nerve: Ethics, values, and the transformation of archaeology. In: Lynott, M. J. and Wylie, A. (eds.). *Ethics in American Archaeology: Challenges for the 1990s.* Society for American Archaeology, Washington DC, pp. 64–7.

3

The Appropriation of Human Remains: A First Nations Legal and Ethical Perspective

James [Sa'ke'j] Youngblood Henderson

Over the centuries, travelers and colonizers have collected the human remains of First Nations (FN) and the practice continues today as an outlandish yet popular activity. The appropriation of FN human remains is undertaken by outsiders who remove buried or stored bodily remains without the consent of FN. The cultural appropriation of Aboriginal human remains is justified under the guise of claims to scientific, academic or heritage goals. FN, however, soundly reject each of these justifications as being the continuing manifestation of race science and its false categories of race. FN asserts that the appropriation and its resulting harms do not benefit either Aboriginal people or science. The anger and torment surrounding the appropriation among FN swell.

In the vast curate of skeletal remains of the colonized, the collectors have divided the remains into human history and medical/forensic applications. The general purpose of cultivating the skeletal remains is said to be for human science to interpret the lifeway and morphological variations of past FN. The activity, however, promotes racial inferiority, racism and oppressive race-based theories of population biology. The collections and the resulting findings deprive FN of their ancestry, Aboriginal and treaty rights as well as human rights. These practices of appropriation seek to denigrate the FN ancestors in order to objectively prove European superiority and justify less than human treatment of FN.

Enormous numbers of human skulls, skeletal remains and other materials of FN and Indigenous peoples exist in collections around the world. Indeed, the exact total of FN skeletal remains is unknown. In Canada, the Canadian

Museum of Civilization has approximately three thousand partial or complete FN skeletons. In the US, at least seventy-one of the Smithsonian collections are from British Columbia and Ontario (G&M 1989). According to reports prepared by the US Congress, the remains of thousands of FN have been stored in the collections of museums and scientific institutions throughout the US. About 18,500 individuals were found in the collection of the Smithsonian Institution alone. These extensive holdings were often gained through illegal means. For example, in British Columbia between 1875 and 1900, grave-robbing and confiscation were so generalized and rampant that by the early 1900s, New York museums housed more FN skulls, skeletons, poles, canoes, baskets, feast bowls and masks from burial sites than remain in British Columbia. (Hume 1989)

The collections of FN human remains raise complex issues of law and ethics. Colonial legal systems have justified the appropriations on the theory that anything found in Indigenous soil belongs either to the colonial government or to the colonial owner of the land. This colonial theory— inconsistent with FN jurisprudence and imperial treaties—permitted archaeologists and other individuals to acquire ownership of skeletons and other materials found in graves of FN not legally designated and protected as 'cemeteries'.

Thomas (2000) and Turnbull (1991) document some instances of the unethical acquisitions. Similar appropriations continue today on a world-wide scale. (Mann 2000; Huxley 2002) The appropriation of FN human remains and buried cultural artifacts has been persistent; it has been con-ducted in multiple sites with overlapping and intersecting dimensions. Some laws, legislation and courts have intervened for the benefit of FN; however, there has been little consistency in the application of legislation and common law. More recently, a new context to the issue has been the trafficking of body parts of murdered Indigenous peoples to medical facilities around the world.

For a variety of legal, ethical and spiritual reasons, most FN strongly believe that the skeletons ought not to be disturbed. FN considers ancestral burial grounds or sites and their contents as 'sacred' and involving freedom of religion (Deloria 1969 and 2000; Byrd 1983). They consider the spirits of such sites to be of central importance, to implicate the order of embod-ied spirits and to be necessary for the maintenance of good relations and harmony. Accordingly, threats to the integrity of these sites come not only from development projects and the impingement of legislation on the sites, but also from the work of the archaeological endeavors. The search for culturally significant objects often leads archaeologists to sacred burial grounds. FN have asked that these objects be left in the ground and that graves not be disturbed out of respect for the dead and in recognition that FN jurisprudence privileges the burial grounds that remain the collective property of all FN.

In years past, US officials have looked at some of the FN perspectives. For example, after following the legally required consultation with traditional Indigenous religious leaders to decide appropriate religious rights and practices, the US Federal Agencies Task Force report acknowledged that the Native people of this continent believe that certain areas of land are holy. These lands may be sacred because they surround and contain burial grounds. (USFATF 1979: 52)

In FN law and jurisprudence, the protection of human remains is the sacred inheritance of particular families and communities—it is essential to the spiritual health of each nation. Restoring health and ending the harmful imbalance that result in *windigo*ism, suicide, mental trauma and physical hurt requires an understanding of the harms and offenses to FN that is interwoven with and connected to the disrespect shown to FN human remains. These harms are ongoing, persistent and crushing. To the outside researchers conducting and creating the harms, it is virtually hidden and unseen.

Academic researchers attempt to provide justification for the appropriation by claiming the need to further knowledge and scholarship. However, this greatly conflicts with the much needed healing and restoration of FN. Researchers who have or who intend to disturb burial skeletons create horrendous harms and offense under the FN law and ethics. Yet, the practices continue under the banner of ethically respectable endeavors. In reality, the practices are privileged in the most abstract terms of colonial privilege. The dichotomy between the stated goal of 'good science' and the resulting harm to FN is ignored, summarily dismissed or scorned. In more recent years, lawyers and academics have begun to think seriously and write about the appropriate legal and moral weighting of the issues surrounding FN human remains. The dialogue, however, has mostly focused upon non-FN or non-Indigenous scholarship in framing the seemingly disparate interests. This creates a hegemonic bricolage, which is amply evidenced by legal interventions into this topic. What is needed instead (as will be discussed later) is Professor Ermine's proposed conceptual framework called the 'ethical lodge', within which the apparent tension and conflicts can be resolved.

Legal Interventions

Canada

Federal and provincial governments and their administrative regimes have ignored Aboriginal and treaty rights that enable FN law to deal with appropriation of human remains. These regimes have engaged in creative avoidance of Indigenous knowledge and heritage, and they have not responded to Canadian constitutional reform in any significant way. Thus, Canadian legislators have not passed any new legislation to protect, preserve or enhance the rights of FN to their knowledge and heritage. One reason for this passivity is the underrepresentation of Aboriginal interests in the federal parliament. (Henderson 1994; Macklem 1997) This creates a chasm in respecting FN knowledge, heritage and dignity that somewhat explains Canada's lack of a centralized system to administer and monitor FN human remains. Currently, no explicit provision in statutory law provides for the repatriation of FN remains and, as such, the resulting legal vacuum creates and encourages opportunities for FN perspectives to be ignored, dismissed and overridden.

Of course, all provinces have addressed the need to protect archaeological resources located on public provincial lands and private lands under the broad category of 'historical resources'. In fact, most provinces provide for designation of historical resources, reporting of funds, government ownership of archaeological resources and control of excavations on public and private lands through a permit system, archaeological impact assessments, stop orders and penalties for non-compliance. Yet, the legislation is silent on the appropriation of FN human remains (unless deemed an archaeological or historical resource).

In those instances where legislation does provide some homage to FN human remains, the provisions are often vague and unclear. In Canada, most provincial heritage acts and cemeteries acts are vague on the protection of Aboriginal burial grounds and skeletal remains. The exceptions are the Saskatchewan *Heritage Property Act* and the Prince Edward Island *Ancient Burial Grounds Act* (1974). In a case decided under the *Heritage Property Act*, the Saskatchewan Court of Queen's Bench granted an injunction to prevent the excavation of an Indian burial site on private land so as to give the local band council an opportunity to investigate and relocate the remains (*Touchwood File Hills Qu'Appelle District Council Inc. v. Davis* 1987). In Prince Edward Island's *Ancient Burial Ground Act*, the burial grounds are vested in the Crown, with protective and administrative duties given to the minister.

United Nations Law

In the past thirty years, five instruments have been created to protect or control the disposition of human remains, some more directly than others. The United Nations Educational, Scientific and Cultural Organization (UNESCO) has created two conventions that indirectly (if at all) address the issue of human remains: the *Convention on the Means of Prohibiting and Preventing the Illicit Import, Export and Transfer of Cultural Property* (1970*);* and the *Convention Concerning the Protection of the World Cultural and National Heritage* (1972). The International Institute for the Unification of Private Law (UNIDROIT) created a convention that deals indirectly with the issue of human remains: the *Convention on Stolen and Illegally Exported Cultural Objects* (1995). These conventions, while laudable in their goals, do not, however, address the issues of FN human remains.

To remedy this gap, Indigenous people have created the *Indigenous Principles and Guidelines for the Protection of the Heritage of Indigenous Peoples* (1995) of the UN Working Group of Indigenous Peoples that protects burials (s. 11 and 29). The UN *Declaration on the Rights of Indigenous Peoples* (2007) is a comprehensive interpretation of how UN human rights covenants apply to Indigenous peoples. The Declaration is concerned with culture, religion and linguistic identity (arts. 3, 5, 11–15, 31–34). Article 11 of the Declaration provides that Indigenous peoples have the right to maintain and strengthen their distinct cultural characteristics, including the Indigenous right to maintain, protect and develop the archaeological and historical sites, and artefacts. Article 11(2) provides that nation states shall provide redress to Indigenous people through effective mechanisms, which may include restitution, developed in conjunction with Indigenous peoples, with respect to their cultural, intellectual, religious and spiritual property taken without their free, prior and informed consent or in violation of their laws, traditions and customs. Article 12(1) provides

Indigenous peoples with the international right to maintain, protect, and have access in privacy to their religious and cultural sites and the right to the use and control of their ceremonial objects. Also, it provides them the right to the repatriation of human remains. Article 12(2) provides that nation states shall seek to enable the access and/or repatriation of ceremonial objects and human remains in their possession through fair, transparent and effective mechanisms developed in conjunction with Indigenous peoples concerned. Article 8(2)(a) provides that nation states shall provide effective mechanisms for prevention of, and redress to Indigenous peoples for, any action which has the aim or effect of depriving them of their integrity as distinct peoples, or of their cultural values or ethnic identities. And Article 40 provides that Indigenous peoples have the right to access to and prompt decision through just and fair procedures for the resolution of conflicts and disputes with states or other parties, as well as to effective remedies for all infringements of their individual and collective rights. Such a decision shall give due consideration to the customs, traditions, rules, and legal systems of the Indigenous peoples concerned and international human rights.

Currently, the existing laws on the appropriation or treatment of human remains attempt to balance an academic interest in the protection of the existing archaeology or cultural record under nationalistic control with an implicit interest in respecting FN toward their burial laws or bioarchaeological remains. However, the Eurocentric tension about ancestral affiliation or identity remains between the secular, the scientific and the FN cultures and communities. Moreover, there is sparse law regarding control over human remains in privately held materials.

The differing interests claiming control of FN human remains create a conflict both in law and ethics. These interests form a transversal ethical space on the issue of harm and offense. Given these interests, it is now apparent that international, national, and tribal laws must work together to protect FN human remains. At the core, however, FN jurisprudence and laws provide the vital cultural context and as such contain the expertise, knowledge and wisdom to serve as the foundation of the new relationships between the interests. Unlike top-down legal systems, FN jurisprudence and laws reflect cultural beliefs and sensitive sacred knowledge in nuanced ways that national and international regimes simply cannot. First Nations must exercise the inherent authority of Aboriginal and treaty rights to exercise their self-determination and define the laws that govern their human remains.

First Nations Remains as Protected by First Nations Heritage and Jurisprudence

The *Constitution Act, 1982*, s. 35 constitutionally protects the human remains of the Aboriginal peoples of Canada. Within the context of the Constitution of Canada, Indigenous knowledge and heritage is an existing Aboriginal right. The 'promise' of protecting Aboriginal rights, as it was termed by the Supreme Court in *R. v. Sparrow* (1990: 1083), recognized not only the ancient occupation of land by Aboriginal peoples, but also their contribution to the building of Canada and the special commitments made to them by successive governments (see *Quebec Secession Reference* 1998, para. 82). The protection of these rights, so recently and arduously achieved, reflects important underlying constitutional values. Accordingly, Aboriginal peoples look to the Constitution of Canada for the protection of their knowledge, ecological relationships and linguistic and heritage rights.

Existing Aboriginal rights created new constitutional contexts for the interpretation of governmental responsibility in protecting Indigenous knowledge and heritage in Canada. In fact, the Supreme Court of Canada in *Van der Peet* (1996) stated that these rights existed pre-contact with Europeans and are integral to a distinctive Indigenous order. The Court acknowledged that these cultural rights arise within the system of beliefs, social practices and ceremonies of the Aboriginal peoples. They are traced back to FN law and thoughts. Indigenous legal systems are *sui generis* to the Canadian order, but are also protected by Canadian constitutional law and the rule of law. The Supreme Court's approach suggests that Aboriginal rights are to be defined by the Indigenous traditions of the Aboriginal peoples in Canada as perceived by them and as supported by evidence. The term *sui generis* categorizes this approach: these rights are found in Aboriginality rather than in Eurocentric traditions and rights deriving from the European Enlightenment.

For the FN, Aboriginal rights perform several vital functions. These constitutional rights are unique bonds that strengthen cohesiveness and identity and raise the quality of life. No systematic collection of FN laws exists, nor has anyone prepared any manuals or handbooks compiling all aspects of FN law covering Indigenous knowledge and heritage. Despite this lack of written law, there is a collection of material in social science literature on Aboriginal traditions and ways of life and on the spiritual relations between these traditions and the land, including detailed studies of kinship, religion and family structures. Although most of these writings are contaminated by Eurocentric bias, once they are decontaminated they may be helpful in understanding the nature and scope of Indigenous knowledge and heritage.

Layered into the *sui generis* approach, the Supreme Court's analysis of Aboriginal rights in *Sparrow* (1990) emphasized that any interpretations of FN culture must be 'sensitive to and [have] respect for the rights of Aboriginal peoples on behalf of the government, courts, and indeed all Canadians'. (1119) Little doubt exists that laws regulating human remains are an integral and distinctive part of their constitutional rights. FN assert the right to enjoy access and privacy in relation to sacred sites, and the right to retain total control of their traditional knowledge and to address and deal with FN human remains as they choose.

These assertions of upholding principles are not without legal precedent. Indeed, the Supreme Court of Canada has affirmed the principle that the Crown cannot expropriate a property interest or right unilaterally without regard to Aboriginal interests. The Crown can no longer act without compensation to FN, including the external regulation of Aboriginal tenure and rights. The Supreme Court of Canada, in its *Sparrow* decision, held that the traditional law or custom of Aboriginal rights was not frozen at the moment of the arrival of Europeans in Canada, and subsequent developments, variations or manifestations of these rights do not extinguish the traditional customs or laws or make them less effective in Canadian law. (1093)

It is also important to note these constitutionally protected rights are embedded within the highest law of Canada. With the creation of a constitutional category of Aboriginal rights in the Constitution of Canada, the courts have placed clear limitations on federal and provincial legislatures. As of 1982, the Crown can no longer maintain that Aboriginal rights exist at the pleasure of the Crown. Additionally, constitutional support for the supremacy of FN law governing human remains over federal and provincial law can be derived from the doctrine of implied repeal under section 52(1) of the *Constitution Act, 1982*. This doctrine states that when the courts determine that there are two inconsistent or conflicting statutes, the later in time is deemed to, by implication, repeal the earlier to the extent of the inconsistency.

FN jurisprudence and law are drawn from a FN heritage and worldview: traditional customary law, tribal belief systems and other contemporary forms of governance. It is also uniquely well-suited to accommodate the religious and cultural beliefs of FN in ways that Eurocentric law cannot. For example, FN laws may better reflect territorial relationship, affiliation and identity of a place, even if a FN is no longer present in the territory. These laws reflect a common belief that the earth is sacred. FN laws create the ability to claim title to the human remains of ancestors, which British common law denies. It therefore reflects not only substantive legal principles, but also the cultural context from which they evolved. Through FN law, FN governance of burial remains will correlate specifically to what tribes seek to protect, allow for forms of punishment consistent with the community's values and properly 'incentivize' behavior that is good for the community at large.

Numerous tribes in the United States have criminal and heritage codes (Riley 2005) specifically addressing the desecration of burial grounds and, in some cases, human corpses. In some instances, the desecration statutes apply to places with religious or historical significance, but to historic places as well. For example, Hopi law (1974) contains provisions devoted to the preservation of 'Places and Objects of Sacred, Historical and Scientific Interest on the Hopi Reservation'. The Eastern Band of the Cherokee Nation has one of the more extensive codes (1999) related to the preservation of human remains and sacred burial grounds.

In the case of human remains, it is common for a great deal of respect to be shown to the wishes of local bands, even when the identity of the deceased is unknown. In some provinces, heritage legislation gives the nearest band council a say in the disposition of such remains. Apart from a statute, however, there is little protection for such human remains. The matter has been the subject of little litigation, so the common law in this area has not developed.

In historical treaties, the FN reserved the right to control their heritage; they did not transfer any authority over human remains. In the modern treaties, the FN are protecting their heritage. The *Yukon Comprehensive Land Claims Umbrella Final Agreement* (1990) provides for cooperation with the FN in the management of heritage resources. The agreement provides for protection of FN resources, giving them a priority over other Yukon heritage resources, and provides for preparation of an inventory of ethnographic resources. It also provides for the protection, care and custody of the resources, and reasonable access to artifacts. The agreement provides for a management scheme consistent with these principles and calls for the formation of a Yukon heritage board composed of

FN and government members. The board will recommend heritage resource policy, designate heritage parks, sites, landmarks and watercourses, manage documentary resources and consult with affected Yukon FN before naming geographical areas. FN approval is required for access to burial sites and FN will be consulted about proper treatment of these sites. The government also agrees in principle to assist in the repatriation of resources originating from the Yukon.

Articles 36 and 37 of the *Nunavut Settlement Agreement* (1990) provide for Aboriginal participation in future heritage resource management, as well as federal assistance in the repatriation of heritage resources. The parties did not agree on the issue of title to heritage resources; this was left to the final negotiations. Chapter 17 of the *Nisga'a Treaty,* entitled 'Cultural Artifacts and Heritage', deals with the repatriation of Nisga'a remains from the Canadian Museum of Civilization and the Royal British Columbia Museum.

Search for Professor Ermine's 'Ethical Lodge'

Professor Leroy Little Bear coined the phrase 'jagged worldviews colliding' to describe the encounter of FN philosophies and European positivist 'scientific' thought (Battiste 2000). This concept of the search for 'ethical lodges' among the jagged worldviews colliding is especially relevant in constructing a conceptual framework. These jagged edges create the protective orbits of distrust that predominate ethical issues.

At this edgy and uneasy juncture of these two worldviews is the proposal of Cree scholar Willy Ermine, a professor at First Nations University, Saskatchewan. Ermine proposes an emergent conceptual framework for generating an 'ethical lodge' as an intermediate zone of confrontation about the appropriation of human remains of FN. The space is nonexistent in the literature, but Professor Ermine articulates it as a deep asymmetrical spiral (or a one-dimensional circle) between Eurocentric and FN knowledge and thought. The ethical lodge straddles these knowledge systems, which are made up of much diversity and complexity and are embedded and formed by discourses, research and policy. It is a space that mediates both sides of the dichotomy. On both sides the researcher has to move into an unfamiliar conceptual framework or paradigm.

The ethical lodge is a cognitive sphere of different 'landscapes'; it is the uncharted realm in which neither FN nor Eurocentric views will have a shared mental map by which to navigate or determine proper conduct or discourse. It is a realm of learning; a space of engagement where incompetence prevails and where existing knowledge systems, and worldviews that filter 'reality' and determine ethics, privacy and consent have to be modified and challenged. It is a space where no single knowledge or way controls an extraordinary realm of change, paradigm shifts and divergent ways of knowing and acting. It is the circle of transformation of consciousness and values. The jagged edges of the ethical lodge exist in policy and in research domains. It operates both as a zone of absence of bad faith and preference, and as a discourse—a way of rationally thinking and talking about the issues. Yet, like all interstices, it shows how light is revealed.

The existing legal and ethical frameworks have not been developed through consultation or accommodation with FN. Canada, the funding agents, and the professions do not have a solid record with respect to research ethics related to FN and values. Little is known about research on FN, the proper guidelines, or their impact on society. Professor Ermine (2004) has reviewed the literature on the ethics involved with research on FN, and the credibility and efficiency of known concerns to FN, and attempts to develop a model of the ethical lodge. He noted that it is difficult for the federally funded research community—academic, governmental, community-based or private—to grasp the negative perception held by FN about researchers and their Eurocentric research product. This raises unique and distinct governance and policy issues on research involving FN.

Professor Ermine drew his initial insights from the term 'ethical space' as developed by Roger Poole in his book *Towards Deep Subjectivity* (1972) and identified the need for an abstract ethical lodge that frames an area of encounter and interaction of two entities with different intentions. Ermine (2004) attempts to bridge the disconnect by first identifying and explicating the elusive centre, and the obstacles of a dividing or fragmenting space, as the theoretical underpinning of a need for cross-cultural linkage that is substantial and ethical. The idea of serrated fractures, produced by contrasting perspectives of the world, entertains the notion of a space where an engaged dialogue sets the parameters for an agreement to interact along with the appropriate ethical forms for that interaction.

Professor Ermine stressed the need for constructing an ethical lodge before any authentic ethical discussion can proceed. I find this particularly insightful in the contested issues surrounding cultural appropriation of human remains. Ermine (2004) applied this idea to the schism between FN and Eurocentrism in health research with all the jagged separation of diverse worldviews, jurisprudence, ethics, and cultures. He conceptualized the ethical lodge as the encounter with the unconstrained schism of misunderstanding that contributes to the tension-riddled enterprise of 'cross-cultural' research involving FN. In FN thought this has been translated as the 'in-between lodge' or the search for 'double understandings'. The duality of the schism is generated by European language and privilege. Euro-Canadian thought views FN law and thought as inferior, while FN are perplexed by the idea of superiority.

The abstract idea of the intersection of two spheres of knowledge, each distinct from one another in multiple forms, in an ethical lodge, inspires an abstract, nebulous space of possibility. Eurocentric thought views cultures and worldviews as differently coloured billiard balls surrounded by European thought. These worldviews are separate and distinct. The in-between space is undefined contexts constructed by Eurocentric thought. Eurocentric thought creates the premises of the separate realities of histories, knowledge traditions, values, interests and social, economic and political imperatives. The construction of these oppositional entities, divided by the void and flux of their cultural distance but existing in a relationship where they are poised to encounter each other, produces significant and interesting approaches to research and policy.

Eurocentric ethics concerning the governance of research involving FN begins with the construction of the other, e.g. the premise that the FN are 'natural objects' of research. This assumption is embedded with claims of superiority. From the Eurocentric paradigm, both the Eurocentric and FN worldviews contain diverse methods and approaches that are brought to the encounter of the two solitudes. Creating contrast by purposefully dislocating and isolating two disparate knowledge systems represented by the diverse FN and European cultures is pursued in the interest of identifying and bringing perspective to the current research context. This contrast provides perspective on a space between consciousnesses that lends itself to clarity about the issues and themes of divergence and convergence in the examination of the ethics in research involving FN. In this space European superiority and race science were constructed.

Most of the ethics discourse applied to the examination of the removal of Aboriginal remains from burial grounds for medical and ethnological research has been filtered by Eurocentrism, its professional organizations and their view of ethics rather than by FN law and ethics. They do not have wide acceptance among FN; they are viewed as intellectual camouflage. The essential and defining element of ethical issues, however, is respect for FN laws and institutions. FN jurisprudence is deeply interconnected with ethical issues. The starting point for any ethical research on human remains must be the laws of the FN involved, which define what constitutes property, who is responsible for keeping the burial grounds and human remains and who has the right to dispose of property.

This presumption of dueling contrasts assembles the positioning of the two entities and creates the urgent necessity for a harmonizing zone of dialogue. In FN thought, this harmonizing zone is the ethical lodge, where a precarious and fragile window of opportunity exists for critical conversations. The spectre of continuing tensions at the contested ground of research ethics, dignity and integrity prompts both worldviews to seize the moment of possibility to create substantial, sustained and ethical/moral understanding between cultures. The ethical lodge provides a context or paradigm for how, at the 'confluence and chance', people from disparate cultures, worldviews and knowledge systems can engage in an ethical and fair manner as we work toward giving substance to what the ethical lodge entails.

Professor Ermine's ethical lodge as a concept is an unfolding process that is inclusive of a series of stages from dialogue to dissemination of results, each played out in many different codes and relationships at the level of research practice. As a process, the fundamental requirements of the ethical lodge include an affirmation of difference. The ethical lodge cannot exist without this affirmation. The affirmation of the space indicates that there is an acceptance of a cultural divide and a direct statement of cultural jurisdictions at play. The ethical lodge also requires dialogue about intentions, values and assumptions of the entities towards the research process. The dialogue leads to an agreement to interact across the cultural divide. With an agreement to interact, the particulars of transcultural engagement, along with all the issues of the research process, are negotiated towards an amicable research agreement between researchers and FN communities.

By Eurocentric construction, the FN view is exotic and distinct. The emerging literature on ethics emphasizes the need to create an innovative ethical lodge and conceptual frameworks for research on FN. The ethical lodge is necessary to construct the growing tension between the interest of Eurocentric scholars in FN human remains and knowledge, and protecting the right of Indigenous peoples to control the dissemination and use of their sacred sites and their knowledge. Other relevant professional associations, such as the Society for Applied Anthropology and the International Council of Museums are unilaterally developing standards of conduct. (SAA 1991; ICOM 1971)

The first attempt to construct an ethical lodge was when the World Archaeological Congress (WAC), with the eight Indigenous peoples and the executive committee from twenty representatives of the archaeological community, created and adopted the *Vermillion Accord on Human Remains* (1989). The Accord centralizes respect for the dead and urges groups or individuals interested in studying human remains to consult with Indigenous peoples prior to undertaking such research. Researchers should demonstrate the value of such research to Indigenous peoples and communities. Such consultations require prior knowledge of the identity of the human remains, 'when they are known or can be reasonably inferred'. The International Law Society (2000) suggests that ethical codes could provide a source such as the *Vermillion Accord* for international law on the protection and repatriation of human remains.

Conclusion

The possession of FN human remains presents intriguing ethical, legal and political issues that make generalization complex. The essential and defining element of the issues, however, is respect for FN laws and institutions. The constitutional rights of the FN pre-empt any philosophical debate and urge for establishing treaty- or Aboriginal-rights-based ethical lodges to resolve these issues.

FN jurisprudence is deeply interconnected with ethical issues. The starting point for any ethical research on human remains must be the law of the FN involved, which defines what constitutes property, who is responsible for keeping of the burial grounds and human remains and who has the right to dispose of property. Unless researchers or professionals are aware of and act consistently with FN law and ethics, removal of human remains are harmful, unlawful, illegitimate and unethical.

Creating ethical lodges in treaty and Aboriginal territories, as conceptualized by Professor Ermine, would be helpful. Ethical research systems and practices should enable Indigenous nations, peoples and communities to exercise control over information relating to their knowledge and heritage and to themselves. These projects should be managed jointly with FN, and the communities being studied should benefit from training and employment opportunities generated by the research. Above all, it is vital that FN have direct input into developing and defining research practices and projects related to them. To act otherwise is to repeat that familiar pattern of decisions being made for Indigenous people by those who presume to know what is best for them.

Some FN communities may want to share their human remains. Most do not. But all want their communities and their knowledge to be consulted, accommodated and respected. This creates innovative forms of dialogical research and ethical lodges.

References

Battiste, M. (2000). *Reclaiming Indigenous Voice and Vision.* Vancouver: UBC Press.

Byrd, R. (1983) In: Hammil, J. and Zimmerman, L. J. (eds.) *Perspectives from Lakota Spiritual Men and Elders.* Forty-first Plains Conference, Rapid City, SD.

Deloria, Jr. V. (1969). *Custer Died for Your Sins: An Indian Manifesto.* Avon Books.

Deloria, Jr. V. (2000). Secularism, Civil Religion and the Religious Freedom of American Indians. In: Devon A. Mihesuah (ed.). *Repatriation Reader: Who Owns American Indian Remains?* University of Nebraska Press.

Ermine, W.J. (2004). The Ethics of Research Involving Indigenous Peoples: A Report to the Indigenous Peoples' Health Centre to the Interagency Advisory Panel on Research Ethics.

G&M (Globe and Mail Newspaper). 1989. Native Remains to be Returned by Smithsonian (12 September), A11.

Henderson, J. Y. (1994). Empowering Treaty Federalism. *Saskatchewan Law Review* 58(2):242.

Hume, M. These Graves Were Robbed under Guise of Science. *Vancouver Sun* (22 September 1989) B5.

Huxley, A. K. (2002). 'Human Remains Sold to the Highest Bidder!' A Snapshot of the Buying and Selling of Human Skeletal Remains on eBay, an Internet Auction Site. Paper presented at the 54th Annual Meeting of the American Academy of Forensic Science, Atlanta, GA.

ICOM (International Council of Museums). 1971. *Code of Ethics.*

International Law Association Committee on Cultural Heritage Law (2000). First Report.

Macklem, P. (1997). Aboriginal Rights and State Obligations. *Alberta L. Rev.* 97: 36.

Mann, B. A. (2000). In Defense of the Ancestors: Ohio Falls Silent. *Native Americas* 50: 17.

Poole, R. (1972). *Towards Deep Subjectivity.* New York: Harper and Row (Torchbook).

Riley, A. R. (2005) 'Straight Stealing': Towards an Indigenous System of Cultural Property Protection. *Washington Law Review* **80**:69.

SAA (Society for Applied Anthropology). Proposal for Ethics Consideration Aspects of Intellectual Property Rights. Drafted by Tom Greaves of Bucknell University (1991).

Thomas, D. H. (2000). *Skull Wars: Kennewick Man, Archaeology, and the Battle for Native American Identity.* New York, Basic Books.

Turnbull, P. (1991). Ramsay's Regime: The Australian Museum and the Procurement of Aboriginal Bodies, c. 1874–1900 15 *Aboriginal Hist.* 108.

USFATF (United States Federal Agencies Task Force) (1979). *American Indian Religious Freedom Act Report.* Washington, DC: US Department of Interior, (1979).

Acts, Statutes, Regulations and Guidelines

Ancient Burial Grounds Act. 1974. R.S.P.E.I., ch. A-9 (Prince Edward Island)

Cherokee Code ant. I, §70–1(a) to -1(b) (1999)

Constitution Act, 1982. Schedule B to the Canada Act (U.K.), c. 11.

Heritage Property Act. 1979–80. S.S. ch. H-2.2 (Saskatchewan)

Hopi Tribe of Ariz., Ordinance No. 26 §§1,2(a) (1974)

Indigenous Declaration on the Rights of Indigenous Peoples. 1993. As Agreed Upon by the Members of the Working Group on Indigenous Peoples at its Eleventh Session. 1993. E/CN.4/Sub. 21/1993/29

Draft Declaration on the Rights of Indigenous Peoples. 1994. E/CN.4/Sub. 21/1994/ Add. 1

Indigenous Principles and Guidelines for the Protection of the Heritage of Indigenous Peoples. 1990–1995. E/CN.4/Sub.2/1995/26 and E/CN.4/Sub. 2/1995/31

Nisga'a Treaty

Nunavut Settlement Agreement in Principle Between Inuit of the Nunavut Settlement Area and Her Majesty in Right of Canada. 1990. Ottawa: Department of Indian Affairs and Northern Development.

UNESCO. *Convention on the Means of Prohibiting and Preventing the Illicit Import, Export and Transfer of Cultural Property.* Nov. 14, 1970.

UNESCO. *Convention Concerning the Protection of the World Cultural and National Heritage.* 7 October to 21 November 1972.

UNESCO. *Convention on Stolen and Illegally Exported Cultural Objects. (1995).*

Vermillion Accord on Human Remains (1989) World Archaeological Congress (WAC)

Yukon Comprehensive Land Claims Umbrella Final Agreement. 1990. Ottawa: Department of Indian Affairs and Northern Development.

Judicial Cases

R. v. Sparrow, [1990] 1 S.C.R. 1075

R. v. Van der Peet, [1996] 2 S.C.R. 507, [1996] 4 C.N.L.R. 177

Touchwood File Hills Qu'Appelle District Council Inc. v. Davis, [1987] 1 C.N.L.R. 180 (Sask.Q.B.)

Reference by the Governor General in Council Concerning Certain Questions Relating to the Secession of Quebec [1998] 2 S.C.R. 217

4

The Repatriation of Human Remains

Geoffrey Scarre

1.

> One ought to act in such a way that, if one ought to do x and one ought to do y, then one can do both x and y. But the second-order principle is regulative. This second-order 'ought' does *not* imply 'can'. There is no reason to suppose, this being the actual world, that we can, individually or collectively, however holy our wills or rational our strategies, succeed in foreseeing and wholly avoiding such conflict. It is not merely failure of will, or failure of reason, which thwarts moral maxims from becoming universal laws. It is the contingencies of this world. (Marcus 1980: 135)

The 'contingencies of the world' have a lot to answer for. There are times when we feel that the world is too replete with values. By doing one thing that we ought, we prevent ourselves from doing something else that we ought. We promote one value at the expense of another, where it is impossible for us to promote both at once. When this happens we feel morally uncomfortable, but there is no ready cure for our discomfort. We want to do our best but the best, as we conceive it, is internally conflicted.

A good example of a clash of values which even the most well-meaning people may find baffling is provided by the long-running and often acrimonious debate over the repatriation of human remains from institutional and museum collections to their place and community of origin. Of all forms of cultural appropriation practised in the last century or two, it would be hard to think of any that has caused greater pain or offense to subaltern communities than the removal and retention of their human physical remains for purposes of study or exhibition. In the days when it was not customary to consider the wishes and feelings of Indigenous peoples in North America, Africa, Australia, Polynesia and other colonial domains, anthropologists and archaeologists tended to look upon human physical remains from these regions as just another morally unproblematic category of fascinating data for research. And so the boxed-up bones of the honoured dead accompanied the crates of art works, weapons, ritual objects and everyday utensils, to begin a new existence elsewhere as laboratory or display objects, sources of information for strangers. From the viewpoint of the Indigenous cultures concerned, this was not merely the stealing of things belonging to the ancestors; this was the stealing of the ancestors themselves.

Scientists, of course, saw the matter very differently. From their perspective, the acquisition of human remains for study purposes was not sacrilegious depredation but praiseworthy service in one of the noblest of all causes, the furtherance of human knowledge. Scientific knowledge was worth acquiring both for its own sake and for the many practical benefits it commonly led to. Allowing for some updating, the nineteenth- and early-twentieth-century collectors of human physical remains from far-flung corners of the globe would readily have agreed with the statement on the scientific importance of such remains recently issued by the British Museum:

> The study of human remains provides one of the most direct and insightful sources of information on different cultural approaches to death, burial practices and belief systems, including ideas about the afterlife. . . . In addition to furthering the public understanding of other cultures, human remains in museum collections also help advance important research in fields such as the history of disease, changing epidemiological patterns, forensics and genetics. Challenging theories about human evolution are being developed from the study of human remains in museum collections such as, for example, the likelihood that there is no genetic basis for modern concepts of race. (BM Newsroom 2004)

This statement, which is typical of many that have been published by institutions and individual scientists in the last few years, forcefully reminds us of what would, or could, be lost if substantial proportions of physical remains currently held by museums, universities and other research centres were returned to the cultures of origin. Research on human remains is (usually) conducted for sensible and important, not idle and frivolous, purposes, and remains that are reburied or otherwise put beyond access can obviously yield no further information. For this reason Dr Richard Foley, of the Leverhulme Centre for Human Evolutionary Studies at the

University of Cambridge, contends that 'We should be learning from skeletons, not reburying them—they are the remains of people still contributing to humanity and its knowledge of itself.' (Science Media Centre 2003: 1) On this view, reburying remains that could yield valuable or useful information is not merely inconvenient but morally wrong, since it impedes the pursuit of a rightly valued end.

It has also been pointed out that, because scientific technologies are constantly evolving, remains which yield no useful knowledge now may do so in the future. For instance, Sebastian Payne, Chief Scientist for English Heritage, records how 'Medieval skeletons from a deserted medieval village in Yorkshire . . . have shown that osteoporosis was just as common among medieval women as it is now, giving fresh insight into the causes of osteoporosis and calling into question ideas that blame our modern lifestyle.' (Payne 2004: 419) Since the methods of analyzing DNA data that produced this result were unavailable when the skeletons were first exhumed, this important discovery would not have been made had the bones not been kept. Reburying or otherwise disposing of remains thus runs the risk of relinquishing repositories of potentially useful information to which science has no access now but may do at a later date.

Another weighty consideration commonly adduced against repatriation is that the genetic and cultural history of most human groups is much more complex than the layman might imagine, and that science offers the only hope of throwing clear light—provided it has the materials—on ancient patterns of migration, assimilation and dispersal of populations. Claims for repatriation, it is claimed, are frequently based on highly oversimplified notions of biological or cultural descent. Even if present-day members of the claimant groups are happy to live with their traditional ideas about their origins, it is possible that their descendants will not be. But by then it will be too late to recover the true story of their ancestry if there are no human remains to examine. Commenting on the pressure by Native Australian groups for the return of all human remains to local communities and the total interdiction of any further research on Indigenous bones, Marta Mirazon Lahr of the Duckworth Laboratory at Cambridge remarks that, if these demands are granted, future generations of Australians will be in the frustrating position of knowing that various people make up their ancestry, but being quite unable to trace it. (Science Media Centre 2003: 3)

Yet for a great many people worldwide, as Philip Walker observes, '[h]uman skeletal remains are more than utilitarian objects of value for scientific research. . . . they are also objects of religious veneration of great symbolic and cultural significance.' (Walker 2000: 3) Professor Sa'ke'j Henderson writes in an unpublished paper that from the standpoint of First Nations people of North America, 'researchers who disturb a burial may . . . be held to do harm to the dead'; and 'they may also be thought to show insufficient respect to the community at large, or to the living descendants who consider themselves owners or protectors of the forbears' remains.' (Henderson 2005: 5) Many Indigenous peoples in Australia, New Zealand, southern Africa and elsewhere possess similar moral and religious traditions which condemn as impious and improper any disturbance of the dead. One widespread belief is that interference with physical remains prevents the soul from finding rest, while in some places (for example, the Hawaiian islands) it is thought that such unquiet spirits become malevolent ghosts who work out their frustration on the living community which has failed to protect them.

In a post-colonial age in which the voices of subaltern cultures which were ignored in the past now find a far more respectful hearing, demands for the repatriation of human remains—the 'bringing home of the dead'— have been taken with ever-increasing seriousness. The US Native American Graves Protection and Repatriation Act of 1990 (NAGPRA), which placed statutory obligations on institutions holding Native remains to return them on request to their cultural or genetic descendants, blazed a trail that several other countries have followed, or at least considered. In the UK, for example, the 2003 government-commissioned Working Group on Human Remains, chaired by Professor Norman Palmer, recommended the consideration of legislative changes permitting British museums to restore human remains when Indigenous communities request them, together with a new standard of good practice in which return in such cases rather than retention would become the default position. Predictably, the position taken by the Palmer Committee rang alarm bells in many academic circles, and several prominent scientists and curators voiced their fear that, were the recommendations to be followed in full, some important research collections could disappear entirely. (Some critics went further and suggested that adoption of a wholesale policy of returning objects collected from lands formerly under British colonial domination could empty several of the country's most prestigious museums.) So far the UK government has not given statutory backing to the more far-reaching proposals of the Palmer Committee, and an advisory panel set up by the Department of Culture, Media and Sport issued in October 2005 a more qualified set of recommendations, on which I shall have more to say below.

Although the debate over repatriation is frequently represented as a conflict between science and religion (or, more tendentiously, as a battle between truth and myth), to think of it merely in these terms would badly oversimplify the issues. For the debate is also about two other crucially important issues, namely justice and 'the politics of identity and recognition' (I borrow the latter phrase from Smith 2004: 406).

The issue of justice arises because of the unsatisfactory circumstances in which many human remains now residing in research collections were initially obtained. Colonial powers normally appropriated what they wanted from the subaltern cultures they controlled, without troubling to say please. The main point of colonization, after all, was to secure access, at the cheapest possible rate, to new resources of all kinds, and, wherever possible, to prevent one's rivals (the other colonial powers) from getting them first. Although the acquisition of items of cultural interest was no doubt often motivated by the purer and nobler aim of the promotion of knowledge, the methods employed by the collectors were sufficiently infected by the spirit of colonialism to be frequently high-handed, grasping, careless of local values and feelings, and in the worst cases downright racist. In fact, a lamentable insouciance about the sensibilities of the Indigenous cultures whose ancestral bones were being removed appears in the records and diaries of anthropologists and archaeologists until well into the twentieth century.

One notorious, though far from unique, example of a scientist whose respect for the people he was studying seems to have been practically non-existent was the Czech-born American physical anthropologist Aleš Hrdlička, who collected many hundreds of skeletons from Kodiak Island and other areas of Alaska in the early decades of the last century. A couple of extracts from Hrdlička's published account of his excavations in 1929–30 give a fair impression of his approach to fieldwork:

> But just as the parts were all gathered, I saw below . . . an old woman who appeared to be provoked at something and was talking rather loudly. On sending the Indian who accompanied me down to see what the trouble was, I learned that the old woman claimed the bones to be those of her long-departed husband.

Although Hrdlička did not dispute the woman's claim, he proceeded with the removal of the bones regardless.

Some of the bones are quite recent. Open three older ones. In two the remains are too fresh yet, but secure a good female skeleton, which I pack in a practically new heavy pail, thrown out probably on the occasion of the last funeral. Then back, farther out, to avoid notice, through swamps and over moss, and against a wind-driven drizzle against which my umbrella is but a weak protection. (Bray and Killion 1994: 21–22)

To judge from his own descriptions, Hrdlička seems positively to have revelled in snatching bones from under the noses of people who deeply resented his sacrilegious and incomprehensible enthusiasm for acquiring skeletons. As one Kodiak Island elder later sadly recalled, 'He had no regard for the people here. And we had no laws, of course. None that we knew about. We just stood by.' (Bray and Killion 1994: 18) Yet Hrdlička only did in a more overt and unembarrassed manner what many other collectors of bones managed more surreptitiously. In the end the result was the same: human remains were removed against the wishes of people who felt impotent either to prevent it or to make any effective form of complaint.

Where one person, or set of persons, has suffered injury at the hands of another, justice demands that some suitable recompense should be made to the injured party. Aristotle speaks of justice in transactions between individuals being 'a sort of equality' and injustice 'a sort of inequality.' Where 'one has received and the other has inflicted a wound, or one has slain and the other been slain, the suffering and the action have been unequally distributed'; therefore it is the role of the just judge 'to equalize things by means of the penalty, taking away from the gain of the assailant.' (Aristotle 1954: 114–15; 1131b–1132a) In the case of human remains appropriated against the will of the community, the least that rectificatory justice would seem to require is the repatriation of the remains. Indeed, it might plausibly be held, on this ground, that repatriation should be proposed by holding institutions even where it has not (yet) been requested; and one of the more notable recommendations of the Palmer Committee was that restoration of remains might in some cases be offered where it was evident that removal had been effected in ethically dubious circumstances. (DCMS 2005: paragraph 384)

The other major aspect to the repatriation debate that needs to be taken into account is closely connected with that of justice, yet sufficiently distinct to merit separate attention. As Laurajane Smith has forcefully argued, 'For many Indigenous communities the control of ancestral human remains is not only about defending their belief systems, but is embedded in wider struggles to control identity.' (Smith 2004: 408) The issue here concerns *who* has the right to say who a people is—whether it is Western anthropologists, archaeologists, historians and other scientific 'experts', or whether it is the people themselves, via their handed-down stories, beliefs and traditions, their first-hand knowledge of their local environment, and their particular experience of interaction with other human groups. Smith contends that nineteenth- and twentieth-century collection of human remains 'was part of racist research that labelled Indigenous peoples as "primitives", objectified them as natural history specimens, and helped to justify and underpin a series of genocidal acts and government policies.' (Smith 2004: 408) This may be overly harsh as a general characterization of the intentions and effects of the older anthropological research (it was not uncommon, for instance, for Westerners to come to feel considerable admiration and respect for the cultures they studied); but it reminds us that scientific characterizations of Native people were typically not value-neutral and measured the subjects they studied according to alien standards. Whilst this inevitably produced a portrait of Indigenous peoples as lacking many of the accomplishments of Europeans, this would not have mattered much had it remained merely an outsider's view, one that could be rejected or regarded with amused or bemused indifference by the people portrayed. But it became more serious when the notion of Indigenous cultures as 'primitive' or 'savage' was absorbed into the worldview of the colonial masters and framed the underlying premise of their policies for 'dealing with the Natives'. For seen in this light, the 'Natives' appeared a suitable case for treatment, with defective ideas of religion, morals and civility that it was a plain Christian duty to correct.

The bullish presentation of alien conceptions of who Indigenous peoples were was liable (and sometimes, no doubt, intended) not only to undermine the subjects' self-understanding but to corrode their self-respect. It is difficult to believe you have the right to hold your head up high when others tell you that you are a sorry specimen of humanity, with the one recourse open to you of trying to become more like them. Self-reassertion therefore requires taking back control of one's own identity and rejecting the claims of outsiders to provide its primary interpretation; but this is harder to do so long as ancestral remains retain their undignified status as research data in foreign institutions. In Western society, as Smith remarks, 'archaeological and other expert pronouncements on Indigenous identity are given authority.' It is therefore vital for the communities in question 'to control how they are understood and viewed if they are to have direct participation in wider negotiations and debates with governments and their bureaucracies over the legitimacy of their claims to sovereignty, land and self-determination.' This involves, amongst other things, taking control of 'material elements, including "the body", that are used to symbolize that identity.' (Smith 2004: 408) Unless and until the bones come home, other people will continue to usurp the people's own prerogative of saying who they are. Appropriation of the bones thus signals a deeper form of appropriation, namely of the right to determine the subaltern culture's identity.

But at this point an uncomfortable thought beckons. Is it always so clear that a people's own characterization of itself should be taken as authoritative? Might not some such self-images be, in some of their aspects, plain wrong? Since to err is human, it seems rash to reject this possibility *a priori*. For example, some members of First Nation peoples of North America assert that their ancestors have occupied their homeland since the dawn of time. Scientific evidence, however, suggests that the human occupation of the Americas began around 12,000 years ago as people migrated across a land-bridge from eastern Asia during the last Ice Age. As 12,000 years is still a very long time, this scientific chronology might not in itself seem to represent much of a threat to First Nation tradition. But because refining the picture of patterns of migration into North America requires scientific study of what few ancient human remains have come to light, it was especially frustrating to researchers when study of the 9,000-year-old 'Kennewick Man' skeleton, which had been washed out of the bank of the Columbia River in Washington State in 1996, was embargoed under the NAGPRA provisions following a demand by a local Indigenous group for possession of the bones for the purpose of reburying their 'ancestor'. Initial tests which suggested that the skeleton lacked close genetic links to the local present-day population were dismissed by the claimants on the ground that they did not need university-trained scientists to tell them who were or were not their ancestors, as their own traditions were quite sufficient to do that.

The bitter (and at the time of writing not finally resolved) battle for possession of 'Kennewick Man' provides a stark example of what the First Nation scholar Professor Leroy Little Bear has vividly termed 'jagged worldviews colliding'.[1] But—to repeat—a dispute like this is not reducible simply to a clash between science, on the one hand, and religion and tradition, on the other (though that element is obviously present here). The demands of justice in regard to the Kennewick case are less clear-cut than in many others, in view of the great age of the remains and the doubts over the existence of genetic or cultural links to the claimant Indigenous group—though it should be said that these factors are not the only relevant ones in the eyes of those Native Americans who see themselves as bound spiritually not merely to their own lineal ancestors but to Native Americans of all eras. But the most prominent strand in the Kennewick case is that of identity politics. The really divisive question is who has the right to interpret the past of the people of the area. The claim by scientists to be the best authorities is felt by upholders of Indigenous rights as a particularly hurtful instance of illicit appropriation. This clash of scientific and traditional approaches to determining past patterns of human relationships is very much more than a mere conflict of theories. Its deeper dimension is a moral one; those who wish to rebury the Kennewick remains resent as the insulting continuation of old colonial habits the claim of the scientific community to 'know best' about the history of the region, and their impatient dismissal of traditional ideas on the subject as risible myth.

It would be nice to think that all disputes where moral issues are at stake were in principle resoluble, if only the parties were willing to discuss them together in a rational and mutually respectful manner. But even the most well-intentioned participants in a moral dispute may fail to achieve a resolution if they disagree about what the core values are, or how to rank them. Given patience and good will, even the sharpest edges of 'jagged colliding worldviews' may eventually be worn down somewhat in the process of debate. Yet where different priorities continue to be assigned to values, consensus will remain elusive.

Even within a single worldview it is not always possible to determine a non-arbitrary ranking of moral demands when, owing to the 'contingencies of the world', these pull us in different directions. The usual assumption is that every moral question has a right answer, if only we are clever enough to figure it out. But this may be an illusion based on wishful thinking. According to Ruth Barcan Marcus, 'there is no reason to suppose on considerations of consistency that there must be principles which, on moral grounds, will provide a sufficient ordering for deciding all cases'. Some moral dilemmas are 'real' in the sense that they have no answers. (Marcus 1980: 135) It is true that we may still have to make some decision in such cases—for practical reasons, doing nothing is often not an option. But we should recognize, thinks Marcus, that where this is so, our decisions are arbitrary in the sense that they are not dictated by any priority principle.

Reduced to its most basic terms, the repatriation debate represents a collision between two fundamental values, *knowledge* and *justice* (for the time being, I shall construe the latter term broadly enough to encompass the politics of recognition and identity). Those who prioritize the value of knowledge will be more sympathetic to the case for retaining (many) human remains in museums and academic institutions; those who prioritize justice will tend to favour a policy of repatriation. But is there some non-question-begging way of deciding between these alternative positions, some standard against which the comparative worth of knowledge and of justice can be assessed? Note that adopting some single-principle ethical theory such as utilitarianism or Kantianism would not take us forward but would only relocate the problem. For we would then face the task of measuring the relative utility of knowledge and justice, or settling the comparative strength of the duties to do justice and to advance knowledge.

2.

Despite the theoretical problems, we are not, I think, reduced to throwing up our hands in despair and declaring that there is no way of resolving the repatriation dispute which is not wholly question-begging or arbitrary. Consider the two propositions:

We should advance knowledge

and

We should do justice.

As Marcus observes, where there are two different things we ought to do (or which it would at least be good to do), we ought to look for a way of doing them both. But, as she also reminds us, our search will not always succeed, and then we will need to choose between our options. Sometimes reflection will reveal to us how the relevant values should be ranked and so what our decision ought to be. But on other occasions we may be unable to locate a plausible ranking principle and be forced to make an arbitrary choice.

Where it is possible to advance knowledge *and* do justice, then we should try to do both. Often there will be no difficulty about this. Indeed, there are cases in which advancing knowledge is actually demanded by considerations of justice, for example where research that will improve the health of a disadvantaged culture helps to redress historical injustices.[2] But the contingencies of the world will not always permit a ready reconciliation of the two objectives. It may be, for example, that justice calls for the return of certain human remains, in an intact state, to Indigenous claimants even though the research potential of those remains is great. This is a moral dilemma, calling for a choice between values. But is it also a dilemma of that particularly intractable sort where no non-arbitrary decision can be made, in the absence of a plausible ranking principle?

Actually, I don't think so. To risk a large generalization, I suspect that most people's moral intuitions will lead them to give precedence to justice over knowledge, when these two values come into competition. And though it might be objected that a general consensus that justice outranks knowledge in the scale of goods is not in itself a *proof* that it really does, it is hard to see what better evidence we could have for this conclusion (assuming that it is sensible to speak at all of an objective hierarchy of values). To feel the force of the intuitions in question, consider the following trio of propositions:

1. Scientists may dig up whatever human remains they like whenever they believe that these will yield valuable theoretical or practical information;
2. The claim 'This is a valuable item of research' is always, when true, sufficient to justify a refusal to return an object to those from whom it was improperly obtained;
3. The members of one society are entitled to treat the members of another as objects of study, even without their consent.

Very few people are likely to accept propositions 1 and 2. These seem to be not just false but *clearly* false. We would have to dispense with some very basic ideas about property and personal rights before we could find either of these remotely plausible. (Anyone who *did* think them acceptable would be committed to approving of the activities of the eighteenth- and nineteenth-century 'resurrection men'.) The third proposition may give us more pause. It touches on the politics of recognition and identity, which are most critically connected with justice where alien views of who the members of a culture are are employed to justify oppression, exploitation, denigration, or forcible suppression of their own self-image. (In the case of former cultures the obtaining of permission to study them is obviously impossible, yet no one argues that history is an immoral discipline. But historians are still under a moral obligation not to misrepresent, traduce or belittle the societies they study.) Some may think that there is nothing wrong in trying to understand another society provided that the research is not subsequently put to unjust uses; others may wish to impose the extra condition that the study should not be regarded by the subjects as an intrusion into their privacy or as breaching their right to control the definition of their own identity. I shall not try to adjudicate between these weaker and stronger positions, the important thing to note being that both acknowledge the priority of the value of justice over that of knowledge.

If the promotion of justice is properly given the precedence over the promotion of knowledge, it follows that many particular claims by communities for repatriation of human remains should be granted by those institutions which hold them. But before we conclude that a policy of wholesale return is the only moral option, there are four things we ought to note.

The first is that not all human remains now held in Western institutions were collected in circumstances of injustice. Some remains were found in deserted spots while others were willingly given, or even sold, to the collectors. Admittedly, the descendants of people who allowed the removal of ancestral remains may, in a post-colonial age, deeply regret the actions of their forbears; but where they do, it is not so easy to say what justice now demands.[3] It would also be hard to argue that considerations of justice have much bearing on a case like that of Kennewick Man, where no one was in possession of, or protected, the skeletal remains before their discovery.

Second, even where justice requires the repatriation of remains to Indigenous claimants, it does not follow that their communities may then do whatever they like with those remains, including reburying or destroying them (e.g., by cremation). One salient consideration here is that future generations within that same culture may take a different view of the status of ancestral remains and wish them to be available for scientific study. Where people recognize responsibilities toward their descendants as well as to their ancestors, they should take seriously the possibility that their children, or their children's children, will think differently about the proper treatment of the dead. (Recall Lahr's observation that future generations of Australians will be unable to trace their ancestry if there are no accessible remains of Indigenous Australians.) Arguably, then, they should consider preserving, in some suitably respectful mode, at least some ancestral remains, even if this would not be their own first choice. It would be unrealistic, though, to suppose that remains will remain long above ground where it is believed that such scientific curiosity on the part of descendants would show a deeply corrupted taste, or that severe harm was being done to the spirits of the dead or to the living community by delaying reburial.

Third, even where human remains were originally removed against the will or without the permission of an Indigenous community, justice may not in all cases demand their return to the community. It may be that present-day people of that culture do not want the remains back, either because they are happy for them to remain in museums and research institutes yielding useful knowledge or because they do not have the means to look after them in the way they deem appropriate (e.g., their former sacred burial ground may have disappeared in the course of urban development).

Fourth and last, to say that the promotion of justice takes priority over the promotion of knowledge is not to imply that the latter must lose all status in the repatriation debate. A community may rightly assert that it has a just claim to the return of certain remains yet choose not to press that claim, or to press it in full. Admission by the holding institutions of the community's entitlement to determine what should happen to contested human remains often goes far towards righting old wrongs and healing old wounds. Where honour has been satisfied by such acknowledgement, negotiation may then be possible on what should actually happen to the remains. At this point the intrinsic and instrumental value of knowledge (something that no one, of whatever cultural background, is likely to dispute) can reappear in the frame. When each side has gained a grasp of where the other is coming from, compromises may be possible which allow *all* the values at issue to be promoted. In a context of mutually respectful debate, while worldviews may continue to differ significantly they will have lost their jagged edges. There is now a prospect of a settlement which offers all parties enough of what they want to be an acceptable alternative to getting exactly what they want, and a preferable alternative to carrying on a bruising struggle.

3.

In this final section, I should like to say some more on the value of compromise in the repatriation debate. Ideally, compromises are not embraced in the grudging, graceless spirit of the combatant who is too weak to achieve his desires but is determined to grant his opponents no more than the minimum concessions that will keep them at bay. A willingness to compromise can be the source of much positive value. People who agree to compromise over a divisive issue may become more self-critical of their own views, and more receptive to the hitherto inadmissible idea that there might be something to be said in favour of their opponents'. The polarization which is characteristic of positions under attack may give way to more nuanced and moderate modes of defence, and opponents cease to be put down as mad or bad. Life for everyone becomes more tranquil and pleasant when confrontation is replaced by constructive dialogue. Over time a sense of human solidarity may come to replace the old antagonisms. Being prepared to compromise should not be regarded as the hallmark of the morally half-hearted—on the contrary, a readiness to compromise can be a mark of moral strength rather than weakness: the strength of those who are prepared to leave their entrenched positions and hold a hand out to their opponents in the name of good fellowship. Most of us, of course, have our sticking-points, issues on which we think we ought never to give way. Some Indigenous groups may feel this way in regard to allowing ancestral remains to continue unburied. Where they do, the priority of justice may give them a right to veto the search for a compromise.

That archaeologists and Indigenous people can engage in effective, mutually respectful dialogue is evident (to cite just one example) in the growing number of archaeological schemes in the USA where representatives of First Nation cultures are involved from the outset in the planning and the day-to-day management of projects. The increasing use of Institutional Review Boards and Community Advisory Boards to vet research proposals and ensure that all relevant interests are taken into account is a positive development to be welcomed and emulated.[4] The kind of cooperative relationship to be found between researchers and Indigenous groups at (to name but two such schemes) the Center for Desert Archaeology in Tucson, Arizona, and the Mohegan Tribe Historic Preservation Society in Conneticut, may, admittedly, be harder to replicate when Indigenous groups seeking repatriation of remains from distant museums are forced to negotiate through lawyers or government officials; there is no substitute for face-to-face meetings and daily contact for developing interpersonal comprehension and trust. Nevertheless, North American experience of relations between researchers and Indigenous communities over the last few years suggests that the prospect of achieving working compromises which both sides can accept is less remote than it might once have seemed.

Speaking of the need for 'a harmonizing zone of dialogue' between proponents of First Nations and 'Eurocentric' outlooks on the proper treatment of the dead, Sa'ke'j Henderson (with acknowledgment to the Cree scholar Professor Willy Ermine) refers to 'the ethical space where a precarious and fragile window of opportunity exists for critical conversations' (Henderson 2005: 15). An ethical space is one in which 'no single knowledge or way controls, . . . the extraordinary realm of change, paradigm shifts, and divergent ways of knowing and acting.' It is a 'circle of transformation of consciousness and values' within which people listen to what others have to say and are prepared to give ground on their own opinions. (2005: 13)[5] Ethical space so conceived is the space in which reconciliation and compromise can happen. It will not always be easy to bring people together in such a space, and some conversations within it may come to nothing, for one may be genuinely open-minded and ready to listen yet remain unpersuaded by another's position. But the possibility of failure is no reason for not trying.

So what might constitute an eligible compromise on repatriation claims? This might be an arrangement whereby some remains are returned for disposal by Indigenous claimants and some, by bipartisan agreement, are retained for scientific study. Particular requests for return would be best negotiated on a case-by-case basis, guided by some general principles. Thus there might be a usual expectation that remains should be returned where they were acquired under conditions that would generally now be deemed unacceptable (those obtained by methods such as Hrdlička's in the Pacific Northwest would obviously come into this category). But there could be some relaxation on the part of claimant groups in their demands for the return of very ancient remains (which are often those of most interest to scientists, on account of their rarity), especially where genetic and/or cultural links with present-day groups would appear to be slight or non-existent (as, seemingly, in the case of Kennewick Man).

Remains of intermediate age are likely to prove the hardest to deal with. The panel set up by the UK's Department of Culture, Media and Sport to advise museums on repatriation issues observes that 'Archaeological and historical study has shown that it is [normally] very difficult to demonstrate clear genealogical, cultural or ethnic continuity into the past'; as a result, in the UK 'claims are unlikely to be successful for any remains over 300 years old, and are unlikely to be considered for remains over 500 years old, except where a very close and continuous geographical, religious, spiritual and cultural link can be demonstrated.' (DCMS 2005: 27) Unfortunately this ignores the important point made by Walker, that '[m]odern Indigenous people often frame . . . disputes over the power to control the interpretation in tribal history in spiritual terms'. When, in the case of First Nation peoples of North America, this belief is coupled with a view that 'space is spherical and time is cyclical', it becomes hard for modern Native Americans to renounce their responsibility for *all* previous inhabitants of their lands, no matter how long ago they lived. (Walker 2000: 18) For compromise to be possible here, it may be necessary for both sides to row back on their starting positions, with Western institutions paying greater attention to alternative ways of reckoning human linkages, and Indigenous cultures acknowledging that it *does* make some relevant difference to connectivity and kinship whether human remains belong to someone who lived 100, or 1000 or 10,000 years ago.

Compromises are often the result of hard bargaining in which each side tries to secure its own maximal advantage, but they may, as we have noted, be motivated by more inspiring objectives too. The DCMS advisory panel, seeking to identify ethical principles to guide repatriation policy, advocates a 'principle of solidarity' which promises to 'further humanity through co-operation and consensus in relation to human remains':

> The principle of solidarity recognises that we all have a shared humanity and an interest in furthering common goals and tolerating differences that respect fundamental human rights. Mutual respect, understanding and co-operation promote solidarity by fostering goodwill and a recognition of our shared humanity. This principle emphasises the importance of rising above our differences to find common ground, co-operation and consensus. It would be reflected, for example, by seeking to find a consensus in relation to competing claims over human remains that all parties can accept. (DCMS 2005: 15)

This is reminiscent of the Kantian idea that we should show our respect for humanity by respecting all human beings and their interests. In Kant's words, 'Humanity itself is a dignity', since 'a man cannot be used merely as a means by any man . . . but must also be used at the same time as an end'. For '[e]very man has a legitimate claim to respect from his fellow men and is *in turn* bound to respect every other.' (Kant 1991: 255) In virtue of our shared humanity, our maxim should be one of 'limiting our self-esteem by the dignity of humanity in another person'; in other words, we should avoid narrow self-centredness and take due account of the legitimate interests of others (what Kant describes as showing 'respect in the practical sense'). (1991: 244)

Admirable though these sentiments may seem, there is one small caveat to enter. Some non-Western cultures may consider the universalizing appeal to *humanity* to be itself peculiarly redolent of Western or Eurocentric values, and questionable in so far as it views human beings in abstraction from the rest of nature. From their perspective, it would be more modest to see human beings as merely a part of the natural whole, and not necessarily the most important one. North American First Nations ethics, in Sa'ke'j Henderson's characterization of it, emphasizes 'the obligation to learn and respect the rules of the earth of which all aspects have life and spirit.' (2005: 24) Compared with what he terms the 'Eurocentric' ethic, this is a much more organic view of man's relationship with nature, and its watchword is 'harmony' rather than 'progress'. Human beings are not the masters of the earth, with the right to do what they want with it, but part of the natural order: significant parts, to be sure, but not the be-all-and-end-all. Humanity exists to serve the ends of nature, not nature those of humanity. Hence the 'principle of solidarity' may be thought to reflect the ambitious universalizing character of Eurocentric thought that, according to Henderson, is absent in First Nations ethics, which rejects the idea that one not only *may* but *ought* to interfere in the lives of others (even of strangers) in order to 'improve' them. (2005: 24) First Nations ethics, by contrast, is more focused on the particular than the universal, on the interests of communities rather than those of mankind as a whole. If this brief sketch of a difference in attitudes is correct, it suggests that the well-meant call to 'further humanity' could receive a less cordial response within some Indigenous cultures than the DCMS advisory panel may have anticipated.[6]

Yet even if the idea of 'furthering humanity', with its associations with questionable notions of progress, human pre-eminence and the superiority of the universal to the particular, may have a rather alien feel to some people, there will probably be more general assent to the panel's claim that 'mutual respect, understanding and cooperation' are goods that deserve to be promoted. Henderson writes that all First Nation cultures, whatever their particular views on 'sharing their human remains', 'want their communities and their knowledge and heritage to be consulted, accommodated, respected.' (2005: 30) In Kantian terms, everyone wants to be treated as an end in himself, and thinks himself entitled to such treatment. And since we are human beings in the world together, we need to find the ethical space to conduct a common ethical conversation in a mutually-comprehensible language. So the 'principle of solidarity', even if it carries certain metaphysical and ethical baggage than some might dislike, incorporates one thought which all might reasonably be expected to embrace: that good fellowship is more readily achievable when our relations are regulated by a spirit of respect for one another's human nature, rather than attitudes of dislike, suspicion, contempt or hostility.

When all this is said, it would be foolish to suppose that compromises over repatriation issues will always be forthcoming, even where negotiation is carried on with the goodwill called for by the principle of solidarity. It can be easier to believe in the virtues of compromise in the abstract than to bring oneself to give up a cherished position. (It is worth pointing out, however, that one can compromise without having to abandon one's beliefs and values; the crucial thing is that one should be prepared not always to press them in practice.) Moreover, rational participants in a bargaining process will be reluctant to give much away until they are persuaded that the other side is willing to reciprocate with concessions of its own (in the terminology of games theory, they are in danger of entrapment in a 'prisoner's dilemma' which blocks effective negotiation at the outset). The achievement of viable compromises can require a lot of goodwill, and a readiness to take risks.

The superiority of compromise to confrontation was notably acknowledged by the World Archaeological Congress at its meeting at Vermillion, South Dakota, in 1989. The fifth principle of the *Vermillion Accord on Human Remains* calls on researchers to negotiate with local communities 'on the basis of mutual respect' for their legitimate concerns about the proper disposition of their ancestors' remains *and* 'the legitimate concerns of science and education'. Thirteen years later, Larry Zimmerman could wryly comment that 'What have mostly not changed since the *Vermillion Accord* are attitudes about the primacy of scientific approaches to the past, accompanied by some rearguard actions.' (Zimmerman 2002: 97) This is probably a more downbeat assessment of the progress in reaching agreements since 1989 than the situation actually merits. But in any case it would be unfair to criticize scientists for believing that their own approach to the past is better than the alternatives. Being scientists, there is no other approach that they could reasonably be expected to adopt. It is not only Indigenous cultures which deserve respect for sticking fast to their distinctive worldviews. The proper target of censure should be the reluctance by some members of the scientific community to concede the strength of the moral and practical arguments for compromise over the disposition of remains. This is the crucial obstacle to settlement, and one that, if it cannot be removed by peer pressure, may call for further legislative and legal action.

The manner of negotiation envisaged by the fifth Vermillion principle is serious, open-minded and open-ended discussion of the options, not posturing or banging the table. How effective such negotiation might prove to be in resolving the many particular disputes remains to be seen in the coming years. But what seems certain is that if it should fail to produce solutions that everyone can live with, then nothing else is more likely to succeed.

Notes

1. This is the title of an essay by Leroy Little Bear included in Battiste. (2000)
2. I am indebted to James Young for emphasizing this point, and for the example.
3. A similar puzzle about justice is raised by the intractable dispute over the fragments of the Parthenon frieze (the so-called 'Elgin marbles') held by the British Museum. Although the sculptures were initially taken by Lord Elgin in 1806 with the consent of the Turkish authority then in control of Athens and against a background of local indifference, modern Greek governments have protested their right to the works, but so far without success. One view, to which I am sympathetic, is that though justice does not *require* return in this case, it would still be more gracious to grant it than refuse.
4. For some critical commentary on the workings of such Boards, see Bendremer and Richman. (2006)
5. Ermine and Henderson credit Poole 1972 with introducing the notion of an ethical space. However, Poole originally used the term 'ethical space' as a label for a place of stand-off rather than negotiation, a barrier and not a meeting ground. It is the place where 'two sorts of space intersect' because two different and irreconcilable sets of intentions are confronting one another. (Poole 1972: 7) I follow Ermine and Henderson in construing the notion of ethical space in a more positive sense, as a place where parties to a dispute meet and try to resolve their difficulties or at least find some common ground.
6. It is sometimes remarked, especially by cultural anthropologists, that ethical outlooks are cultural constructions. This is true if it is taken to mean that ethics have their origin in particular cultural settings. In any society, people need to settle their values and a conception of the good, together with the ground-rules of communal life. But it is false if it is read as the relativistic claim (made

explicitly by, for example, Goldstein and Kintigh) that 'no particular system of ethics can be said to be absolutely right or wrong', and that there is no objective way of choosing between different systems since standards of ethical judgement are always internal to specific systems. (Goldstein and Kintigh 1990: 585–86) As Douglas Lackey has emphasized, the fact that there are different views about ethics no more establishes that there are 'many' ethics than the fact that there are different theories in science shows that there are 'many' sciences. (Lackey 2006: 149) Commenting on the disputes that have arisen in the USA in the wake of NAGPRA, Lackey rejects the familiar analysis that represents the conflict as a clash of different systems of ethics, relativistically conceived; the 'real conflict' is, rather, a 'tension between the various dimensions of human good: political, cognitive, aesthetic, material'. Ethics is not a party to this contest but its referee. (2006: 149) This account by Lackey of the structure of the debate seems to me exactly right.

References

Aristotle (1954). *Nicomachean Ethics*, tr. by Ross, Sir David (London: Oxford University Press).

Battiste, M. (ed.) (2000). *Reclaiming Indigenous Voice and Vision* (Vancouver: UBC Press).

Bendremer, J. C. and Richman, K. A. (2006). Human subjects review and archaeology: A view from Indian country. In Scarre, C. and Scarre, G. (eds.) The Ethics of Archaeology (Cambridge: Cambridge University Press), pp.97–114.

BM Newsroom (2004). Human Remains. http://www.thebritishmuseum.ac.uk/newsroom/current2005/humanremains.html.

Bray, T.L. and Killion, T.W. (eds.) (1994). *Reckoning with the Dead: The Larsen Bay Repatriation and the Smithsonian Institution* (Washington and London: The Smithsonian Institution).

DCMS [Department for Culture, Media and Sport] (2005). *Guidance for the Care of Human Remains in Museums*. http:www.culture.gov.uk/Reference_library/Publications/archive_2005/guidance_chr.htm.

DCMS (2003) *Working Group on Human Remains Report* [aka *The Palmer Report*]. http:www.culture.gov.uk/Reference_library/Publications/archive_2003/wgur_report2003.htm.

Goldstein, L. and Kintigh, K. (1990). Ethics and the reburial controversy. *American Antiquity*, **55**: 585–91.

Henderson, Sa'ke'j (2005). The appropriation of human remains, unpublished.

Kant, Immanuel (1991). *The Metaphysics of Morals*, tr. by Gregor, Mary (Cambridge: Cambridge University Press).

Lackey, D. P. (2006). Ethics and Native American reburials: a philosopher's view of two decades of NAGPRA. In: Scarre, C. and Scarre, G. (eds.) *The Ethics of Archaeology*. (Cambridge: Cambridge University Press), pp. 146–62.

Marcus, R. B. (1980). Moral dilemmas and consistency. *The Journal of Philosophy*, **77**: 121–36.

Payne, S. (2004). Handle with care: thoughts on the return of human bone collections. *Antiquity*, **78**: 419–20.

Poole, R. (1972). *Towards Deep Subjectivity* (London: Allen Lane: The Penguin Press).

Scarre, C. and Scarre, G. (eds.) (2006). *The Ethics of Archaeology* (Cambridge: Cambridge University Press).

Science Media Centre (2003). Collections of human remains 'lost to science forever'. http:www.sciencemediacentre.org/press_releases/03-11-07_remains.htm.

Smith, L. (2004). The repatriation of human remains – problem or opportunity? *Antiquity*, **78**: 404–13.

Vermillion Accord on Human Remains (1989). www.worldarchaeologicalcongress.org/site/about_ethi.php.

Walker, P. L. (2000). Bioarchaeological ethics: a historical perspective on the value of human remains. In: Katzenberg, M. A. and Saunders, S. R. (eds.) *Biological Anthropology of the Human Skeleton* (New York: Wiley-Liss), pp.3–39.

Zimmerman, Larry (2002). A decade after the Vermillion Accord. In: Forde, C., Hubert, J. and Turnbull, P. (eds.) *The Dead and their Possessions: Repatriation in Principle, Policy and Practice* (New York: Routledge), pp.91–98.

5

'The Skin Off Our Backs' Appropriation of Religion

Conrad G. Brunk and James O. Young

Introduction

The appropriation of religious beliefs and practices, with the possible exception of the appropriation of human remains, is the most contested form of
appropriation from Indigenous people. The book would be incomplete
without a chapter on the appropriation of religious beliefs. One can easily
confirm that passions run high when appropriation of religious beliefs is at
issue by a review of the literature on the subject. Christopher Ronwanièn:
te Jocks is typically passionate when he writes that when outsiders 'pretend
to use . . . ceremonies away from their proper setting, it really is like stealing
the "skin off our backs."' (Jocks 1996: 420) Another writer has compared
the appropriation of religious belief and ceremonies to sexualized violence:
both result in particularly horrific violation. (Smith 2005)

Any discussion of the ethics of the appropriation of religious belief must
be particularly sensitive to the experience of Indigenous people. There are
important reasons for this. One of the most obvious is that the colonization
of Indigenous peoples around the world, and certainly in North America,
has involved the massive appropriation of their land, art objects and ceremonial artifacts, and extinction or near extinction of their languages, practices, the flora and fauna of their habitats, and, not least, of their spiritual
beliefs and practices by the missionizing practices of the colonizing culture.
All of this continues to constitute a massive erosion of Indigenous cultural
identity, amounting to what could be termed near cultural extinction. The
self-identity of many Indigenous peoples hangs on the fragments of their
culture that survive this onslaught. Seen in this context, the appropriation
of one more remaining fragment—spiritual and religious practice and
ritual—has an impact that it would not have if the appropriation acted in

the reverse direction, from the dominant to the struggling, colonized culture. It is easy to see how this appropriation feels from the inside like the very 'skin off our backs'.

On the other side of the equation, however, is the commitment most people share, on all sides of these cultural and colonial divides, to the value of liberty of conscience and its corollary, freedom of religious belief and practice.

This chapter is an attempt to balance liberty of conscience with recognition of the potential harm and the undoubted profound offense that can result from the appropriation of the various aspects of religion. Our conclusion is that while liberty of conscience and freedom of religious practice are a fundamental right of persons in free society, nevertheless there are important moral obligations owed by those who appropriate the religious ideas and practices of others that may place limits on the exercise of these rights.

At the outset, we must be clear about the sort of appropriation under consideration in this chapter. We are concerned solely with appropriation that occurs when outsiders from one culture (often a settler culture) adopt religious beliefs, rituals or ceremonial practices from an Indigenous culture, often, but not always, over the protests of the insiders, in this case members of an Indigenous culture. (For the sake of economical expression, when we speak of the appropriation of religious belief, we also refer to the appropriation of ceremonial and spiritual practices. In this chapter, reference to religious beliefs includes reference to what are often called 'spiritual' beliefs).[1] We are not concerned here with the appropriation of tangible artifacts such as sacred regalia, ceremonial items and sacred sites (such as medicine wheels). We recognize that this sort of appropriation is widespread and poses serious ethical issues. These issues, however, are dealt with elsewhere in this volume. We simply wish to focus on adoption of religious beliefs and ceremonial practices. While the appropriation of the sacred regalia and other tangible property is often obviously unethical, the appropriation of religious beliefs and ceremonial practices raises a series of different and perhaps even more complex questions. The answers to these questions are not obvious and, because they are not obvious, they need to be addressed in this separate essay.

We must also make clear that we are concerned with an ethical question. We are not concerned with the question of whether people who appropriate the religious beliefs and practices of Indigenous peoples commit a social *faux pas* by appearing to be faddish, superficial or even silly. Perhaps the adoption of a mish-mash of half-understood beliefs, originating in a variety of unrelated cultures, is a sign of ignorance, confusion, intellectual hubris or foolish-ness. Sherman Alexie, the distinguished Spokane First Nation writer, seems more inclined to ridicule than to accuse morally those who appropriate Indigenous religious beliefs. (Alexie 1992) We are concerned only with the question of whether people who adopt the religious beliefs and practices of other people engage in some kind of wrong. People can have silly, half-digested and inconsistent beliefs without necessarily acting unethically.

The appropriation of religious beliefs from Indigenous cultures is wide-spread. Advocates of the 'deep ecology' movement or 'radical environmen-talism' have explicitly appropriated many Indigenous religious conceptions. Gary Snyder, author of the Pulitzer Prize-winning book *Turtle Island* (1974), is an example of such a deep ecologist.[2] Members of the so-called men's movement and other 'New Age' thinkers have also appropriated Indigenous religious beliefs. This process of appropriation can be traced back at least as far as *Iron John* (1990) by Robert Bly, the guru of the men's movement. Even before deep ecology and the men's movement, appropria-tion of religious beliefs was common. We have in mind Carlos Castaneda's *The Teachings of Don Juan: A Yaqui Way of Knowledge* (1968), a book that had, within a decade of its publication, sold four million copies. Castaneda purports to reveal the spiritual secrets of a Yaqui shaman from Mexico.[3] These authors and others have not simply adopted various religious or spiritual beliefs. Non-Indigenous people have also practiced what they regard as vision quests, Lakota sun dances, Navajo crystal and herbal healing techniques, medicine wheel ceremonies, sweat lodge ceremonies, and a variety of other ceremonies and spiritual practices appropriated from a variety of Indigenous cultures.

While the focus of this essay is on the appropriation of religious belief from North American First Nation cultures, such appropriation from the Indigenous cultures of Australasia has also proved controversial. An example of such appropriation is found in Marlo Morgan's *Mutant Message Down Under* (1994). This book purports to be the record of a journey through Australia in the course of which Aboriginal people shared sacred knowledge with the author. Many authorities are skeptical about whether Morgan actually undertook a journey anything like the one described in the book, but she certainly appropriated elements of Australian Aboriginal religious beliefs.

The appropriation of religious belief and practice has been widespread, and so too has the opposition to it among many Indigenous people. When, in 1993, the Dakota, Lakota and Nakota nations adopted a 'Declaration of

War Against Exploiters of Lakota Spirituality' their resolution acknowledged that 'there are certain ones among our own people who are prostituting our spiritual ways for their own selfish gain.' (Churchill 1994: 276) Sometimes this point is put in a more positive light. Vine Deloria, Jr., a prominent Hunkpapa Lakota activist and writer, has opposed appropriation of religious belief, and yet he has written a glowing introduction to *Black Elk Speaks*. This book is, in the words of its subtitle, 'The Life Story of a Holy Man of the Ogalala Sioux.' (Neihardt 1932) It reveals a great deal about Sioux spirituality and yet Deloria seems to recommend that everyone, including non-Indigenous people, adopt Black Elk's beliefs.

However, not all Aboriginal people object to religious appropriation by others, or at least to all forms of it. One investigator reports that some Indigenous people believe that others need to adopt the religious beliefs of Indigenous people 'if humans are to reharmonize life on earth.' (Taylor 1997: 187) To those trained in the Euroamerican intellectual tradition, this seems to be a reasonable stance to take with respect to one's deeply held beliefs. In this tradition it would, in fact, seem odd *not* to think that others should believe what one takes to be the truth. Still, as will be apparent from the Indigenous people quoted in this essay, objections to appropriation of religious beliefs are commonplace among members of Indigenous cultures.

What ethical issues are raised by this practice? On the face of it people would seem to have the right to adopt whatever beliefs make sense to them, regardless of their origin or who else holds them, and regardless of the unique cultural or other significance these beliefs may hold for others. And, if they have the right to adopt the beliefs, they would seem also to have the right to adopt ritual, ceremonial and other practices that express these beliefs and engage them in the world. Those who object to appropriation of religion and aim to persuade appropriators of its morally objectionable nature need to identify those aspects of the practice that constitute a harm or injustice sufficient to overcome this presumption in favour of freedom of religious belief. We turn now to a consideration of arguments that have been put forward to overcome this presumption.

Appropriation and the Distortion of Cultures

One common argument holds that outsiders who appropriate religious belief distort the beliefs they adopt. For example, M. Annette Jaimes has stated that, in appropriating a belief from Indigenous peoples, outsiders 'tend to deform it beyond all recognition.' (Quoted in Churchill 1994: 139) This is an entirely plausible claim. Euroamericans and others who have appropriated religious beliefs from North American First Nation cultures have certainly tended to conflate them with, and integrate them into, systems of belief from a variety of other religions and cultures that are inimical to the original system of belief from which they were taken. The conflation invariably leads to a misrepresentation of the spiritual beliefs of First Nation cultures, beliefs that are often quite distinct. The conflation does not end there. Ward Churchill describes the spiritual beliefs of Robert Bly as

> A strange brew consisting of roughly equal parts Arthurian, Norse, and Celtic legend, occasional adaptations of fairy tales by the brothers Grimm, a scattering of his own and assorted dead white males' verse and prose, a dash of environmentalism, and, for spice, bits and pieces of Judaic, Islamic, East Asian, and American Indian Spiritualism. (Churchill 1994: 209)

Writing in the same vein, Rayna Green notes that the ceremonies conducted by appropriators of Indigenous American spiritualism

> are often a hodge-podge of generic Plains ritual combined with holistic healing and 'human potential movement' language. (Green 1988: 45)

A particularly common view holds that First Nation spiritual beliefs are fundamentally continuous with Buddhism and other Eastern religions. While there may be similarities between certain beliefs of Indigenous North American and certain Eastern religions, amalgamation of the distinct traditions does not do justice to Indigenous spirituality. Indeed, it likely does lead to serious distortion of the nature of Indigenous spirituality in the minds of those who engage in this appropriation and also in the dominant cultural understanding of Indigenous culture.

The fact that outsiders distort the religious beliefs they appropriate provides the basis for one moral argument against such appropriation. A central premise in this argument is that the distortion of the religion and spirituality of Indigenous culture by the dominant culture constitutes *in itself* a direct harm to the former. To misrepresent and distort the character of other people, and especially of their cultural identity, with the consequence that this distortion becomes the widespread understanding in the dominant culture is, without doubt, a form of harm to people and to a culture.

In the dominant ethics of Euroamerican culture this recognized harm is seen as necessarily having to be balanced against the good, even the right, of freedom of belief and expression. Hence, liberal societies in the tradition of John Stuart Mill are loath to condemn or restrict forms of speech that are viewed as false, distorting or misrepresentative of others, unless this speech can be shown to intend harm or is motivated by malice or hatred. Libel and 'hate speech' laws, always controversial in liberal societies, are based upon this moral balancing.

The privileging of free speech and belief over the harm of misrepresentation, subject only to the limits of malicious intent and motivation is justified in the liberal Millian ethical framework because of its assumption that the moral relation is among 'free and equal' persons in society, each able to respond to the abuse by free speech of others with free speech of their own that counters the misrepresentation. This assumption, however, is seriously challenged in the argument of Indigenous peoples that the relationship between a colonized and nearly extinguished culture and a dominant, colonizing or settler culture is hardly between 'free and equal' parties. This argument surely is correct in most post-colonial societies. It provides reason, even within the ethics of the dominant liberal culture, to give weight to the claim by Indigenous peoples that the appropriation (and attendant distortion) of their spirituality constitutes a significant harm to the cultural identity of individuals and to the culture itself.

Another crucial (and related) premise in the distortion argument is that appropriation (and distortion) of religious beliefs actually *deprives* Indigenous people of an important part of their own culture. Appropriation deprives Indigenous people of their culture in so far as they are influenced to see their culture in the distorted way that outsiders see it. (This argument is essentially the same as one of the arguments against the appropriation of subject matters, discussed in the chapter in this book by Young and Haley.) Deloria has worried that outsiders will set themselves up as authorities on Indigenous religions and presume to correct Indigenous people about the nature of their religious beliefs. He adds that

> when a real Indian stands up and speaks the truth at any given moment, he or she is not only unlikely to be believed, but will probably be publicly contradicted and 'corrected' by the citation of some non-Indian and totally inaccurate 'expert' . . . Moreover young Indians in universities are now

being trained to view themselves and their cultures in the terms prescribed by such experts *rather than* in the traditional terms of the tribal elders. (Quoted in Churchill 1994: 219)

Here Deloria seems to have in mind academics who set themselves up as experts on Indigenous religious belief, but his argument could be adapted to apply just as well to anyone who adopts Indigenous religious beliefs and makes inaccurate public claims about them. These appropriators may have access to the media not available to Indigenous people. Their writings may have wide distribution, and be consumed by young Indigenous people, with the results that Deloria fears.

This objection must be taken seriously given the near unanimous view that a people's culture is essential to their well-being. Will Kymlicka maintains that membership in a culture is, in John Rawls' sense of the word, a primary good. (Kymlicka 1991: 167) Charles Taylor has adopted a similar position. He maintains that the preservation of a cultural identity is absolutely essential. Nothing, he writes, 'is more legitimate than one's aspiration that it never be lost.' (Taylor 1994: 40) Avishai Margalit and Moshe Halbertal hold that all people have a right to their culture. (Margalit and Halbertal 1994)

We agree fully with these affirmations of culture as a primary good. Two questions then need to be addressed. The first is whether, or under what conditions, appropriation of religious beliefs and practices in fact poses the threat to Indigenous cultures that Deloria and others believe it does. We also need to ask whether the fact that appropriation of religious belief can threaten the authentic identity of another culture might provide sufficient moral grounds for the limitation on the liberty of conscience of the appropriator. Or, perhaps the question could be posed another way. Perhaps it could be asked whether ethical restrictions on the exercise (say, the public expression or advocacy) of appropriated religious beliefs, ceremonies and rituals in order to respect the authenticity of the culture from which they are taken actually constitute an infringement of the right to liberty of conscience. Liberty of conscience, like all other rights, needs itself to be defined in terms of its impact upon other rights. In Justice Holmes' famous dictum in this regard, the right to freedom of speech does not include the right to shout 'fire' falsely in a crowded theatre. It's not that the right to free speech is legitimately limited in this case; instead, there is no right to speak in that way. If, for example, the right to freedom of belief implies the right to appropriate the beliefs held by others, it does not imply the right to *represent* the beliefs as authentically those of the appropriated culture, as we argue below.

Before we ask these questions, a preliminary question needs to be addressed. This is the question of who has the responsibility for preserving the integrity of Indigenous cultures. Arguably, members of Indigenous cultures themselves have primary responsibility for the preservation of their cultures. They ought, if they wish to see their cultures preserved, take all reasonable steps to ensure that their cultures are maintained. Even Deloria seems to grant as much. His entry in the *Encyclopedia of World Biography* states that he 'insists that young Native Americans receive traditional teachings before exposing themselves to the philosophies of the dominant Euro-American culture.' This seems exactly right. If Native Americans wish to preserve their culture and, in particular, their religious culture, then they have the primary responsibility to devote themselves to the study and teaching of their traditions. They are better equipped to recognize when outsiders have not fully understood or have distorted the beliefs and practices they have appropriated.

While those whose culture is threatened have this primary responsibility, this does not imply that outsiders to the culture bear no responsibility at all to refrain from representations of their appropriated beliefs that make the Native task difficult or impossible. This can be made impossible when members of a dominant outsider culture represent their appropriated beliefs and practices as authentically those of the appropriated culture. It is one thing to adopt a belief about the sacredness of the natural environment inspired by a particular Aboriginal world views, or to adopt a 'sweat lodge' practice as a spiritual ceremony. This in itself does not pose a threat of misrepresentation of the appropriated culture. However, when the belief or practice is publicly represented as 'Ogalala Sioux' or 'Haida', it may well pose this threat. Thus, in cases of severe inequalities between the appropriating and the appropriated cultures, the appropriators of the beliefs and practice of others have an obligation to refrain from the *representation* of these as the beliefs or practices of the culture of origin. We intentionally say 'representation' here instead of 'misrepresentation', because outside appropriators are not in a position to decide whether the beliefs they have appropriated are authentically preserved in their own cultural setting. That is a judgment the members of the originating culture are in the best position to make.

Understood this way, the deep-seated moral commitment to freedom of belief and conscience in liberal society is still respected. If outsiders truly believe certain beliefs (that originate in an Indigenous culture), they can hardly be thought to act wrongly in adopting the beliefs and engaging in corresponding practices. Indeed, such sincere adoption is a profound honoring of the culture insofar as it affirms its validity.

We are not arguing that the right to freedom of religious belief and conscience ends wherever any form of harm to others begins. The free expression of religious belief can, and often does, cause various forms of offense to others who hold other beliefs. For example, if a person comes to believe that her prior religious convictions are in error and publicly declares this to be the case, members of her former group may well be offended by her new view of the matter, and, if they have some economic or other interest in the prosperity of the group, they may well be materially harmed. This is one of the consequences of affirming liberty of conscience as a right. The idea of freedom of belief is premised upon a judgement that the typical offenses and harms caused by such freedom are vastly outweighed by the benefits of its exercise. Or, put conversely, the value lost by the suppression of free conscience is far greater than the values typically lost by its exercise. The offense caused by public expressions of disagreement is clearly of this typical kind of harm.

But, there are at least three reasons why this argument does not lead to the conclusion that freedom of belief justifies the unqualified appropriation of religious belief and practices. The first is simply the obvious but often neglected point that the assertion of a right to do X leaves open the question of whether it is a morally good thing to exercise the right, or to exercise it in any way one may choose. With respect to the appropriation of religious beliefs and practices, we agree that anyone has the right to adopt the beliefs or practices of others, but there certainly is no implied auxiliary right to represent those as authentically the beliefs and practices of others, and in many circumstances there are good moral reasons for not doing so. In addition, where the appropriated culture has an understanding that certain of its cultural creations, such as stories, songs, rituals or ceremonies, are a form of tribal, family or individual property, there may be a moral obligation to respect these claims.

The second reason for qualifying the right is that there are conditions under which the strongest arguments for an unqualified right to freedom of conscience simply do not obtain. Among these conditions are those to which we have already alluded—where there is not the equality of power and of equal access to the means of communication and persuasion that is assumed in the typical liberal arguments for the right. Under conditions in which a culture, already under serious threat of extinction from the pressures of the dominant culture in which it struggles to maintain itself, cannot reasonably protect itself from the distortion resulting from the appropriation of the culture by that dominant culture, the right to freedom of conscience runs up against another right—that of the right of persons to their cultural identity.

The third reason is that, while the right to freedom of belief comes as close as any putative moral right to being unqualified by other conflicting values, this is clearly not true of the right to religious *practice*. Modern legal jurisdictions such as those of many North American and European nations, which affirm a fundamental constitutional right to freedom of religion and conscience, have all had to place restrictions on actions done in the name of freedom of religion and conscience. In most of these legal jurisdictions, the right to free exercise of religion does not extend to the refusal to give vital blood transfusions to one's children, the practice of polygamy, refusal to be conscripted into a war considered on religious grounds to be unjust, or the proclamation of one's religious beliefs via loudspeaker in a park. The right of religious exercise gives way to the legitimate rights of others and to the fundamental responsibilities of citizenship.

The right to freedom of religious belief and practice, as fundamental as it is in a liberal society, clearly goes only so far in establishing a right to the appropriation of the religious beliefs of others. It would seem evident, then, that where a culture whose beliefs and practices have been appropriated is able to make a reasonable claim that the manner of that appropriation threatens the identity of that culture within the larger dominant culture, then the moral obligations of respect for cultural identity and integrity would take precedence over a simple declaration of the religious rights of the appropriators.

It can be argued that the views one holds are not completely voluntary. To hold certain beliefs is often to do so because one is compelled by the available evidence to hold those beliefs. This is particularly true with respect to religious beliefs. They are often accompanied by a 'Here I stand, I can do no other' sort of commitment. There is no reason to believe that individuals whose religious beliefs involve the appropriation of Indigenous beliefs are unlike others in this regard. This is another good reason for respecting fully the right of people to adopt beliefs and live in accord with them (consistent, of course, with the rights of others), regardless of the origin of these ideas. It is not often appropriate to blame people for adopting views they feel compelled to espouse, even less demand that they should abandon those views. But, we can ask them to take care in the public expression and representation of those views and the practices that may follow from them. Insensitivity in this regard *is* blameworthy. It is one thing to adopt the metaphysical, social or psychological assumptions involved in an Indigenous 'sweat lodge' ceremony, or even to engage in the activity itself. It is quite another to make the claim that one is practicing the religion of the group from which it has been appropriated—even calling the practice a 'sweat lodge'.

Appropriation as Theft

The appropriation of Indigenous religious beliefs and practices is commonly objected to on the ground that it is a kind of theft. We have already noted Jocks' view that appropriation of religious beliefs is a particularly brutal form of theft. Others adopt a similar view. Margo Thunderbird, a Shinnecock Nation activist, has stated that, after stealing the land from Indigenous peoples, settlers have

> . . . come for the very last of our possessions; now they want our pride, our history, our spiritual traditions. They want to rewrite and remake these things, to claim them for themselves. The lies and thefts just never end. (Quoted in Churchill 1994: 216)

Anecdotal evidence suggests that this view is quite widespread. If appropriation of religious beliefs and practices is theft, then it is wrong. It can be theft, however, only if religious beliefs can be property. But can religious beliefs, or any beliefs, be property? Is a belief the kind of thing over which a person or culture might claim the exclusive rights of control and disposition normally conferred by property rights?

One can easily understand why members of Indigenous cultures regard appropriation of their religious beliefs as a form of theft. Indigenous people often have religious or spiritual beliefs that are closely associated with their own kinship group. If their religious beliefs include belief in the existence of supernatural beings, these beings are often regarded as the ancestors of members of the Indigenous culture. The supernatural beings are no one else's ancestors. Often the ceremonies of a culture are associated with specific sites. Usually, Indigenous cultures have taken care to ensure that knowledge of its spiritual beliefs and practices are restricted to initiated members of a culture. In many cases, however, the secrets of a culture have been deliberately violated. For example, the Mennonite missionary H.R. Voth intruded on Hopi religious ceremonies, either by direct coercive threats or simply by taking advantage of the coercive power of the dominant culture. (Talayesva 1942: 252) On top of all this, as the above quotation from Margo Thunderbird indicates, Indigenous people often feel that their religious beliefs are all they have left after the depredations of settlers. The O'odham-Chicano activist Dennis Martinez echoes this sentiment. He notes that it often seems religion is 'the last thing [Indian] people have left that's theirs.' (Quoted in Taylor 1997: 1993)

All of this said, at least two reasons can be given for thinking that religious beliefs cannot be owned. The first reason is that, whether or not they are true, they are simply general knowledge claims about the world and such claims can be made by anyone, for whatever reason or from whatever source or authority. It is difficult to see what basis there could be for exclusive rights to such a claim.

Consider, for example, the religious belief, held by the Ganalbingu culture of Australia's Northern Territory, that Barnda, a long-neck tortoise, created the world. If we supposed the belief to be true, then it is just a fact about the world, similar to the fact, believed by many, that the universe originated with a Big Bang 12 billion years ago. If these are both facts, then they are, of course potentially knowable by anyone who has the appropriate epistemological tools, and they might be the object of (true) belief even on completely irrelevant grounds. Being knowable in these ways, coming to know (and thus believe in) them can hardly violate anyone else's exclusive right to them. So, no one owns knowledge of (or beliefs about) these facts. Some people might know either of the (supposed) facts, and try to keep them secret. But the desire to keep to oneself knowledge about a fact in the world—e.g., that there is a white sand beach in a quiet cove that no one else knows about—does not create ownership or entitlement of any kind in that knowledge. Someone else's discovery of that fact ends one's exclusive knowledge, but does not steal anything from her.

It might be objected at this point that this argument is simply imposing a Western conception of intellectual property on quite different Indigenous conceptions that do make sense out of the ownership of certain kinds of knowledge or belief. In Western theories of intellectual property, only specific expressions of an idea can be owned. General ideas cannot be owned and even copyright in specific expressions of an idea expires after a time. Conceptions of intellectual property vary from one Indigenous culture to another, but often Indigenous people believe that more can be owned than Western theories allow. Certain spiritual beliefs are regarded as the property of a specific culture or even as the property of a particular clan within the culture. Sometimes in Indigenous cultures spiritual knowledge is held to belong to the female members of a clan, while the male members own other spiritual knowledge. Usually, spiritual knowledge is thought to be owned in perpetuity. This 'ownership' of certain forms of knowledge includes the right to maintain it in secrecy—to be shared only with those whom the 'owner' chooses, sometime in accordance with well-defined rules.

We might conclude that we simply are up against an insurmountable cultural divide here—a hard choice between two competing ethical conceptions—with no shared philosophical criteria for deciding between them. But before conceding to the relativist case, it might be worthwhile to take a closer look at the matter. Things might not be as incommensurable as they seem at first blush. It is not so clear that the various Indigenous claims about the ownership of religious 'beliefs' are really very different from the claims of the Western tradition of intellectual property. The Western conception makes (at least) two very important exceptions to the general rule that knowledge itself cannot be the property of anyone. The first, as we have seen, is that specific *expressions* of ideas and knowledge can be owned, at least for periods of time, and this is the whole point of copyright. The second is that *applications* of knowledge to the world, including techniques for obtaining knowledge, can be claimed as intellectual property and protected under patent law.

Both these exceptions are premised upon a distinction between pure knowledge of a truth about the world that is discernible by anyone seeking to understand the world and hence available to anyone, and a specific articulation or application of the ideas by an individual or group. In the first case, the truth is thought to exist in itself, apart from anyone's understanding of it, whereas in the second case, the specific form of articulation or application of the truth is the product, in part, of the creative activity of the individual. It is a kind of 'added value'. Certain Indigenous cultures may not share some of the epistemological assumptions inherent in this Western view (e.g., the objectivity of 'truth'), but, nevertheless, most, if not all, of the typical claims made by these cultures about the rights of property they claim for aspects of their Native religion would be defensible in the very terms laid out in the Western view.

Religious beliefs, and certainly the religious beliefs of many traditional cultures, are rarely viewed simply as abstract beliefs about what is 'true' about the world. Without doubt, religious beliefs and practices make certain assumptions about the nature of the world, but these cognitive beliefs are not the dominant aspect of religion. Western religion, and particularly Christianity, does tend to put dogma (true belief) at the center of religious sensibility, but most other religions place much greater emphasis upon praxis (action) than upon dogma. When Indigenous people claim rights to protect aspects of their spirituality, it is not primarily the cognitive beliefs about the world underlying their religion to which they are laying claims. Traditional religion is embodied in stories, rituals and practices, all of which can be understood as ways of understanding the world, and more importantly, ways of understanding how to *be* and *act* in the world. And these understandings, these practices and disciplines, are clearly the creations ('added value', to use the crassly utilitarian Western concept) of the culture. There is no essential difference between the claims of these cultures (or clans or families within them) to their spiritual myths and stories (which are their *way* of expressing truths about the world) than the claims of Western scholars to copyright of their ways of expressing an idea.

Certainly, when it comes to the issue of rituals and practices the case for Indigenous religion is even stronger in terms of the Western intellectual property conventions. Here the claim clearly is not to property rights in ideas or beliefs about the world, but to what is more closely analogous to the *applications* of knowledge claimed under patent law in the Western intellectual property regime. In many traditional cultures, rituals and practices play roles analogous to that of *technologies* in modern cultures in the sense that they are ways of manipulating the world, which includes, of course, the metaphysical or spirit world. It is not assumed that the ritual or practice should be universally adopted (in the way Western religions and philosophies tend to think). In fact the opposite is assumed—that it is the reserved possession of the family, clan, tribe or culture. Why shouldn't this be viewed as analogous to the Western *patent* right?

Clearly, neither the Western copyright nor the patent is conceived within that conceptual framework as a limitation, to say nothing of a *violation*, of the rights to freedom of conscience or belief. Neither prevents or limits anyone's right to believe whatever one chooses. Copyright and patent laws, however, do not prevent others from quoting copyrighted material or using patented processes as long as proper acknowledgement or compensation is given. In this sense the Western intellectual property regime does not seem as restrictive as certain Indigenous claims to property rights in religious expressions. Even so, this difference is simply a difference of opinion about the conditions under which a right of intellectual property can be relinquished ('alienated'), not about whether there are such rights and whether they restrict freedom of belief and conscience.

So, it appears that the Indigenous objection to certain forms of religious appropriation as 'theft' is entirely intelligible, even within the terms of Western conceptions of intellectual property. Under what conditions would the claim of 'theft' have the most merit? We are brought back to the same kinds of appropriation of religion that seemed to us ethically unjustified in the previous section of this chapter—namely those that take on the religious beliefs and practices *in the same or similar form* they take within their original cultural settings, failing to respect the culture's own sensitivities and rules about how these beliefs are expressed and practiced.

For example, a story that may be told only by a shaman or spiritual healer within a tribe or clan in order to teach or illustrate a religious or spiritual belief should be respected as a creative expression of that culture to which those authorized within the culture have certain entitlements. Those entitlements include the conditions, if any, under which the story can be told or the ritual or practice engaged in, and by whom. Respecting those entitlements is a moral obligation of anyone within the culture or outside it, on essentially the same grounds that respect for copyright, or the avoidance of plagiarism, is a moral obligation within the cultural conventions of Western society. Just as plagiarism is a form of theft in Western culture, so the appropriation of religious stories and practices is theft. Respecting this right does not inhibit anyone from adopting the underlying belief about the world or the moral teaching, and thus does not in any way restrict any rights to freedom of belief of others, whether inside or outside the originating culture. Those who wish to adopt the belief may do so without appropriating the particular cultural expressions of those beliefs—and if they respect the culture, they will respect its norms of exclusive use.

A similar analogy to Western intellectual property conventions can be made about the appropriation of religious rituals and practices, such as sweet grass ceremonies or sweat lodges. As we have argued, such things are effective strategies of interaction with the physical, psychological and spiritual worlds. They too are the creative 'techniques' (in the broad sense of this term) of a culture, to which they may reasonably claim rights of exclusive use, just as a patent achieves in Western intellectual property law. No controversial norms about the obligations to respect other cultural practice even if they contradict one's own are required here. There are shared values between Indigenous and Western culture on these issues, and these support the conclusion that there is a moral obligation to refrain from the appropriation of rituals and practices if they are claimed as the exclusive right of another culture. Of course, like most moral norms, this one needs to be carefully nuanced. The extent to which others can engage in what looks like a ritual or practice claimed by another culture will depend upon the expectations of that culture. The more the ritual is *represented* as the practice of another culture, the more problematic it is likely to be. And the more it will be appropriately characterized as 'theft'.

Of course it must be recognized that cultures have been interacting for a very long time. As a result of this interaction, the expressions of belief, and even practices, of one culture can often have a great deal in common with the beliefs of other cultures. A culture may claim ownership of certain religious expressions when these are quite similar to those of other cultures, which also claims ownership. The interaction between cultures makes it impossible to say a single culture is the sole repository of certain beliefs, expressions or practices. In such circumstances, it becomes increasingly ambiguous who has the moral entitlement to these things, and attempts to give control over certain ones to one culture would constitute an unfairness to others' cultures.

The line of argument just advanced does not address one of the additional ways in which Indigenous people appropriately feel robbed by the appropriation of their religion. Many outsiders set themselves up as authorities on the religious beliefs and practices of Indigenous people. These outsiders then charge substantial sums of money to instruct others in these religious beliefs or to have them participate in vision quests or sweat lodge ceremonies. The commercial exploitation of Indigenous religious beliefs adds an additional insult to the appropriation. We will return to a discussion of this matter in a subsequent section.

Offensive Appropriation of Religion

Perhaps at the root of Indigenous objections to the appropriation of religion is the sense of a profound offense. Here the phrase 'profound offense' is used in the sense laid out by philosopher Joel Feinberg in his landmark book. (Feinberg 1985) When outsiders adopt their spiritual expressions or mimic their religious ceremonies, many Indigenous people feel violated or experience a kind of revulsion. One could argue that this reaction to the appropriation of religion provides the basis for an argument against this practice. There is a *prima facie* argument against causing people to feel violation or revulsion. Nevertheless, we take it that freedom of belief is not undermined by this argument.

Certainly sometimes the very offensiveness of an act is the basis for an argument against the act. Consider, for example, the infamous application of the American Nazi Party for a permit to march through Skokie, Illinois, a neighborhood with a large Jewish population. Even if the Nazis may have a moral (as well as legal) right to hold such a march, they act wrongly in doing so. Holding the march is wrong simply because it is so offensive to so many people. Moreover, it is intended to be offensive and has no counter-balancing social value. It is easy to imagine acts that would be similarly wrong simply because they were so offensive to Indigenous people. A march celebrating Columbus Day, that wends past an impoverished Indian reserve, would be an example of such an unjustified offense.

For reasons we have put forward earlier in this chapter, the appropriation of abstract religious beliefs or ideas (or better, the espousal of identical ideas, which ought not to be called 'appropriation' at all) is never wrong for this reason. One cannot be expected to tailor one's views according to whether or not other people find the views offensive. Consider, for example, atheists living in a deeply conservative theistic religious community, say, certain areas of Iran or the American south. Most members of these communities will find the atheists' views deeply offensive, but this is no reason at all for the atheists not to maintain their views on religion. This is a simple corollary of the principle of the absolute liberty of conscience. The same point applies to individuals who, exercising their liberty of conscience, adopt religious beliefs shared by some Indigenous people. They do not act wrongly, even if some Indigenous people are offended by such adoption.

But it is not adoption of an abstract idea, or even the appropriation of it from an Indigenous people, that is generally objected to as 'offensive'. It is the *representation* of the idea—in its public expression and practice—that in nearly every case is the occasion for offense. It can be offensive because it misrepresents the culture, which is not morally acceptable for reasons we put forward earlier. It can be offensive simply and only because it is being publicly expressed as authentically Indigenous, when the person expressing it is not a member of the culture. The objection here is that the religious expression has been torn from its appropriate cultural context, and this in itself distorts it and makes it inauthentic. It is the inauthenticity of the expression that causes the offense. It is probably similar to what many devout Roman Catholics would feel if the traditional Catholic mass were celebrated *as an authentic sacrament* by a group of people who held what Catholics would consider heretical or anti-Catholic views on other religious matters. The 'heretical' group owes a duty of respect to Roman Catholics not to practice and represent their ritual as an authentic Catholic ritual.

Not every offense is a form of harm that anyone else has a duty to avoid. It is impossible to avoid offending everyone and people can be offended by anything. There is reasonable offense and unreasonable offense. Offense at the mere adoption of one's beliefs by another is, in our view, an unreasonable response in any society that values freedom of thought, as both Western liberal societies and most modern Indigenous cultures do. But offense at the inauthentic, commercialized or distorted representation or practice of one's religion is not always unreasonable, and where it is not, there is a moral wrong involved.

Summary

We have argued in this chapter that, while the mere adoption of religious (or any other) beliefs that may have originated in one culture by members of another does not in itself constitute an unethical appropriation, there are many ways in which religion can be, and often is, unethically appropriated. There are ways in which such appropriation can constitute morally unacceptable harm and disrespect for cultural rights of property and identity. And, we have argued that respect for such ethical considerations does not constitute an unwarranted restriction upon the generally held right of freedom of religious belief or conscience.

We argued that, even when viewed from the perspective of the classical Western liberal tradition in moral theory, as articulated in the case of rights of liberty in the philosophy of John Stuart Mill, the objections often raised to the appropriation of religion are well founded. The three objections we considered are that it threatens cultural identity through distortion and misrepresentation, that it constitutes a form of cultural theft and that it constitutes a form of unacceptable offense. We attempted to show that, to the extent that these objections are not simply to the adoption of abstract ideas or beliefs by others, but to the public expression of beliefs and the engagement of rituals, ceremonies and practices in certain ways, they carry great moral weight, and they impose upon outsiders significant obligations of respect.

Outsiders ought not to misrepresent their knowledge of the Indigenous religious beliefs they appropriate and they ought not to misrepresent the nature of their beliefs. Outsiders will generally not be experts on the religious beliefs of Indigenous peoples and they ought not to represent themselves as such. To do so is dishonest at worst and arrogant at best. Outsiders should not presume that they know more about Indigenous religious beliefs than those who have had the benefits of being educated in the context of a culture and who have made a careful study of its religious beliefs. If they are appropriately humble, they will not be tempted to correct statements about the beliefs of an Indigenous culture made by someone educated within the culture.

When we say that outsiders ought not to misrepresent the nature of their beliefs we mean, in part, that they ought to be clear that they are not people who have been raised in the Indigenous culture from which they appropriate. In most contexts they should not say that they subscribe, for example, to 'the Lakota belief about p' or 'the Navajo belief about q'. It would be more accurate and honest to say that they believe 'the Lakota-inspired belief about p' or 'the Navajo-inspired belief about q'. Perhaps even better, they should simply maintain that they believe p or q and not make any reference to the cultural origins of their beliefs. (In some contexts, failing to acknowledge the origin of one's beliefs may seem like plagiarism and may cause avoidable offense to Indigenous people.) By taking care in describing one's beliefs and practices and their origins, appropriators of religious belief can avoid misrepresenting (in a potentially harmful and probably offensive manner) what members of Indigenous cultures actually believe.

Individuals who appropriate religious beliefs ought to be suitably deferential towards the culture from which they appropriate. Outsiders owe to the other culture every reasonable effort to understand precisely what the culture believes. By taking care in this way, outsiders minimize the chance that they will offend insiders by distorting their views. When outsiders attribute certain religious beliefs to the members of a culture, they ought to take reasonable steps towards ensuring that the views that they attribute are actually held within the culture. This is a fundamental tenet of respect. This said, if people wish to appropriate part of a culture's religious beliefs, combine this part with other religious traditions or make any other changes, liberty of conscience leaves them free to do so, as long as they do not claim to be engaged in the authentic practice of the Indigenous religion, and as long as they have respected the rightful claims of ownership of expressions and practices in the ways we have defended above.

It is important to recognize that there are illegitimate ways for outsiders to derive commercial benefits from the appropriation of the religious beliefs of Indigenous people. It is dishonest and offensive for, say, a non-Lakota person to advertise that he offers instruction in the 'Lakota sweat lodge ceremony'. To profit monetarily from offering instruction under such a rubric compounds the offense that is offered to Indigenous people. Only Lakota (and perhaps those they have authorized) can offer instruction in *Lakota* religious beliefs and practices. Native artists are protected by a variety of pieces of legislation. The US has the *Indian Arts and Crafts Act* of 1990, which made it illegal to market any artwork or craft as Indian unless it was produced by a member of an Indian group recognized by the US government. Similarly, the (Australian) National Indigenous Arts Advocacy Association has taken steps to protect Indigenous artists from fraud. Artists who demonstrate that they are of Aboriginal or Torres Strait Islander origin are entitled to mark their works with a label of authenticity and others may not. Crafting legislation that protects Indigenous religious beliefs as legislation can protect Indigenous artists would prove difficult, if not impossible. Still, from a moral point of view, it is clear that outsiders ought not to profit by representing their teachings as conveying the religious beliefs and practices of a culture to which they do not belong. Of course, there is nothing wrong, other things being equal, with offering something described as, say, 'New Age vision quests'.

All this may seem to leave those who appropriate religious beliefs without many responsibilities. We believe, however, that those who have benefited from the appropriation of Indigenous people's lands have important obligations to Indigenous people. Of course they have the obligation to offer fair restitution or restoration of land, but there are more specific obligations. In particular, there may be obligations to assist Indigenous people in the preservation of their cultures. After all, the invasion of Indigenous people's lands has placed their cultures under duress. An obligation to assist, where possible and desired by Indigenous people, in the preservation of cultures will include an obligation to assist in the preservation of a culture's religious beliefs and practices. There are many obligations of restitution and restoration that the benefactors of colonizing ancestors owe to the colonized peoples in their societies. The obligations of respect for religious belief and practice are only reinforced by these larger obligations.

Notes

1. The term 'spiritual' has come to be used widely to refer to metaphysical beliefs or personal practices and disciplines that are not part of any traditional institutionalized religion, theology or ideology. So-called 'New Age' spirituality is an example.
2. For a discussion of the appropriation of religious beliefs by radical environmentalists, see Taylor (1997).
3. For a skeptical discussion of Castaneda's writings see Churchill (1998: 27–65).

References

Alexie, Sherman (1992). 'White-Men Can't Drum.' *New York Times Magazine*, 4 October 1992, 30–1.

Bly, Robert (1990). *Iron John: A Book About Men*. Reading, Mass, Addison-Wesley.

Castaneda, Carlos (1968). *The Teachings of Don Juan: A Yaqui Way of Knowledge*. Los Angeles, University of California Press.

Churchill, Ward (1994). *Indians Are Us? Culture and Genocide in Native America*. Toronto, Between the Lines.

Churchill, Ward (1998). *Fantasies of the Master Race: Literature, Cinema and the Colonization of American Indians*. San Francisco, City Lights Books.

Feinberg, Joel (1985). *The Moral Limits of the Criminal Law*, Vol. 2, *Offense to Others*. New York and Oxford, Oxford University Press.

Green, Rayna (1988). The Tribe Called Wannabee: Playing Indian in America and Europe. *Folklore*, **99**, 30–55.

Jocks, Christopher Ronwanièn:te (1996). Spirituality for Sale: Sacred Knowledge in the Consumer Age. *American Indian Quarterly*, **20**, 415–31.

Kymlicka, Will (1991). *Liberalism, Community, and Culture*. Oxford, Oxford University Press.

Margalit, Avishai and Moshe Halbertal (1994). Liberalism and the Right to Culture. *Social Research* **61**, 491–510.

Mill, John Stuart (1859). On Liberty. In: *Three Essays*. Oxford, Oxford University Press, 1975.

Morgan, Marlo (1994). *Mutant Message Down Under.* New York, Harper-Collins.

Neihardt, John G. (Flaming Rainbow) (1932). *Black Elk Speaks.* Lincoln, University of Nebraska Press, 1979.

Smith, Andrea (2005). Spiritual Appropriation as Sexual Violence. *Wicazo Sa Review,* **20**, 97–111.

Snyder, Gary (1974). *Turtle Island.* New York: New Directions.

Talayesva, Don C. (1942). *Sun Chief: The Autobiography of a Hopi Indian.* New Haven, Yale University Press.

Taylor, Bron (1997). Earthen Spirituality or Cultural Genocide?: Radical Environmentalism's Appropriation of Native American Spirituality. *Religion,* **27**, 183–215.

Taylor, Charles (1994). *Multiculturalism: Examining the Politics of Recognition.* Princeton, Princeton University Press.

6

Genetic Research and Culture: Where Does the Offense Lie?

Daryl Pullman and Laura Arbour

Introduction

In 1984 a government census team from Papua New Guinea (PNG) visited the remote Hagahai tribe for the first time. (ETC Group 1996; Bhat 1996) The team was accompanied by representatives from the PNG Institute of Medical Research, including Carol Jenkins, an American medical anthropologist. The visitors were alarmed by the low birth rate and high disease mortality observed in this isolated group of some 260 inhabitants. Jenkins subsequently received funding from the US National Geographic Society to conduct research on the Hagahai. (Jenkins 1987) Her initial research project, titled 'Cultural History and Adaptation of the Hagahai of the Western Schrader Mountains, Papua New Guinea', was submitted to the PNG's Medical Research Advisory Committee, which provided ethics clearance. In an interview with the *Los Angeles Times* in 1987 she stated that her intention was 'to monitor and promote improvement in [the Hagahai's] health status [and] ... aid their adaptation to the inevitable modernization of their biology and culture.' (*Los Angeles Times* 1987)

Over the next several years the PNG Institute of Medical Research collected biological samples from members of the Hagahai and sent some to Australia for testing. However, the samples that were to gain international notoriety were collected from twenty-four Hagahai men and women in May 1989. Previous testing had confirmed that all twenty-four were infected with the HTLV-1 retrovirus, of potential value in the development of diagnostic tests and vaccinations for leukemia-related diseases. These samples made their way eventually to the laboratories of the US National Institutes of Health (NIH) in Washington DC, where scientists confirmed that the retrovirus carried by the Hagahai was unique.

In April 1990 the NIH filed a patent application for a cell line derived from one of the Hagahai donors, a healthy twenty-year-old male. That cell line became US Patent No. 5,397,696, which was granted in March of 1995. According to RAFI (Rural Advancement Foundation International), a Canadian-based activist group concerned about technological development in the developing world, at no time had the Hagahai or the government of Papua New Guinea been consulted about whether they approved of Hagahai cells becoming US government property. Furthermore, beyond the letter of ethics clearance provided to Carol Jenkins for her initial 1985 anthropological study, RAFI claims the NIH has no record on file of any additional ethics approval for subsequent medical research on the Hagahai. (ETC Group 1996) A RAFI press release issued subsequent to the granting of the patent stated in part: 'the United States Government has issued itself a patent on a foreign citizen. On March 14, 1995 an Indigenous man of the Hagahai people . . . ceased to own his genetic material.' (Taubes 1995).

Carol Jenkins, one of the 'inventors' listed on the US patent application, disputes RAFI's account of these events. (Taubes 1995). She claims to have discussed the idea of the patent with the Hagahai and proceeded only with their approval. According to Jenkins, the Hagahai have a solid understanding of the concept of ownership, and were willing to proceed with the understanding that the tribe would receive any royalties that might accrue to the researchers should a marketable product result from research on this cell line. Others rallied to the defense of Jenkins and the NIH. In an interview with the journal *Science*, law professor Henry Greely, a leading expert in intellectual property law and chair of an ethics subcommittee for the Human Genome Diversity Project, maintained that any claim that this patent gave the US government ownership over this Hagahai person or his genetic material is 'absolute rubbish'. According to Greely the patent covers only a viral preparation derived from the cell line and three different bioassays to determine whether or not people are infected by the virus. (Taubes 1995) Nevertheless, despite the lack of agreement among various parties about the sequence of events that led to US Patent No. 5,397,696, and ongoing confusion among the legally uninformed about what exactly is covered by such a patent, significant pressure from the international community eventually forced the US government to drop its claim to the Hagahai cell line. (Shaw 2003)

The Hagahai example is but one in a series of controversial cases involving human genetic research that transpired throughout the 1990s. Many of the most troubling cases involved genetic materials taken from Indigenous populations from remote locations like the Solomon Islands, Panama and Tristan da Cunha, several of which also resulted in the withdrawal of patent applications in the face of substantial international pressure. (Rifkin 1998) Like the case of the Hagahai these others bear all the hallmarks of what has come to be called 'biocolonialism' or 'biopiracy', in which members of a dominant outside culture visit an Indigenous group for the purpose of expropriating genetic materials. Concern about cases such as these was part of the impetus for the *Universal Declaration on the Human Genome and Human Rights* developed by the United Nations Educational, Scientific and Cultural Organization (UNESCO). Article 4 of the declaration states, 'The human genome in its natural state shall not give rise to financial gains.' (UNESCO 1997) A subsequent recommendation by UNESCO's International Bioethics Committee states in part, '. . . there are strong ethical grounds for excluding the human genome from patentability.' (UNESCO 2001) Such declarations have done little, however, to deter the drive for patents on human genetic materials. A recent study found that 20 percent of the estimated 24,000 to 30,000 genes in the human genome have been patented in the US, with the majority being held by private companies and universities. One California-based pharmaceutical company alone holds patents on some 2000 human genes. (Lovgren 2005)

It is clear that the practice of issuing patents on human genetic materials gives rise to a variety of ethical, legal and social concerns. Some of these, such as the need for prior ethics review and approval of research protocols that lead to the collection of biological samples in the first place, and the need for free and informed consent of research subjects who donate their genetic materials, are not unique to human genetic research. Others, however, are more narrowly focused on genetic research. What are the nature and extent of intellectual property rights over living organisms? Who has the right to consent or to refuse consent on behalf of a community when the research involves extraction of human DNA? Is there a need to engage in some form of benefit-sharing with those who provide biological samples? These and related issues have generated a large and expanding literature in recent years, particularly as they pertain to research on Indigenous peoples.

The remainder of this essay will focus more narrowly on what it might mean to claim that human genetic material is in some sense 'cultural property'. Should we interpret the activities of cultural outsiders like Carol

Jenkins and researchers from the NIH, who collect genetic samples from discreet populations for the purpose of exploiting the information contained therein, as 'cultural appropriation of human genetic information'? If not, what might constitute 'cultural appropriation' in the context of genetic research? In what follows we consider the ethical and legal status of human DNA, and examine whether there are circumstances in which it is meaningful to treat it as the cultural property of an identifiable group. Our general conclusion is that although 'cultural appropriation' of genetic information may be a risk in certain circumstances, most cases discussed widely in the literature raise different kinds of concerns. Hence an over-emphasis on the notion of cultural appropriation may do more to obfuscate than illuminate the various ethical, legal and social issues involved in the debate about human genetic research on Indigenous populations in general, and on the granting of patents on human genetic materials in particular.

Setting aside the issue of patents on human genetic materials for a moment, it is clear that genetic research has the potential to alter the manner in which various cultural groups understand their heritage, and can affect how they think about themselves as distinct groups. Concerns about such matters have played a role in the backlash against the Human Genome Diversity Project (HGDP), and they continue to bedevil the more recent Genographic Project (GP) sponsored by National Geographic. Both the HGDP and the GP aim to use genetic information to trace migration patterns of distinct populations. Subsequent findings of these projects could lead to a conflation of biology and culture (Juengst 1998), might undermine cultural narratives about a people's origins that have been held for generations or centuries and could alter perceptions of who's in and who's out of particular cultural groups. (Elliott and Brodwin 2002) In these latter cases, however, the effects of genetic research might be equally considered the 'genetic appropriation of culture', as well as the 'cultural appropriation of genetic information'. Insofar as the outcomes of such 'genetic appropriation' could undermine or otherwise alter a community's or group's understanding of themselves as a people, the research could cause 'cultural offense'. Here we argue it is important to distinguish between 'cultural property' and 'traditional knowledge' in the narrow sense in which those notions function in discussions of intellectual property law and more general discussions of cultural appropriation, and 'knowledge of a tradition' and 'cultural identity'. The latter are somewhat more amorphous notions but they nevertheless capture some of the broader concerns raised by Indigenous peoples intent on preserving their cultural narratives, and who may be offended by certain types of genetic research or by the treatment of their genetic materials. This latter knowledge is experiential in nature and includes the lived experience of those who share a particular cultural history and tradition. Hence, 'cultural appropriation' is generally associated with some notion of property, is descriptive, and may not imply wrongdoing. 'Cultural offense', on the other hand, is better thought of in terms of the law of persons and associated notions of group or communal identity, and more clearly identifies that such action can be 'culturally offensive', at least to some. While these latter cases may not have the same legal traction as do cases in which identifiable cultural objects are absconded, they nevertheless raise significant and enduring moral concerns.

Human DNA as Cultural Property

International conventions aimed at the protection of cultural property predate the advent of the genetic age in medicine and associated debates regarding the status of human DNA. Thus neither the *Convention for the Protection of Cultural Property in the Event of Armed Conflict* (1954), nor the UNESCO *Convention on the Means of Prohibiting and Preventing the Illicit Import, Export and Transfer of Ownership of Cultural Property* (UNESCO 1970) include human genetic material under their respective definitions of cultural property. This is not to say that human genetic material or the information derived from it cannot or should not be considered cultural property in some instances, but establishing its status will require reference to policy decisions and case law from other contexts.

In order to appreciate the broader context in which the controversy regarding the Hagahai and other cases involving patents on human genetic materials transpired, we must go back to 1980 and the landmark US patent case of *Diamond v. Chakrabarty.* (1980) In that year the US Supreme Court upheld an earlier ruling by the Court of Customs and Patent Appeals which allowed that living things are in fact patentable. The case in question concerned an application by Ananda M. Chakrabarty, an engineer with General Electric, to file a patent on a single strain of *Pseudomonas bacterium* that was effective in breaking down oil slicks. Chakrabarty had filed his patent application initially in 1972, but it was denied at that time on the grounds that products of nature or live organisms cannot be patented. However, Chakrabarty did his original work before recombinant DNA splicing methods had been developed, relying upon more traditional methods to coax the bacterium to accept plasmids (rings of DNA) from other strains with the desired properties. By the time his appeal was heard in 1980 the splicing of DNA from one organism to another was commonplace, and patents had already been issued on technologies for the manipulation of DNA. As one commentator describes it, 'technological boosterism was in the air.' (Stix 2006) In this context the Supreme Court decided that Chakrabarty's bacterium was indeed 'an artificially made composition of matter', and in a narrow 5 to 4 decision it ruled that his patent application should stand.

The Chakrabarty ruling opened the floodgates for patents on all manner of living organisms, from bacteria to genetically modified plants and animals, to human genes and gene fragments. A quarter of a century and literally tens of thousands of patents later, however, the debates continue with regard to whether or not such patents admit of any moral justification in the first place, even as the legal wrangling over the extent of the intellectual property rights covered thereby continues to enrich patent lawyers. Indeed, so numerous are patents on various biological materials that the very process developed to ensure innovation in biotechnological development now threatens to hamstring it. As a recent report from the US National Research Council (2006) notes: '. . . confusion and delays may ensue when the intellectual property rights necessary to arrive at a commercial end product are held by patentees too numerous or heterogeneous to agree on licensing terms . . .'

It is not our intent to canvass the broad and diverse range of issues and accompanying arguments pertaining to intellectual property and gene patents here. Suffice it to say that although still controversial, patents on biological life forms in general, and human genetic materials in particular, are the reality of international trade law. (Resnik 2004) While the United States Patent and Trademark Office continues to offer refinements to the patent process to ensure that patent examiners have clearer criteria by which to guide their judgments about what can and cannot be patented, and to curtail the practice of bioprospecting in which patents are sought over gene sequences for which no utility is currently known, there is nothing to suggest that the patent regime will be replaced. The United States has negotiated bilateral agreements with a number of countries in order to secure stronger intellectual property protection, granting favored-trading status only to nations that meet rigid intellectual property right protections. (Jong and Cypess 1998)

Those bodies most concerned about maintaining biological diversity and the cultural integrity of Indigenous communities seem now to accept this reality. Although the 1997 *Universal Declaration on the Human Genome and Human Rights* and subsequent statements of UNESCO's International Bioethics Committee speak against patents on human genetic materials and commercialization, the subsequent *International Declaration on Human Genetic Data* (UNESCO 2003) is silent on this matter. While the latter document acknowledges that human genetic information 'may have cultural significance for persons or groups', the emphasis has shifted to the need to share genetic information and to ensure fair compensation and benefit sharing with those who provide genetic materials. (National Research Council 2006)

Although the United States Patent and Trademark Office does not discriminate between human and non-human biological materials in the review and granting of patents, various international bodies concerned with the protection of biodiversity and benefit sharing continue to do so. While the reasons for this are never stated explicitly, the implicit assumption is that human genetic material is distinct and unique, and ought to be managed differently. Inasmuch as the question of the unique nature of human DNA has some bearing on its status as cultural property and on whether it can be the object of cultural appropriation, it is worth dwelling for a moment on the different manner in which human and non-human DNA are treated in various international agreements.

The United Nations Environmental Programme's *Convention on Biological Diversity* (CBD) is the key international instrument for conserving and utilizing global biological diversity. The CBD became a legally binding document in 1993. Although it is stated that the CBD represents 'the international community's effort to define principles for the use of genetic resources from all sources, including plants, animals, fungi and microorganisms' (United Nations Environmental Program 2002), subsequent references state that the scope does not include human genetic resources. Again, no direct explanation is provided as to why human DNA is excluded from the scope of the CBD; however, the implicit rationale can be drawn from the underlying principle invoked to establish the legal status afforded non-human DNA.

The rationale in question is found in the discussion of the historical and structural context for the CBD's provisions on genetic resources. There it is noted that prior to the negotiation of the CBD most discussions of genetic resources focused narrowly on plants used in agriculture. Early attempts to negotiate international agreements with regard to plant genetic resources 'reflected the then widely accepted understanding that plant genetic resources were "a heritage of mankind [*sic*] and consequently should be available without restriction."' At the time the CBD was negotiated, however, it was felt that the common heritage doctrine failed to provide a mechanism to ensure that countries and farming communities that provided genetic resources for the development of 'elite' varieties of plants and animals would be able to share in the benefits derived from their use. Like the air we breathe, if plants and animals are the common heritage of humanity it is difficult for any individual or group to assert a claim that a particular type of plant or animal represents their intellectual or cultural property. Thus the CBD 'represents the international community's effort to redefine the principles governing access and benefit-sharing, starting from the principle that parties have sovereign rights over their genetic resources, rather than from the "common heritage" principle.' Insofar as one can claim a sovereign right over an entity, one can negotiate fair compensation from those who want access to it.

While the principle of a 'sovereign right' over genetic resources may be appropriate for plants and non-human animals, it presents a problem to speak of human genetic material in this manner. That is, to have a sovereign right over something implies proprietary control such that one can do with it as one pleases. But to speak of human genetic materials in this way is considered by many to connote commodification of the human genome such that some persons or entities might claim ownership over others or over some significant aspect of their genome. (Lavoie 1988; Caulfield 2003) Although both India (Indian Council of Medical Research 2000) and China (People's Republic of China 1998) have claimed an ownership interest in human genetic materials on behalf of their citizens, many find such a notion objectionable, especially in countries that have experience with slavery and trafficking in persons or human body parts. (Dickenson 2004) It was just such concerns that animated the initial international outrage expressed against US patents on the Hagahai and other human genetic materials, and which are reflected in statements to the effect that the human genome is 'the heritage of humanity', even if only in a symbolic sense. (UNESCO 1997)

In light of the number of patents that have been issued in recent years, however, it seems the symbolism in question may be little more than an idle gesture. Given this reality some have argued that the only way to ensure that individuals and groups receive just compensation for the use of their genetic information is to accept commodification as a reality and to sell their biological samples at fair market value. One commentator has suggested that US $50,000 per sample would be appropriate in this regard, and that it would be prudent for individuals to start demanding payment for their DNA rather than to donate it to enterprising researchers. (Bear 2004) Indeed one community in Newfoundland and Labrador views the genes of their relatively homogenous population as a valuable natural resource that could be exploited in the international market place, and has taken out suggestive ads in international trade journals that invite prospective industry sponsors to 'get into [their] genes'.

At issue here is the legal character of human genetic material, and despite a quarter century of moral angst, legal wrangling and international negotiation, this remains an open question. As Canadian legal scholar Moe Litman (1997) has noted, legal taxonomy is a purposive and normative process, and as such it is the antithesis of a technical or objective exercise. It is rooted in value judgments that entail fundamental policy choices. Objects are treated as property under the law, not because of some intrinsic quality or objective characteristic that identifies them as property *per se*, but because 'labelling them as property, and thereby subjecting them to property law, best effectuates a broad range of social, philosophical, psychological and economic goals.' Hence the legal character of human genetic material will vary depending on the context and the purposes for which it is being characterized; it might be regarded as private property, common property, person or information, or some combination of these. Litman summarizes his legal opinion on the matter as follows: '. . . in law human genetic material is *sui generis*, that is legally unique. Its legal uniqueness emanates from the fact that this material is unique in its social implications. It is my view that human genetic material is best classified as a flexible legal hybrid with the character of a number of traditional juristic categories, including property and person.'

The hybrid legal characterization of human genetic material manifests itself in different forms depending upon the parties involved and their respective value priorities and purposes. The patent system treats the information contained in human genetic material as intellectual property. Those who hold a patent thus have a right to exclude others from accessing, using or selling that information for a limited term (typically twenty years). Patent holders, in turn, are guided by their own value priorities. Public bodies that hold patents do so ostensibly to ensure that valuable information is accessible rather than suppressed as 'trade secrets'. Private companies, on the other hand, use patents as a means of protecting their economic investments. (National Research Council 2006) On yet another hand, those who advocate the selling of genetic samples (at US $50,000 a pop, for example), view DNA as an individual's private property to be disposed of in any manner he or she finds acceptable. By way of contrast, the Newfoundland community that wants to attract investors by inviting them to 'get into their genes', views the local genetic resource as a kind of common property to be exploited for the economic benefit of members of that community.

Each of the foregoing examples treats human genetic material as some form of property, be it private, communal, intellectual or otherwise, and thus subject to the dictates of property law. A growing literature on the subject of 'benefit-sharing' in human genetic research is devoted to ensuring that the competing interests represented in the various notions of property are adequately addressed, and that vulnerable communities are fairly compensated if their genetic materials are exploited for commercial purposes. (Pullman and Latus 2003a,b; Sheremeta and Knoppers 2003; Dickenson 2004)

If Indigenous or other communities are concerned primarily about the protection of some sort of property interest in their genetic materials, then property law and effective benefit sharing arrangements are the appropriate tools by which to protect those interests. However, for many Indigenous communities it is not primarily economic exploitation that worries them, but rather the very processes of human genetic research that often fail to recognize and respect the manner in which Indigenous cultures think about biological materials. The concern is summarized nicely in this statement from the Indigenous Peoples Council on Biocolonialism (2000):

> Many Indigenous peoples regard their bodies, hair, and blood as sacred elements, and consider scientific research on these materials a violation of their cultural and ethical mandates. Immortalization, cloning, or the introduction of genetic materials taken from a human being into another living being is also counter to many Indigenous peoples' cultural and ethical principles. Indigenous peoples have frequently expressed criticism of Western science for failing to consider the inter-relatedness of holistic life systems, and for seeking to manipulate life forms using genetic technologies.

Given this perspective, some maintain that international instruments such as the Trade-Related Intellectual Property System (TRIPS) and the

World Intellectual Property Organization Patent Law Treaty of 2000 are just the latest means by which First World governments and firms impose their values upon the developing world. As such, informed consent is perceived not as protection from exploitation but further evidence of dominance. Benefit-sharing agreements in turn are simply a means by which to bribe developing countries into treating their genetic materials as commodities. (Dickenson 2004)

Indigenous peoples are not the only ones to raise concerns about emerging genetic technologies and the potential they hold to manipulate the biological basis of life or to alter how we think about ourselves as human beings. There have been numerous critiques of the new biotechnology in recent years and its potential to alter fundamental human nature (Rifkin 1998) or to undermine human dignity. (President's Council on Bioethics 2002) However, in the context of cultural studies it is often Indigenous peoples who have the most at stake. Genetic information can be used to trace the lineage of particular groups and to identify those who are related biologically to a particular population, even though they may not have shared a cultural history with that group. (Elliott and Brodwin 2002) Population studies in the West Indies, for example, have shown that settlement was from the West and not from the Americas as traditionally thought. (Clegg 1994) Later we will discuss the Lemba tribe of Southern Africa which has used Y-chromosome markers to stake a claim to its Jewish heritage. (Spurdle and Jenkins 1996)

Genetic ancestry tracing can threaten the very identity of a cultural group that has evolved over many generations through on-going historical narratives and associated cultural practices. With the advent of the Human Genome Diversity Project and the more recent National Geographic Genographic Project, such cases are becoming more common and can be the source of stress and dissension within and between cultural groups. In this context it is not so much human DNA as cultural property that is at issue, but rather the manner in which genetic information can affect cultural identity. If we were to apply a legal analysis to these latter concerns, we might say the law of persons takes precedence over property law. Here the main concern is no longer intellectual property, patents and fair benefits, but rather the ability to control or manage information that is materially important to how members of a cultural group define and think of themselves as a people. In these cases the discussion of 'cultural appropriation' may indeed be relevant in that the information derived from the genetic research may be in conflict with the long-standing cultural beliefs. But more clearly, the 'cultural offense' arises from the use of the DNA of a tribe or community without their knowledge, for purposes that might undermine their own beliefs.

Summing up, our characterization of the moral and legal status of human DNA suggests that human genetic material is *sui generis*, or legally unique. As such it admits of a variety of interpretations. Depending on context human genetic material may be treated as individual, communal or intellectual property, and various aspects of property law including patents, licensing agreements and negotiated benefit-sharing arrangements are the means by which to manage the complexities involved. Such legal instruments are available to various communities whether defined geographically, culturally or otherwise, in order to protect their property and related economic interests if necessary. In our view, however, the property category—private, intellectual, cultural or otherwise—fails to capture the fundamental concerns of cultural groups who have broader non-economic worries about the manner in which their genetic materials are collected, stored and utilized. Here the very notion of cultural identity is often at stake, which can at times manifest itself in terms of cultural offense.

The Genetic Appropriation of Culture

The Lemba, or Belemba, are a Bantu speaking people of some 50,000 to 70,000 in number who live in Zimbabwe and South Africa. They consider themselves to be one of the ten lost tribes of Israel who left Palestine some 2500 years ago. They practice circumcision, keep one day of the week holy and avoid eating pork. Their concept of the divine, method of burying the dead, and various other cultural beliefs and practices are quite similar to those of Jews. (Heppner 1999)

Skeptics of the Lemba's claims regarding their Jewish ancestry have pointed out that there are numerous groups around the world who practice religious rites similar to those of the Jewish tradition, and who make similar ancestry claims. However, Y-chromosome tracing has indicated that there may be something to the Lemba claim after all. In particular, one of the Lemba clans carries, at a very high frequency, a Y-chromosome type which is called the 'Cohen modal haplotype'. This haplotype is known to be characteristic of the paternally inherited Jewish priesthood, and is thought more generally to be 'a potential signature haplotype of Judaic origin.' (Thomas *et al.* 2000)

The Lemba case is a powerful example of the ambiguity that obtains when biology is confused with culture. To this point the discovery that they are 'genetically Jewish' has helped to confirm the Lemba's aural tradition, but it has not resulted in thousands of claims for Israeli citizenship. Israel offers the 'right of return' to all Jews, so it is conceivable that some members of the Lemba community might make such a claim. What would happen if they did? What should happen if they did? Conversely, what if the research had failed to establish a genetic connection between the Lemba and ancient Israel, as it has, for example, in the case of the Mormon Church? (Southerton 2004) Would Israel be justifiably offended by the Lemba's misappropriation of their history and cultural practices? Should they demand that the Lemba (and the Mormons) cease and desist from such misappropriation? Might such 'scientific discomfirmation' lead to the breakdown of cultural beliefs and practices that constitute, to some degree, the Lemba identity?

In an age in which genetic science plays an ever increasing role in how we think about ourselves both individually and corporately, and where identity claims can have significant legal and social ramifications, the question of what constitutes 'legitimate belonging' and the criteria by which to establish it are of tremendous importance. Anthropologist Paul Brodwin observes that 'to claim a certain social identity always implies certain rights and obligations.' To specify what counts as legitimate belonging will affect how people respect such rights or enforce these obligations. (Brodwin 2002) Elsewhere Elliott and Brodwin (2002) have noted, 'It is worth remembering that genetic ancestry tracing has the potential to disrupt identity claims as well as to corroborate them. Given the imprimatur of science carried by genetics, those disruptions may be hard to repair.'

Issues such as these are at the heart of the protests that have plagued the Human Genome Diversity Project (HGDP) since its inception in the early 1990s. The HGDP followed in the wake of the Human Genome Project (HGP), the largely successful international effort to map the entire human genome. But while the HGP focuses on genetic similarities of the human species as a whole, the HGDP trades upon genetic differences within the species. Thus the HGDP aims to collect DNA samples from between 400 and 500 distinct populations (many of them Indigenous communities) around the world, in addition to European populations which would be handled separately. (Roberts 1992) Promoters of the HGDP consider these samples to be a resource to promote worldwide research on human genetic diversity with the ultimate goal of understanding how and when patterns of diversity were formed. In their view the utilization of renewable samples from well-chosen populations will facilitate studies of the genetic geography and history of the human species. (King and Motulsky 2002; Cavalli-Sforza 2005)

Although even critics of the HGDP acknowledge that it is 'an undertaking of great scientific interest' that will provide a rich source of material for those who study human populations (Alper and Beckwith 1999), the HGDP has faced significant resistance from the outset. Many see it as yet another tool by which dominant cultures will exploit those who are most vulnerable. In particular concerns have been raised about commercial exploitation of the genetic materials collected from Indigenous populations (Liloqula 1996) and that the information gathered might be used for racist ends. (Alper and Beckwith 1999) Indigenous peoples are particularly incensed that they were not consulted in the planning of the project, even though it is their genetic materials that will constitute the bulk of the data collected and stored for future research purposes. (Lock 1999) Of particular relevance to the present discussion are concerns about the genetic reification of cultural/ethnic groups, leading, as we have termed it here, to the genetic appropriation of culture.

Such ongoing worries resulted in a negative decision by the US National Research Council in 1997 with regard to the provision of public funds to support the HGDP. (Harry and Kenehe 2006) Despite a lack of significant funding, however, the project continues to limp along, even as its supporters persist in their assertions that the ethical concerns are largely unfounded. 'This project has survived with little support until now', states one of the original founders of the HGDP in a recent article. 'Its potential uses in medicine, science and social problems such as racism are sufficiently important that the project should be continued and expanded.' (Cavalli-Sforza 2005)

In 2005 the National Geographic Society launched its own genetic diversity project, titled the Genographic Project (GP). Although this project has attempted to distance itself from the HGDP and the intractable ethical problems associated with it, critics maintain it shares similar goals and intellectual leadership. (Harry and Kanehe 2006) National Geographic has secured major funding for the GP through private partners such as IBM Corporation and the Waitt Family Foundation, and has thus avoided the degree of public scrutiny directed at the HGDP. Nevertheless the Indigenous Peoples Council on Biocolonialism maintains the GP raises many of the same ethical concerns. Although they acknowledge once again that the collection of blood from Indigenous peoples may be of interest scientifically, their concern is that such research will fail to protect Indigenous cultures. In particular it is noted that the consent form for participation in the GP states 'it is possible that some of the findings that result from this study may contradict an oral, written or other tradition held by you or by members of your group.' (Harry and Kanehe 2006)

The key shortcoming of both the HGDP and the GP as it concerns issues of genetics and culture is the reductionist approach that assumes that 'social, linguistic, and political factors associated with decent patterns, genealogy making, ethnic affiliation, ideas about race, and racism are layered as a flotsam over the biological truth.' (Lock 1999) The naive assumption seems to be that if people only understand the biology involved, political and social problems associated with group identity and difference will somehow evaporate. But as philosopher Eric Juengst (1998) has observed, 'No matter how great the potential of population genomics to show us our interconnections, if it begins by describing our differences then it inevitably will produce scientific wedges to hammer into the social cracks that already divide us.' In the end there are no solid connections between biology and culture, and the tendency to reduce the latter to the former should be resisted. As one Native commentator has observed, 'It is one matter for tribes, scientists, and government to look for cultural affiliation in cultural artifacts or for cultural identity in cultural practice and in voiced assertions of that identity. However, there are no concrete answers in DNA about cultural affiliation, cultural identity, or about the morality or justice of any one decision regarding the fate of ancient remains and claims to cultural and political autonomy and rights. Even with DNA analysis, Indian people, scientists, and lawmakers are still left looking for answers that lie in the "imprecise" sciences of ethics, religion, and legal jurisdiction.' (Tallbear 2000)

What is at issue here is the matter of how we define ourselves as persons, both individually and corporately, and the politics of identity associated with such self-understandings. This begs the question of whether genetic heritage is either a necessary or a sufficient condition for cultural group membership, and the answer will depend on the particular interests of those who either ask or answer that question. Outsiders who want to establish disputed membership in a group will answer one way, while insiders who want to maintain some exclusive control may answer otherwise.

So while international guidelines acknowledge that 'genetic data itself may be the subject of moral, social or religious beliefs', and may instruct those who collect such data to 'give these convictions all due respect, endeavoring to do nothing . . . that would give offense to those from whom the samples and the data have been obtained' (UNESCO 2001), the questions of to whom the researcher owes this due respect, and who might be legitimately offended in this regard remains ambiguous. For as the case of the Lemba graphically illustrates, it is not only the identity and culture of those who donate genetic samples that is at risk, but also that of other cultural groups who may unwittingly be biologically implicated in the science.

Community Identity, Cultural Offense and Control of Genetic Information

Much of the recent controversy regarding the legal and moral status of human genetic material has treated it as some form of property, and has applied various elements of property law in order to ensure that the interests of all parties are adequately protected. Various communities, whether defined geographically (Pullman and Latus 2003a,b), by disease (Terry 2003), ethnically (Barkham 2000) or otherwise, have appealed to property law as a means to protect their economic interests. Although there is still much controversy and concern about the moral legitimacy of the commodification of human genetic material inherent in the notion of property, this is the reality of current international law.

While property law has become the *de facto* means by which to protect various economic interests in human genetic material, we have argued that it fails to address the broader cultural concerns raised by the collection and use of this material for research purposes. This is because it is difficult to characterize human genetic material as cultural property in any meaningful sense. The human genetic material of the Hagahai, the Lemba, or any other identifiable cultural group, is neither cultural object, cultural subject, nor does it represent cultural content *per se*. This is not to say that the manner in which genetic material is treated does not have significant implications for a cultural group as a whole, however that group is defined. Research on human genetic material has the potential to alter profoundly the manner in which a community understands itself, and may have implications for the determination of who's in and who's out as far as membership in the community is concerned.

Indigenous communities themselves have sponsored legislation aimed at establishing genetic criteria as a means of determining group membership. (Tallbear 2000) In this respect genetic research might lead indirectly to cultural appropriation or misappropriation, as it could be used to deny rights of membership, exclude from participation in cultural practices or prevent access to genuine cultural objects to some individuals. The recent case of the genetic exclusion of some who had long considered themselves members of the Seminole Nation of Oklahoma is a case in point. (Johnston 2003) Conversely it could grant these privileges to others who had never participated in the community historically.

What is at stake in such identity claims is not so much 'traditional knowledge' but rather the more amorphous notion of 'knowledge of a tradition'. The latter knowledge is experiential in nature and is acquired over time through the lived experience of a community and its members. It can include shared histories, ceremonial practices, customs, beliefs and a myriad of other tangible and intangible elements. The question of cultural identity pertains for the most part to questions of inclusion in or exclusion from an identifiable community, and while the core of any given cultural community may be easily recognizable, things are often less distinct as one moves further toward the edges. Genetic information is not irrelevant to the question of cultural identity, but it is only one element in this diverse complexity. Given the common observation that genetic variation within groups is generally greater than that between groups, genetic information should be of limited relevance when compared to the experiential knowledge members of cultural communities acquire over time.

There are no quick and ready solutions to how disputed identity claims should play out in the international arena. Given the experience of the HGDP, however, one can hope there will be sustained pressure on any domestic or international court to avoid the conflation of cultural and genetic identity. Although the recent case of the Seminole Nation is not all that encouraging, we are still in early days in this regard and one can hope that this case will serve as an exception rather than set the rule.

Assuming, for the moment, that questions of cultural identity and group membership have been resolved, how should we think about the matter of cultural offense? The notion of offense figures prominently in discussions of cultural appropriation in general, (Young 2005) and although we have argued that the latter notion fails to capture the essence of the controversies surrounding the collection and use of human genetic material, it is nevertheless the case that such collection and use can be the source of cultural offense. As noted previously, those who conduct research on human genetic materials are reminded that genetic data can be the subject of moral, social or religious beliefs, and are instructed 'to do nothing . . . that would give offense to those from whom the samples and the data have been obtained.' (UNESCO 2001)

'Offense' is a rather slippery and subjective notion, and it is not immediately clear how much weight to give to such concerns in the context of human genetic research. Science has a way of undermining long held traditional and cultural beliefs, and if the standard is 'zero tolerance' in this regard, it is likely that a great deal of valuable research will be curtailed. Christians who accept a literal interpretation of the creation account of Genesis may be offended by research in evolutionary biology, but few would argue that such research must thus be halted. In the same vein, while the Indigenous Peoples Council on Biocolonialism makes explicit reference to the warning contained in the consent document for participation in National Geographic's Genographic Project to the effect that 'the findings that result from this study may contradict an oral, written or other tradition held by you or by members of your group' (Harry and Kanehe 2006), this is not a sufficient reason to end that project. Individuals or communities may consider the possibility of such a result offensive to their beliefs, and may for this reason choose not to participate, but this potential offense in itself does not make the project morally suspect.

The imperative to avoid cultural offense in genetic research must be interpreted to apply to the process of research, and not to the results *per se*. Indigenous communities want to be partners in the planning process whenever possible, want to be informed of the reasons for supplying genetic samples and want to be apprised of how those samples are used and any results forthcoming from the research. If studies on ancestry are carried out with the tribe or community, and the tribe or community is in support of the information to be derived, no cultural offense will occur. Indeed, cultural appropriation of genetic information is offensive only when conducted without the knowledge and consent of the tribe or community and when they do not support the use of the information derived.

The manner in which research on Indigenous populations can go awry is clearly illustrated in the now infamous case of the Nuu-chah-nulth community of Vancouver Island. (Dalton 2002) When first approached in the 1980s by University of British Columbia researcher Ryk Ward to participate in genetic research on rheumatoid arthritis, the Nuu-chah-nulth enthusiastically embraced the research. More than a third of the adult population eventually provided blood samples. When Ward was unable to find the hoped for genetic marker predisposing to arthritis, however, he used the samples to explore the ancestry and geographic origins of the Nuu-chah-nulth. In conjunction with other anthropological methodologies, this emerging method utilizes human DNA markers to trace the migration patterns of peoples around the world. By using DNA isolated from the Nuu-chah-nulth blood samples Ward identified mitochondrial DNA markers to trace the genetic origins of some of the earliest inhabitants of North America. (Ward *et al.* 1991) In the process of doing this research, Ward took the Nuu-chah-nulth samples first to Utah and then to Britain, where he continued to use them for anthropological research until 2000. (Peters *et al.* 2000) It was years before the Nuu-chah-nulth learned of what had happened to their genetic samples and years more before they were able to have the samples returned. (Wiwchar 2004) In the interim they developed their own research ethics guidelines relevant to their community, and through Canadian Institutes of Health Research-funded workshops on genetic research in Aboriginal communities, they contributed to the CIHR (2007) *Guidelines for Health Research Involving Aboriginal People.*

While the Nuu-chah-nulth case is a paradigm example of how not to conduct genetic research with an Indigenous community, there is much that can be learned from their response throughout and subsequent to this ordeal. The research was implemented in an accepted 'participatory model' of community-based research, with active participation from community members, promises of benefit sharing and the development of community research capacity. However the secondary use of the samples for research unrelated to health illustrates the disconnect between expectations of the community that consents to research, and the researchers who often consider the samples theirs to use for any research once individual identifiers have been removed.

The practice of archiving samples and using them for secondary health research has been a common practice among biomedical researchers, and still occurs in some places. Consider, for example, the recent lawsuit against a researcher at Arizona State University by the Havasupai of Arizona.

(Dalton 2004) According to their claim, the Havasupai sought help in 1989 for research on diabetes. Unbeknownst to them, however, further research was conducted on schizophrenia and 'inbreeding', research areas to which they had not consented and ones which could well lead to further stigmatization and discrimination. The lawsuit for $75 million dollars has been supported by a resolution by the National Congress of American Indians. Cases such as these raise concerns on several fronts. Not only can they be the source of profound offense to the communities involved, but the subsequent legal action may curtail much needed research to address well known disparities that often involve genetic research.

The moral requirement that communities have a measure of control over research conducted among their members has garnered considerable interest in the genetics era. Much has been written on the notion of 'community consent', and the means by which to acquire and maintain it. There are numerous challenges in this regard at both the conceptual and pragmatic levels. (Weijer 1999) It is somewhat paradoxical, for example, to claim that genetic information has little to do with cultural identity on the one hand and yet to insist that culturally defined groups should exercise a degree of control over genetic research, on the other. (Juengst 1998) Nevertheless, as the World Business Council for Sustainable Development (2002) observed in a recent report, the foremost concern of Indigenous peoples is 'to have their own rules and values, as embodied in their customary laws, acknowledged and applied in dealing with these questions.' Given the historical record of exploitation of these peoples it would seem somewhat disingenuous to exclude these communities from discussions about the kind of genetic research that is planned or not to allow them some input into how such research might be conducted, on the technical point that genetics really has little to do with culture after all.

Much effort has been made in recent years to develop guidelines for genetic research in Indigenous communities that ensure appropriate community participation in all aspects of the research project. In Canada the Canadian Institutes of Health Research has taken the lead in developing standards for health research on Indigenous populations. Central to the guidelines on genetic research is the notion of 'DNA on loan', which connotes that the community never relinquishes control of DNA that is collected for genetic research. This concept requires that any new research must be agreed to by the research participant. It also includes a mechanism for return of the DNA for cultural purposes such as culturally appropriate burial, as well as for other reasons related to the research. (Arbour and Cook 2006)

Like the Nuu-chah-nulth, many Indigenous communities have established governance structures to review proposed research, to assess the potential impact upon the community and to provide 'community consent' where appropriate. But as Arbour and Cook (2006) observe, 'Even when the community does not have an established structure, or the research does not lend itself to a community approach, the researcher's commitment to an on-going research relationship is essential in providing integrated accountable governance of the research. . . . The overriding principles include respect for Aboriginal individuals, families and communities, and the cultural, social and political milieu in which they live.'

Conclusion

The mapping of the human genome has ushered in a new era of human genetic research and with it a myriad of ethical challenges. In this essay we have canvassed a variety of those issues as they pertain to the ethical and legal status of human genetic material, questions of gene patents and intellectual property and broader social and cultural concerns associated with engaging in various types of genetic research. All of these issues are complex, and none admits of a quick or precise solution. As the various examples discussed throughout illustrate, how the ethics question is defined in most cases is contingent on how the parties involved understand the ethical and legal status of human DNA. Given the *sui generis* nature of human DNA we should not expect settled answers to many of the issues raised any time soon. Nevertheless, on the matter of 'the cultural appropriation of human genetic material' we have argued that there is an answer to be had, namely that the notion does not really capture the essence of the controversies that surround human genetic research as it pertains to distinct cultural groups. Human DNA does not function as 'cultural subject', 'cultural object', or 'cultural content' in the sense usually associated with those terms. Hence, while there have been numerous cases in which identifiable cultural groups have been treated unethically in the course of conducting genetic research, it is better to characterize such transgressions as violations of more traditional concepts within research ethics, and not as matters of 'cultural appropriation' *per se*.

References

Alper, J.S., and Beckwith, J. (1999). Racism: A central problem for the Human Genome Diversity Project. *Politics and the Life Sciences* **18**,2: 285.

Arbour, L., and Cook, D. (2006). DNA on loan: Approaches to carrying out research on Aboriginal families and communities. *Community Genetics* **9**: 153–60.

Barkham, P. (2000). Faraway Tonga cashes in on its gene pool secrets. *The Guardian*, November 23.

Bear, J. (2004). What's my DNA worth, anyway? A response to the commercialization of individuals' DNA information. *Perspectives in Biology and Medicine* **47**,2: 273–89.

Bhat, A. (1996). The National Institutes of Health and the Papua New Guinea cell line. *Cultural Survival Quarterly* **20**.2. Available at: http://www.culturalsurvival. org/ourpublication/csq/article/the-national-institutes-health-and-papua- new-guines-cell-line

Brodwin, P. (2002). Genetics, identity, and the anthropology of essentialism. *Anthropology Quarterly* **75**,2: 322–330.

CIHR (2007). Guidelines for Health Research Involving Aboriginal People. Available at: http://www.cihr-irsc.gc.ca/e/documents/ethics_aboriginal_ guidelines_e.pdf

Caulfield, T.A. (2003). From human genes to stem cells: new challenges for patent law. *Trends in Biotechnology* **21**,3: 101–3.

Cavalli-Sforza, L. (2005). The Human Genome Diversity Project: past, present, and future. *Nature Reviews Genetics* **6**: 333–340.

Clegg, J.B. (1994). Travels with DNA in the Pacific. *Lancet* **344**: 1070–1072. Convention for the protection of cultural property in the event of armed conflict (1954) available at http://www.icomos.org/hague/

Dalton, R. (2002). Tribe blasts 'exploitation' of blood samples. *Nature* **420**: 111.

Dalton, R. (2004). When two tribes go to war. *Nature* **430**: 500–502.

Diamond v Chakrabarty 447 US 303 (1980)

Dickenson, D. (2004). Consent, commodification and benefit-sharing in genetic research. *Developing World Bioethics* **4**,2: 109–24.

Elliott, C. and Brodwin, P. (2002). Identity and genetic ancestry tracing. *BMJ* **325**: 1469–71.

ETC Group (1996). New questions about management and exchange of human tissue at NIH: Indigenous person's cells patented. Available at: http://www. etcgroup.org/en/materials/publications.html?pub_id=468

Harry, D., and Kanehe, L.M. (2006). Genetic research: Collecting blood to preserve culture? *Cultural Survival Quarterly* **29**.4. Available at: http://www. culturalsurvival.org/ourpublications/csq/article/genetic-research-collecting- blood-preserve-culture

Heppner, M.A. (1999). Science ties the Lemba closer to mainstream Jews. *Kulanu* **6.2**: 1,13.

Indian Council of Medical Research (2000). *Ethical Guidelines for Biomedical Research.* Available at: http://icmr.nic.in/ethical_guidelines.pdf

Indigenous Peoples Council on Biocolonialism (2000). Available at: http://www.ipcb. org/publications/primers/htmls/ipgg.html

Jenkins, C.L. (1987). Medical anthropology in the Western Schrader Range, Papua New Guinea. *National Geographic Research* **3**,4: 412–30.

Johnston, J. (2003). Resisting a genetic identity: The Black Seminoles and genetic tests of ancestry. *J Law, Med, Ethics* **31**,2: 262–71.

Jong, S-C., and Cypess, R.H. (1998). Managing genetic material to protect intellectual property rights. *J Industrial Microbiology and Biotechnology* **20**: 95–100.

Juengst, E. (1998). Group identity and human diversity: Keeping biology straight from culture. *Am J Hum Genet* **63**: 673–77.

King, M-C., and Motulsky, A.G. (2002). Mapping human history. *Science* **298**: 2342–3.

Lavoie, J. (1988). Ownership of human tissue: Life after *Moore v. Regents of the University of California.* 75 *Virginia Law Review* 1363–1367.

Liloqula, R. (1996). Saving genes versus saving indigenous peoples. *Cultural Survival Quarterly* **20**, 2. Available at: http://www.cs.org/publications/csq/csq-article.cfm?id=1584&highlight=Liloqula,%20Ruth

Litman, M.M. (1997). The legal status of genetic material. In Knoppers, BK. (ed.) *Human DNA: Law and Policy.* Cambridge, MA.: Kluwer Law International.

Lock, M. (1999). Genetic diversity and the politics of difference. *Chicago-Kent Law Review* **75**,83: 83–111.

Los Angeles Times (27 Dec 1987). Disease threatens survival of remote, stone age folk.

Lovgren, S. (2005). One-fifth of human genes have been patented, study reveals. *National Geographic News.* Available at: http://news.nationalgeographic.com/news/2005/10/1013_051013_gene_patent.html

National Geographic *Genographic Project.* Available at: https://www3.nationalgeographic.com/genographic/

National Research Council (2006). *Reaping the benefits of genomic and proteomic research: Intellectual property rights, innovation, and public health.* Washington, DC: The National Academies Press.

People's Republic of China (1998). General Office of the State Council, *Interim Measures for the Administration of Human Genetic Resources.* Available at: http://www.cal-china.org/documents/Trainees%20%20Paper/Zheng%20 Xiao/Veronica%20Paper.doc.

Peters, A., Coulthart, M.B., Oger, J.F. *et al.* (2000). HTLV Type I/II in British Columbia Amerindians: A Seroprevalence Study and Sequence Characterization of an HTLV Type IIa Isolate. *AIDS Res Hum Retroviruses* **16**,9: 883–892.

President's Council on Bioethics (2002). *Human Cloning and Human Dignity*. New York: Public Affairs.

Pullman, D. and Latus, A. (2003a). Benefit sharing in smaller markets: The case of Newfoundland and Labrador. *Community Genetics* **6**: 178–181.

Pullman, D., and Latus, A. (2003b). Reconciling social justice and economic opportunism: Regulating the Newfoundland genome. In Knoppers, B-M. (ed.) *Populations and Genetics: Legal and Social-Ethical Perspectives*. Leiden: Martinus Nijhoff: 543–564.

Resnik, D. (2004). *Owning the Genome: A Moral Analysis of DNA Patenting*. Albany: State University of New York Press.

Rifkin, J. (1998). *The Biotech Century*. New York: Penguin Putnam.

Roberts, L. (1992). Anthropologists climb (gingerly) on board. *Science* **258**: 1300–1.

Shaw, J. (2003). Bioprospecting: Corporations profit from indigenous genes. *In These Times*. Available at: http://www.inthesetimes.com/comments. php?id=467_0_1_0_C

Sheremeta, L., and Knoppers, B.M. (2003). Beyond the rhetoric: population genetics and benefit-sharing. *Health Law J* **11**: 89–117.

Spurdle, A.B., and Jenkins, T. (1996). The origins of the Lemba 'Black Jews' of Southern Africa: evidence from p 12f2 and other Y-chromosome markers. *Am J Human Genet* **59**: 1126–33.

Stix, G. (2006). Owning the stuff of life. *Scientific American* (Feb) **294**: 2.

Southerton, S.G. (2004). *Losing a Lost Tribe: Native Americans, DNA, and the Mormon Church*. Salt Lake City, Utah: Signature Books.

Tallbear, K. (2000). Genetics, culture and identity in Indian country. Seventh International Congress of Ethnobiology, Athens, Georgia, Oct. 23–27.

Taubes, G. (1995). Scientists attacked for 'patenting' Pacific tribe. *Science* **270**: 17.

Terry, P.F. (2003). PXE International: Harnessing intellectual property law for benefit-sharing. In Knoppers, B-M. (ed.) *Populations and Genetics: Legal and Social-Ethical Perspectives*. Leiden: Martinus Nijhoff: 377–93.

Thomas, M.G., Parfit, T., Weiss, D.A. *et al.* (2000) Y chromosomes traveling south: The Cohen modal haplotype and the origins of the Lemba—the 'Black Jews of Southern Africa'. *Am J Hum Genet* **66**: 674–686.

United Nations Environmental Program (2002). UNEP/CBD/COP Bonn guidelines on access to genetic resources and fair and equitable sharing of the benefits arising out of their utilization. Sec. 9.

UNESCO (1970). *Convention on the Means of Prohibiting and Preventing the Illicit Import, Export and Transfer of Ownership of Cultural Property*. Available at: http://portal.unesco.org/en/ev.php-URL_ID=13039&URL_DO=DO_TOPIC&URL_SECTION=201.html

UNESCO (1997). *Universal Declaration of the Human Genome and Human Rights*. Available at: http://portal.unesco.org/shs/en/ev.php-URL_ID=1881&URL_DO=DO_TOPIC&URL_SECTION=201.html

UNESCO (2001). *Proceedings of International Bioethics Committee of UNESCO* (Eight Session, September 2001). Available at http://portal.unesco.org/shs/en/ev.php-URL_ID=2145&URL_DO=DO_TOPIC&URL_SECTION=465.html

UNESCO (2003). *International Declaration on Human Genetic Data.* Available at: http://portal.unesco.org/shs/en/ev.php-URL_ID=1882&URL_DO=DO_TOPIC&URL_SECTION=201.html

United States Patent and Trademark Office (2001). Revised Examiners Guide. Available at: http://www.uspto.gov/web/offices/pac/dapp/opla/presentation/focuspp.html

Ward, R.H., Frazier, B.L., Dew-Jager, K., and Paabo, S. (1991). Extensive mito-chondrial diversity within a single Amerindian tribe. *Proc Nat Acad Sci USA* **88**: 8720–24.

Weijer, C. (1999). Protecting communities in research: Philosophical and prag-matic challenges. *Cambridge Quarterly of Health Care Ethics* **8**: 501–13.

Wiwchar, D. (2004). Nuu-chah-nulth blood returns to west coast. *Ha-Shilth-Sa* **31**: 25.

World Business Council on Sustainable Development (2002). *Intellectual property rights in biotechnology and health care—Results of a stakeholder dialogue* 18. Available at: www.wbcsd.org/plugins/DocSearch/details.asp?type=DocDet&ObjectId=MjI1Ng

Young, J.O. (2005). Profound offense and cultural appropriation. *Journal of Aes-thetics and Art Criticism* **63**,2: 135–46.

7

Appropriation of Traditional Knowledge: Ethics in the Context of Ethnobiology

Kelly Bannister and Maui Solomon (Part I)
Conrad G. Brunk (Part II)

> To what extent can law control the movement of ideas? Does it make sense for ethnic groups to define their cultural practices as property that cannot be studied, imitated, or modified by others without permission? How far can democratic states go to provide Indigenous peoples with cultural protections without violating the rights of the general public? What is the future of the public domain, which is squeezed on one side by the privatizing logic of the world's corporations and on the other by native-rights activists promoting novel forms of collective copyright?[1]

Knowledge appropriation is by no means a new phenomenon, and in the broadest sense, one can argue it is a necessary aspect of the successful adaptation and evolution of human societies, past and present. By this we mean that little, if any, of the technologies, customs, understandings, beliefs, or cultural practices that underlie a way of life are created out of nothing. As in Young and Haley's chapter (this volume) 'nothing comes from nowhere'. Rather, these emerge from or are influenced by pre-existing ideas, experiences and other forms of knowledge within, between and among different cultures. This 'intercultural play', as noted by anthropologist Michael Brown (2003: 251), 'highlight[s] the complexity and moral ambiguity of the kinds of borrowing and imitation dourly summarized by a term like "cultural appropriation". . . . The fluid dance of imitation and contrast, reticence and disclosure is an essential part of social life in pluralistic societies. It is suppressed only with difficulty and some cost in creative freedom.'[2] We add that even non-pluralistic societies are a part of this same 'fluid dance of imitation' with other societies.

Given the unbounded and intangible nature of 'knowledge' as a concept, and the mutability and fluidity with which it can move across visible and invisible boundaries (e.g., persons, communities, cultures, and nations), it would be impossible and misleading to profess to cover a topic so broad as the ethics of knowledge appropriation within a single chapter of this volume. Knowledge appropriation, directly or indirectly, is an element of most of the other topics discussed, thus its separate treatment in this volume is somewhat artificially (although justifiably) imposed to facilitate a deeper analysis.

We focus on one small and highly controversial context for knowledge appropriation: the traditional knowledge of Indigenous peoples, particularly as this knowledge relates to biological and cultural heritage, referred to as 'collective biocultural heritage'.[3] In Part I of this chapter we draw heavily on academic and lay writings, international law and policy, international discussion fora, and our direct experiences as scientific and legal practitioners in the field of ethnobiology, which is the study of interrelationships between human societies and their biological environs. We also integrate perspectives and illustrative examples from the personal experience of one of us (Solomon) as a person of Indigenous Moriori and Maori ancestry. The appropriation of traditional knowledge related to collective biocultural heritage is one of increasing notoriety and interest to all sectors of society, providing a useful context from which to draw out and assess key ethical and philosophical issues of wider application. In Part II of this chapter, some of the philosophical and ethical arguments are laid out that support a developing international consensus among ethnobiologists and others concerned with the research and development that raises questions of knowledge appropriation. We argue that the 'ethical space' in which cultures can create a conversation moving toward mutual understanding and agreement begins with the attempt to build upon shared concepts and understandings.

Part I: Ethnobiology as a Case Example

Kelly Bannister and Maui Solomon

What is traditional knowledge?

Traditional knowledge is also commonly referred to as 'Indigenous knowledge' or the 'cultural knowledge of Indigenous peoples'. Not surprisingly given the diverse and dynamic nature of traditional knowledge, a singular and exclusive definition of the term does not exist. It is not a concept uniformly held by all Indigenous peoples and is problematic to generalize, especially within Eurocentric frameworks. Moreover, some western-trained philosophers and political scientists debate whether Indigenous knowledge even constitutes a form of knowledge.[4]

Recognizing the lack of international consensus on the term within legal and policy fora, as well as tensions inherent in ongoing efforts to evolve a definition that meets a diversity of needs (academic and non-academic; Indigenous and non-Indigenous; domestic and international)[5], for the purposes of this chapter we adopt the following 'working understanding' of traditional knowledge adapted from Bannister and Solomon (2009)[6]:

> The traditional knowledge of Indigenous peoples is part of a complex *system* that arises from Indigenous cosmologies and is based on Indigenous epistemologies. Traditional knowledge refers to the inter-generational accumulation of the collective stories, experiences, practices, genealogies, legends, mythologies, customs, laws, lore, spiritual teachings, wisdom, values and knowledge that have been passed down from one generation of Indigenous peoples to the next. Traditional knowledge systems share the commonly held belief that there is an inter-dependence and holistic relationship existing between the physical and spiritual worlds, such that the physical and spiritual wellbeing of present and future generations depend upon the health and vitality of the environment in which they live. Traditional knowledge is generally understood as collective in nature and usually utilized and practiced for the benefit of the wider group and authorized individuals or groups within the collective. Although rooted in specific lands and traditions, traditional knowledge is not seen as limited in time or space but continually evolving in response to the modern world. Although commonly discussed in the singular (traditional *knowledge*), the plural (traditional *knowledges*) better acknowledges the diversity across different communities and cultural groups.

Further to this understanding of traditional knowledge, we underscore two points. First, we are purposeful in our choice *not* to use the common acronym 'TK' (or any abbreviation at all) as in our view this facilitates reification and enables the concept of traditional knowledge to be conveniently delimited in ways that further impede adequate understandings. Second, as indicated above, we recognize traditional knowledge as part of a *system* of cultural knowledge embodied within Indigenous and traditional communities. Understanding appropriation of traditional knowledge, therefore, requires understanding the cultural context from which it emerges, which in turn requires recognition of the underlying social, ecological, political and other factors that may threaten or in some cases have collapsed these living systems.

Framing the issues

Unlike questions of monetary reparations or the return of Indigenous lands, struggles over intangible resources lead to vexing questions of origins and boundaries that are commonly swept under the rug in public discussions, which tend to treat art, stories, music and botanical knowledge as self-evidently the property of identifiable groups.[7]

Acts of taking and using traditional knowledge beyond the cultural context where it originated have become increasingly complex and contested, particularly when commercial exploitation is involved. For example, in the last couple of decades there has been a concerted effort by government, academe and industry to identify traditional knowledge related to biological diversity, such as medicinal plant knowledge that may lead to new drugs, health-care products, health foods, or other useful consumer goods. A complex of ethical, legal, political, and ecological issues revolve around the use, misuse and commodification of traditional knowledge.

In framing the issues, it is helpful to examine the two extremes of a diverse spectrum of actors and interests in traditional knowledge appropriation. Proponents (largely within academe, government, and the private sector—especially herbal, biotechnology, and pharmaceutical companies) argue that scientific validation and exploitation of traditional medicines or other traditional knowledge will bring prestige and vital economic opportunities to Indigenous and local communities and/or national governments of 'developing' countries, provide new cures and other advancements to wider society, and offer incentives for the conservation of disappearing ecosystems. For example, this is the underlying rationale of the International Cooperative Biodiversity Groups (ICBG) Program administrated by the Fogarty International Centre (FIC), US National Institutes of Health, which has funded international drug discovery projects since 1993:

Efforts to examine the medicinal potential of the earth's plants, animals and micro-organisms are urgently needed, since enduring habitat destruction and the resulting diminishment of biodiversity will make it increasingly difficult to do so in the future. Forty to fifty percent of currently used drugs have an origin in natural products. The FIC-managed Biodiversity Program is designed to guide natural products drug discovery in such a way that local communities and other source country organizations can derive direct benefits from their diverse biological resources. Benefit-sharing may provide clear incentives for preservation and sustainable use of that biodiversity.[8]

In contrast, opponents of appropriation argue that knowledge and resources are being 'stolen' from Indigenous communities, eroding their cultures and the ecosystems upon which they depend, interfering with cultural responsibilities (e.g., to past and future generations) and undermining Indigenous rights to traditional resources, intellectual property and cultural heritage. For example, a collective statement submitted to the United Nations Permanent Forum on Indigenous Issues in 2004 makes the following assertion:

> Indigenous knowledge is the foundation of Indigenous cultures. This knowledge permeates every aspect of our lives and is expressed in both tangible and intangible forms. Indigenous knowledge reflects the wisdom of our Ancestors, and we have a responsibility to protect and perpetuate this knowledge for the benefit of our future generations. . . . Indigenous peoples are greatly concerned over the application of intellectual property rights over genetic resources and traditional knowledge. We continue to maintain and protect biologically diverse ecosystems for the collective good. We hold knowledge about our environments that is potentially valuable to bioprospectors or others seeking to profit from our knowledge and exploit our resources.

> There is urgent need to halt the misuse and misappropriation of traditional knowledge and associated biological resources, innovations and practices. Indigenous peoples are seeking international standards and mechanisms that ensure equity, justice and respect for our collective rights. We recognize that our traditional knowledge constitutes the collective heritage and patrimony of our peoples, and the genetic material contained within the flora and fauna around us constitutes our sustenance. Thus, we are refusing to place economic value on these things for the exploitation by others.[9]

While some Indigenous peoples are clearly opposed to any form of appropriation or commodification, others choose to develop their knowledge and resources commercially for their own benefit, considering this choice consistent with their rights to self-determination and ability to make decisions in their own best interests.

One well-known example is the Indigenous San who signed a benefit-sharing agreement with South African's Council for Scientific and Industrial Research (CSIR) in 2003 to develop the appetite-suppressing properties of species of the succulent plant Hoodia, which grows in the semi-arid areas of Southern Africa, primarily the Kalahari desert. Hoodia has been used for generations by the Indigenous San peoples of Southern Africa (South Africa, Namibia, Botswana and Angola) as a thirst and appetite suppressant in times of low food availability. Documentation of the traditional uses of Hoodia was made in the academic literature by White and Sloane (1937: 1002)[10] and by Watt and Breyer-Branwijk (1962: 138).[11] The latter work is thought to have stimulated the laboratory investigations that eventually led to the isolation and patenting of active components of the plant as an appetite suppressant[12] and exploration of its commercial potential by CSIR in conjunction with pharmaceutical companies Phytopharm, Pfizer (initially), and, more recently, the multinational food corporation Unilever. Originally the commercial development interests were pursued without involvement of the San peoples (who reportedly were thought to be 'extinct' by representatives of the original companies involved). Subsequently, the San people through two representative organizations (the South African San Council and the Working Group on Indigenous Minorities in Southern Africa, WIMSA) were included in a landmark benefit-sharing agreement, which was widely believed would bring an unknown but likely substantial amount of revenues to the San (through a Trust Fund), if commercialization within the multi-billion dollar 'obesity market' were successful.[13]

Beyond the Hoodia experience, in 2004, the South African San Council signed a more general bioprospecting[14] agreement with the CSIR 'to work together in researching the Indigenous knowledge of the San people on the usage of Indigenous plants, to the benefit of both parties.'[15] Through WIMSA, they have also negotiated a second benefit-sharing agreement with growers and traders of Hoodia. Not surprisingly, the San Council's agreements have been applauded by some actors and interest groups as revolutionary (e.g., securing financial and other benefits for highly impoverished San communities, having traditional knowledge formally recognized as intellectual property, and developing new frameworks for informed consent, benefit-sharing, and equitable bioprospecting), while condemned by others as 'selling out' (e.g., reaching an agreement prematurely that resulted in securing fewer potential benefits than could have been negotiated if the San held out for longer in the negotiation process, selling out on cultural values by selling traditional knowledge, and accepting compensation for traditional knowledge only, without securing rights in the Hoodia plant itself).

From the latter camp, Indigenous right activists Debra Harry and Le'a Malia Kanehe (2005) express the following views:

> . . . it is outrageous to promote selling a monopoly on traditional knowledge to a Western corporation so that marginalized communities can earn recognition as Indigenous peoples. The San do not even possess complete decision-making power over their minute share of the royalties, royalties to be deposited in "their" Trust. It is instructive to note that although "their" Trust includes representatives of various San communities, the CSIR and the Department of Science and Technology also sit there, apparently as paternalistic trustees.

> The intent here is not to criticize the San for their participation in the benefit sharing agreement. In hindsight, it is clear that the only option presented to the San was to accept a share in the deal, or get nothing at all. And had CSIR and Phytopharm not been "caught red-handed" with the appropriation of San knowledge, the San may have simply remained unknown victims of theft. We see the case as a recent, very instructive example of the power dynamics typical when Indigenous peoples are forced to contend with the actions of colonial states and multinational corporations. The San case also illustrates how the profit potential of genetic material tends to evoke unscrupulous practices.[16]

While the San's negotiated revenues from successful commercialization of Hoodia have been actualized only to a limited extent due to delays in the commercialization process, substantial revenues are changing hands in the marketing of Hoodia within the much less regulated herbal and food supplement markets. Within these market economies, 'unbelievable' claims about Hoodia's weight-loss potential abound, along with consumer warnings about false claims by competitors.[17] Despite evidence of widespread and blatant acts of appropriation and commodification of traditional knowledge and resources within the herbal, natural foods, and related industries, generally these corporate activities have received far less scrutiny and media attention than the biotechnology and pharmaceutical industries.[18]

In the case of Hoodia and the San, however, a new precedent may be in the making with a profit-sharing agreement in March 2007 on 'San authorized' Hoodia (complete with logo) between the San and the Southern African Hoodia Growers Association.[19] Furthermore, written appeals have been initiated to national governments (South Africa, Switzerland, and Germany) by the San to halt the sale of Hoodia products produced outside the agreement in those countries, arguing the sales are in contravention of international agreements on biodiversity, namely the Convention on Biological Diversity.[20] The letter to the ministers responsible in South Africa, Germany and Switzerland submitted by the Working Group of Indigenous Minorities in Southern Africa and supporting nongovernmental organizations states:

> Through the CSIR agreement only the license holders Phytopharm (UK) and Unilever have legitimate access to the knowledge and the genetic resource, and for the moment the license holders are not selling any hoodia products. The Hoodia Growers Association will market their products with a clear logo showing that the San have received a benefit from the growing of hoodia. No products have yet been placed on the market bearing this logo. Therefore all hoodia products currently on the market are not part of the abovementioned two San benefit sharing agreements. The San have not negotiated ABS-agreements with anyone except the CSIR and the South African Hoodia Growers. It seems safe to conclude therefore, all commercially traded hoodia products today contain illegally acquired resources and traditional knowledge according to the CBD [Convention on Biological Diversity].

Beyond the moral and legal benefit-sharing concerns of the San as traditional knowledge holders, CSIR as the patent holder and Phytopharm and Unilever as the licensees, the Hoodia case also raises a myriad of important issues related to the impact of traditional knowledge exploitation on associated biological resources, particularly wild plant populations. As noted, multi-billion dollar profit projections in the obesity market have been made for Hoodia plants generally, stimulating a massive trade (legal and illegal) in *Hoodia gordonii* and other *Hoodia* species. In 2004, a proposal was adopted to include the entire genus of *Hoodia* in Appendix II of the *Convention on International Trade in Endangered Species of Wild Fauna and Flora* (CITES), and currently all trade in specimens of *Hoodia* spp. requires the issuance of CITES permits or certificates.[21]

The issues that arise when a traditional plant resource is brought into the mainstream and subjected to global market forces are not limited to Hoodia. There is a growing list of plants in high demand for the botanical industry that have become endangered or at risk as a result, such as Goldenseal (*Hydrastis canadensis*), American ginseng (*Panax quinquifolium*), Black Cohosh (*Cimicifuga racemosa*), Blue Cohosh (*Caulophyllum thalictroides*), Slippery Elm (*Ulmus fulva*), and Echinacea (*Angustifolia* spp.).

The inextricable links between biological resources and the integrity of knowledge systems are described in a 2005 submission to the *Working Group on Indigenous Populations* (International Institute for Environment and Development, 2005; emphasis in original):

> *Biological resources* cannot be separated from knowledge for a number of reasons. Firstly, thousands of traditional crop varieties (or 'landraces'), are themselves the product or embodiment of knowledge of past and current generations of farmers which have developed, conserved and improved them. Secondly, according to the worldview of many Indigenous societies, knowledge and resources, ie. the intangible and tangible components, cannot be separated. Knowledge and resources are used and transmitted together. Knowledge is derived from biological resources and landscapes, through spiritual beliefs and rituals, eg. from sacred plants, forests or mountains. Areas which have been degraded of their biological wealth lose their "sacred" character and hence ability to impart knowledge. Thirdly, the maintenance and creation of knowledge depends on the customary use of biological resources and their informal exchange between individuals and communities.

The same submission argues that integral links of equal importance are also found at the landscape level (International Institute for Environment and Development, 2005):

> *Landscapes* provide the physical space for interaction with natural and biological resources, and for sharing of knowledge and resources between individuals and communities. Knowledge is often acquired from particular sites in the landscape of spiritual significance such as sacred lakes, rivers, forests or mountains. Furthermore, traditional forms of governance and belief systems often operate at landscape scales, through customary institutions for management of common property resources. Where peoples have lost their traditional territories or no longer have access to sacred wilderness areas, the processes which sustain and create traditional knowledge and beliefs are likely to be severely weakened or lost, thus putting traditional knowledge at serious risk.[22]

Moreover, landscapes are not just physical in character but have been shaped and influenced by human interaction with them, the naming of land features, and the stories that have become associated with and etched into the land. In this way, landscapes can be viewed as social constructs upon which traditional knowledge has evolved and developed over time. As New Zealand archaeologist Susan Forbes notes, 'Landscapes are the way we *perceive* environment. . . . What we perceive is a product of knowledge, experience, beliefs and biases. Landscapes give us a sense of place or belonging. They reveal our relationship with land over time—whether we are directly aware of their influence, landscapes have a profound effect on human life.'[23] When someone from one culture endeavors (through research or otherwise) to interpret the stories within another's cultural landscape, what that 'outsider' sees or perceives is necessarily based on her/his own knowledge and biases, which may be quite different from the stories of the land as understood by the traditional inhabitants belonging to that landscape.

Thus any interpretation or reinterpretation of that 'traditional' landscape by an 'outsider' runs the risk of either missing the point or placing her/his own cultural biases of what s/he has perceived the landscape to represent. For example, the labeling of vast areas of land by early English colonists to Aotearoa/New Zealand as 'wastelands' unoccupied by the natives disregarded the fact that these lands were used for seasonal hunting, planting and gathering, and were vital in sustaining the livelihoods and knowledge systems of the Indigenous inhabitants. Labeling the lands as unoccupied wastelands facilitated their appropriation by the settlers. Although motives for colonial appropriation of lands may not be the same as motives for appropriation of traditional knowledge, there are comparable impacts on Indigenous peoples. And, as we shall see later, the rationalizations used by the appropriators are similar.

The story of non-Indigenous academic experts documenting and interpreting the cultural landscapes of Indigenous peoples is known throughout the world. One example is found in the case of anthropologists, archaeologists, geologists and ethnologists who have studied the culture and landscape of the Moriori peoples of Rekohu (Chatham Islands) over the past 200 years. The hypotheses, research methodologies and conclusions invariably are rooted within the researchers' own academic disciplinary framework and 'cultural values'. Typically, research about Moriori peoples has taken place without active involvement or participation of local Moriori people who hold generations of knowledge of the environmental and cultural landscapes, which the researchers may be experiencing for the first time. Thus any research outcomes, while having value in recording the researchers' observation of what they saw or thought they saw, is seriously impoverished as an *accurate* record of the old stories and values associated with that landscape. These records have become the basis upon which new, and often misleading, stories have been told about Moriori and Rekohu, including damaging claims that Moriori people are an extinct race.[24]

The latter point was publicly acknowledged by the Governor-General of New Zealand, Sir Paul Reeves, in his 1989 public speech launching the first widely accepted history of the Moriori people written by Michael King, *Moriori: A People Rediscovered*:

> I did not find it easy to read *Moriori*. It was a painful experience. Not simply were you ravaged by the aggressive Maoris and deprived of your land by successive decisions of the Land Court, you have also been wounded by the opinions of pseudo scientists who said Morioris did not exist or came from some early and inferior Pacific people. The insidious impression spread that to be a Moriori was something shameful, something to be denied and hidden. Many of us have had to struggle with issues of identity and who we are. From my own experience, I can understand a little of what this has meant for Moriori people.[25]

Moriori people have recently embarked on a project to redress the inaccuracies documented about their culture and landscape by undertaking their own cultural evaluation process and building a database based on their traditional knowledge and values of the land. This work is being undertaken by the Hokotehi Moriori Trust (Chatham Islands) using a collaborative team of Moriori elders and experts who have lived in and with the land for generations alongside archaeologists, and is guided by Moriori social, cultural, environmental, scientific, economic, spiritual, and ethical imperatives.[26] Interim findings from this project have significantly changed the way heritage landscapes were defined by earlier archaeological surveys that were carried out without Moriori input. The interim results have invalidated and overturned these previous studies, which defined Moriori as seasonal, transitory occupants of temporary occupation areas. The collaborative project has recorded evidence that clearly shows sustained, large-scale occupation. These findings are being used by Moriori to support their arguments for return of waahi tapu (sacred lands) in negotiation of the settlement of their treaty claims with the New Zealand government.

In addition, Moriori have been compiling their own traditional knowledge database using as a model, database software developed for the Traditional Knowledge Revival Pathways initiative in Australia.[27] The purpose of the Moriori database is to capture and retrieve elements of traditional knowledge that are at risk of being lost forever so that they may be utilized by present and future generations of Moriori and Chatham Islanders for the better management of their environment using sustainable cultural practices. Importantly, this traditional knowledge database will be owned and controlled by the local community and decisions to share knowledge will be under the direct control of the knowledge holders themselves. An important aspect of the knowledge retrieval project is the reclamation and maintenance of an Indigenous identity and its importance for living in relationship with the land.

While loss of territory goes hand in hand with loss of knowledge, without a focus on the *people* being located within the landscape, the emphasis may fall on preserving traditional knowledge so it is not lost (to future research or other endeavors and generations to come) rather than what can be done to ensure that the people continue to inhabit their traditional lands and to maintain their customary practices. Arguably, the latter is what will be more likely to result in maintenance of a peoples' traditional knowledge base. However, an over-emphasis on preserving traditional knowledge for its instrumental value has predominated among researchers from academia, government and industry alike.

The example of bioprospecting is particularly revealing in this regard. A popularized conservation-based argument for saving the world's remaining rainforests is premised on the assumption that biodiversity is 'nature's medicine chest' and that rainforests are worth more when alive and functioning than for their timber value if cut down. But as lawyer Brendan Tobin (2004) indicates, by focusing on the instrumental value of traditional knowledge, the bigger point may be lost:

Awareness of the plight of traditional knowledge has risen dramatically during the last fifteen years or so. Ironically, this has been the result not so much of concerns to protect Indigenous cultures but an indirect result of increased interest in the potential of traditional knowledge to provide leads for new product development.

While the international debate has tended to focus primarily on the question of biopiracy, there are many more immediate threats to traditional knowledge which require attention if it is to be conserved and strengthened. These include loss of land and language, insensitive educational and health policies, agriculture and fisheries extension programs, and the impact of organized religion, amongst others. Development of any effective global program for protection of [traditional knowledge] should, therefore, include not only a means for the recognition of ownership rights but also a system for strengthening the continued use and development of [traditional knowledge] as part of the global body of science, and a mainstay of the populations in developing countries, where local sustainability and development opportunities are closely linked to the integrity of [traditional knowledge] systems.[28]

While some bioprospecting programs, such as the ICBG program (mentioned previously), support the direct involvement of Indigenous or local communities or organizations in drug discovery projects, most bioprospecting takes place on the basis of the published literature, far away from such involvement. Downstream use and commodification of published information by third parties is a significant and contentious issue related to traditional knowledge appropriation, largely because once information enters the so called 'public domain' through publications or open access databases it is considered 'free game for free enterprise'.[29] Placing traditional knowledge in the public domain commonly diminishes the context from which the knowledge was created, and therefore the sense of responsibility to source communities. Third parties from the commercial sector (e.g., biotechnology, pharma, herbal, floral) all too often lack sufficient awareness or incentives to address the inequities and potential harms to source communities and ecosystems that result from traditional knowledge appropriation and unfettered use.

The Hoodia example is particularly noteworthy in two ways. First, academics had a key role as facilitators (wittingly or unwittingly) of traditional knowledge appropriation through their publication of traditional Hoodia uses by the San, which informed the research by CSIR that led to the discovery of appetite-suppressing compounds. Second, it was only after significant international attention was drawn to the fact that the San had been left out of the equation that CSIR initiated a benefit-sharing agreement with the San.

Today, Indigenous intellectual property and cultural heritage rights have become a central issue for ethnobiologists and many other academics whose research involves traditional knowledge. However, scientists were largely caught off-guard by widespread and vehement accusations of 'biopiracy' in the early 1990s, the peak of bioprospecting efforts by university-industry-community consortia. The late Darrell Posey (1947–2001), a well-known ethnobiologist, author and Indigenous rights advocate, observed (Posey 1999: 225):

> The publishing of information, traditionally the hallmark of academic success, has become a superhighway for transporting restricted (or even sacred) information into the unprotectable "public domain". . . . As a result, ethnoecologists are increasingly seen by Indigenous, traditional and local communities not as allies but as instruments of corporate interests. Scientists are not accustomed to playing the role of the villain, and they find the lack of trust in their activities to be of profound puzzlement. They see themselves as seekers of the truth, and if anything, victims of a system that exploits their efforts by low pay, reduced research funds, and precarious infrastructural support.[30]

An analysis of the flow of Indigenous medicinal knowledge into the public domain through academic publication during the 1990s by legal scholar Russel Barsh led him to conclude that 'academic activity poses a much greater immediate threat to Indigenous knowledge systems than the patent system.'[31] He suggests that 'standard setting by academic and professional associations would have a greater impact if coupled with rigorous screening by the ethics panels of universities, by government agencies, and by foundations that finance university research, including pharmaceutical industry foundations.'

We suggest it is not enough to seek solutions only from within dominant Western institutions and frameworks, as these will continue to perpetuate historical power inequities, no matter how well-intentioned. What is needed is both the *will* and the *way* for all parties, Indigenous and non-Indigenous, academic and non-academic, to actively engage in a process of transforming relations that leads to mutually agreed standards to guide behaviour in a post-colonial era. This is new and unfamiliar territory for all involved. Cree scholar and philosopher Willie Ermine has proposed the concept of 'ethical space' as 'a common space of retreat, reflection and dialogue' for this purpose. In Ermine's (2005) words, the concept of ethical space is 'the analogy of a space between two entities, as a space between the Indigenous and Western spheres of culture and knowledge'.[32]

> The positioning of these two entities, divided by the void and flux of their cultural distance, their histories, values, traditions and national imperatives,

produces a significant and interesting notion that has relevance in research thought. The affirmation for the existence of two objectivities, each claiming their own distinct and autonomous view of the world, and each holding a different account of what they are seeing across the cultural border, creates the urgent necessity for a common space of retreat, reflection and dialogue.

The entrenched differences of the two entities can fragment and interfere with real communication between individuals, nations and even different parts of the same organization because the hidden values and intentions can control behaviors, and these unnoticed cultural differences can clash without our realizing what is occurring. These distinct, unseen, unspoken differences create disparity between the West and Indigenous worlds and without an appropriate exploration of the social constructs and inhibitions that affect communications, there will no understanding of how thought functions in governing our behaviors. The act of dialogue is the act of resolving the confrontation and is itself an ethical act.

Just as Youngblood Henderson (this volume) considers the relevance of ethical space to appropriation of human remains, so too do we reflect on this 'abstract, nebulous space of possibility' in the appropriation of traditional knowledge. We use ethnobiology as the context for our reflections. Specifically, we examine a unique process spanning more than a decade, undertaken by the International Society of Ethnobiology to develop a Code of Ethics to address traditional knowledge appropriation and related issues.

Creating ethical space in ethnobiology

The International Society of Ethnobiology recognises that culture and language are inextricably connected to land and territory, and cultural and linguistic diversity are inextricably linked to biological diversity. Therefore, the right of Indigenous peoples to the preservation and continued development of their cultures and languages and to the control of their lands, territories and traditional resources are key to the perpetuation of all forms of diversity on Earth.[33]

Ethnobiologists are intermediaries between scientific and Indigenous cultures, catalyzing change and facilitating appropriation of traditional knowledge and associated biological resources. While ethnobiology is primarily academic in nature, it is well established that academic data often flow into the private sector for commercial purposes. Before his death, Darrell Posey argued that a lack of relationship between researchers and traditional knowledge holders facilitates commodification of the sacred. He challenged researchers in the ethnosciences to develop higher levels of awareness and commitment to respect and protect Indigenous rights and cosmologies in research, explaining the potential harm in ignorance: 'the plant, animal, or crystal that an ethnopharmacologist wants to collect may, in fact, encompass, contain, or even be the manifestation of an ancestral spirit— even the healer's grandmother.'[34]

Posey did more than simply promulgate his convictions about research relations; he inspired a new wave of intellectual and political debate on research ethics and set in motion a cascade of events that have fundamentally influenced how the appropriation of traditional knowledge is conceptualized, from local to international levels. In 1988, Posey was key in organizing the first international gathering of ethnobiologists, called the International Congress of Ethnobiology, held in Belém, Brazil. With a small number of others, he founded the International Society of Ethnobiology, launching a new course for ethnobiologists the world over by creating an umbrella for scientists, environmentalists and Indigenous peoples to work together to protect the world's endangered biological and cultural diversity. Over 600 delegates from thirty-five countries, including representatives from sixteen Indigenous organizations participated in the first Congress. At the close of the Congress, founding members joined together to forge the first statement of guiding principles to represent the goals and ideals of ethnobiologists and ethnobiology in an international context— the *Declaration of Belém*.

The *Declaration of Belém* explicitly recognizes the continuing destruction of ecosystems throughout the world, and both the devastating biological and human implications of these developments. Recognizing that Indigenous peoples 'have been stewards of 99% of the world's genetic resources', the *Declaration of Belém* underscores the point that the knowledge underlying the resource management practices of the world's Indigenous peoples is directly tied to the maintenance of the biological diversity of the planet. Loss of traditional knowledge is inextricably linked to loss of biological diversity and *vice versa*. The *Declaration of Belém* was the first international declaration to call for mechanisms to be established to recognize and consult with Indigenous specialists as proper authorities in all activities affecting them, their resources, and their environments, and that procedures be developed to compensate Indigenous peoples for use of their knowledge and their biological resources.[35] The *Declaration of Belém* has served thereafter to encourage members of the Society and its International Congresses in ethical practices that lead to equitable and meaningful dialogue between Indigenous peoples and those trained in Western scientific traditions.

A formal Ethics Committee, led by Posey, was established in 1992, with a specific mandate to develop a Code of Conduct for the Society. Open hearings over the course of the next four years led to development of a draft Code of Ethics and Standards of Conduct in 1996, intended to provide ethnobiologists with guiding principles developed in conjunction with Indigenous peoples. In 1998, the first half of the Code of Ethics (consisting of fourteen principles) was finalized during an intensive pre-congress workshop and adopted by the membership at the sixth International Congress in Aotearoa/New Zealand. Completion of the second part of the Code of Ethics (research practices) was deferred to the next congress. However, the following Congress in 2000, held at the University of Georgia (USA), was largely embroiled in an international controversy surrounding the host university, which at that time was leading an ICBG-sponsored bioprospecting project in Chiapas, Mexico labeled as 'biopiracy' by activist organizations and eventually cancelled. A special session of the Ethics Committee was organized during the Congress to debate issues of prior informed consent, intellectual property rights and benefit-sharing, which were not only at the heart of the Chiapas bioprospecting controversy but at the very forefront of ethnobiology everywhere. Agreements were made to call together a 'Crucible type group' to debate these important topics and to formulate a policy statement.

Posey's untimely death in 2001 significantly hindered these efforts and ethnobiologists worldwide were divided on issues of appropriation of traditional knowledge as related to their apparently conflicting dual role of both promoting and protecting biological and cultural diversity. Formal discussions about the ISE Code of Ethics remained in abeyance until the ninth Congress in Canterbury, UK, in 2004 when a special session was held to discuss and renew the commitment of the membership to complete the Code of Ethics. Internet-based discussions ensued for a further two years and the final Code of Ethics was completed after an intensive three-day pre-Congress workshop followed by a Congress working session as part of the tenth International Congress in Chiang Rai, Thailand in 2006. The final Code of Ethics, consisting of a preamble, purpose, seventeen principles and twelve practical guidelines, was unanimously approved by the membership, thereby completing a remarkably long, complex and divisive journey in search of a unifying formula to address traditional knowledge appropriation and related issues in ethnobiology.

The Code of Ethics is founded upon the single underlying value of 'mindfulness', which invokes 'an obligation to be fully aware of one's knowing and unknowing, doing and undoing, action and inaction.' It is characterized by a number of progressive principles that extend well beyond contemporary biomedical and social science research ethics standards:

- Indigenous prior proprietary rights and cultural responsibilities are explicitly acknowledged.
- Active community participation in all stages of research from inception to implementation and interpretation is encouraged.
- The concept of 'educated prior informed consent' is promoted, which recognizes informed consent not only as an ongoing process but as requiring an educative component that employs bilingual and intercultural education methods and tools to ensure understanding by all parties involved.
- The precautionary principle is supported through promoting proactive, anticipatory action to identify and to prevent biological or cultural harms resulting from research activities or outcomes.
- Researchers are expected to incorporate reciprocity, mutual benefit and equitable sharing in ways that are culturally appropriate and consistent with the wishes of the community involved.
- Research is viewed as a cycle of continuous and on-going communication and interaction, which should not be initiated unless there is reasonable assurance that all stages can be completed.
- Supporting Indigenous communities in undertaking their own research based on their own epistemologies and methodologies is a priority.
- The importance is underscored of acknowledgment and due credit in accordance with community preferences in all agreed outcomes (e.g., publications, educational materials) including co-authorship when appropriate, and extending equally to secondary or downstream uses and applications such that researchers will ensure the connections to original sources of knowledge and resources are maintained in the public record.
- Research is expected to be conducted in the local language to the degree possible, which may involve language fluency or employment of interpreters.

- Researchers are expected to have a working understanding of the local context prior to entering into research relationships with a community, which includes knowledge of and willingness to comply with local governance systems, cultural laws and protocols, social customs and etiquette.

The value and the principles noted above are innovative in that they underscore additional layers of duty in research that compel researchers to be concerned about the dignity and autonomy not only of *individuals*, but also of *collectives* or *groups*. Moreover, the concept of research ethics is extended beyond just humans to the surrounding environment upon which human well-being depends, and includes rights and responsibilities to the living and non-living, and extends into past, present and future. One consequence is that researchers are obliged to think beyond project-based timeframes (i.e., a few years) and consider larger temporal scales, whether years, decades or generations. Another implication is that time and resources are needed to understand or establish protocols and develop agreements that reflect mutual expectations around the research (e.g., obtaining appropriate consent or permission, informing and involving local people, defining and sharing outcomes and benefits of research in meaningful and useful forms, and adequately protecting community knowledge or property from misrepresentation or misappropriation).

This evolution of thought in research ethics seems inherently an exercise in democratization and decolonization of the research enterprise, which presents significant challenges to power hierarchies and decision-making structures embedded in dominant Western institutional frameworks and academic models of knowledge production that are based on linear, extractive conventions for documenting and publishing traditional knowledge.[36] It is important in this regard to note that the Code of Ethics is explicit in its target sphere of influence as well as its limitations in this regard. It is seen as an internationally agreed-upon standard that is meant to meet, support and enable but *not trump* community-level processes and structures:

> This Code of Ethics recognizes and honors traditional and customary laws, protocols, and methodologies extant within the communities where collaborative research is proposed. It should enable but not over-ride such community-level processes and decision-making structures. It should facilitate the development of community-centered, mutually-negotiated research agreements that serve to strengthen community goals.

At least in the abstract, the Code of Ethics appears to address (to greater or lesser degrees) each ethical issue that we have raised in relation to appropriation of traditional knowledge. Rather than a stance against appropriation, its guidance focuses on how traditional knowledge and expertise ought to be approached to prevent *mis*appropriation (acquisition of knowledge without the consent of the knowledge holders), implying that there are losses to society in the absence of appropriation (e.g., conservation incentives, new medicines and other useful products, economic opportunities, training and technological advances for source communities). The purpose of the Code of Ethics can be seen as ensuring appropriation occurs in respectful and culturally appropriate ways that benefit (rather than harm) the source communities involved and support (rather than sever) interrelationships with biological and cultural diversity and the protection of Indigenous peoples' collective biocultural heritage.

It remains to be seen whether the Code of Ethics is an effective tool to foster an ethical space for ethnobiological research and beyond. However, we suggest that the extraordinary process of developing the Code of Ethics, which involved several hundreds of individuals (Indigenous and non-Indigenous, academic and non-academic) from a diversity of backgrounds and from all corners of the globe, has inherently been one of creating ethical space. In our interpretation, this includes respect for parallel or multiple processes that stem from different beliefs and worldviews, i.e., finding ways to work together while maintaining the integrity of one's own epistemology and being mindful of necessary self-limits, such that one belief, process or system of knowing does not take precedence over the other. As noted by Bannister and Hardison (2006),

> Respect for parallel processes requires sufficient awareness and understanding of the "other", *i.e.*, a level of cross-cultural "competency", and is fundamentally about sharing of power to make decisions. The idea that "I can respect other beliefs without believing them, but first I need to know they exist".[37]

Apart from the ISE Code of Ethics, a considerable amount of work has been undertaken over the last decade at national and international levels in the area of 'protecting traditional knowledge' through recognition of traditional resource rights, tangible and intangible cultural heritage rights, and intellectual property rights. Initiatives of both the Convention on Biological Diversity (CBD) and the World Intellectual Property

Organization (WIPO) have received the majority of attention, specifically the Working Group on Article 8j (Traditional Knowledge, Innovations and Practices) of the CBD,[38] the Working Group on Access and Benefit Sharing in relation to Article 15 of the CBD,[39] and the WIPO Intergovernmental Committee on Intellectual Property and Genetic Resources, Traditional Knowledge and Folklore (IGC).[40] However, other international bodies and agencies such as the United Nations Conference on Trade and Development (UNCTAD), the United Nations Educational, Scientific and Cultural Organization (UNESCO), the World Conservation Union (IUCN) and the World Bank are also developing policy positions in this area.

The fora, legal structures, language of discourse, political agendas and unequal status of the parties involved in the ongoing international debate over 'protection of traditional knowledge' inevitably result in an unequal playing field. Thus, the values and aspirations of those whose knowledge is the subject of so-called 'protection' are relegated to minor players and subjugated to the political posturing and often conflicting agendas of nation states. This environment is unlikely to cultivate the confidence of Indigenous peoples that they are being listened to, or that their traditional knowledge will be 'protected' beyond a commercial, monocultural paradigm, from within a construct based on Indigenous values and assumptions. As noted in Solomon (2004),

> . . . [traditional] knowledge is not just an intellectual pursuit or outcome, it encompasses the physical and metaphysical, the tangible and the intangible. For Maori, the traditional knowledge of a 'thing' cannot be separated from its culture or context. The same or similar values and attributes of traditional knowledge are held by Indigenous and traditional peoples the world over. The *values* associated with the knowledge cannot be separated from the knowledge itself.[41]

It is a valid point to convey from the perspective of Indigenous people, who often feel alienated in the various urban fora in which they are required to articulate their cause and justify themselves, that the spaces for dialogue in relation to traditional knowledge ought to be in the places where that knowledge is best understood and appreciated. If traditional knowledge cannot be adequately comprehended in isolation from its values base, and if that values base is firmly rooted in the sand, sea and soil of the lands and waters where the knowledge emerged, it follows that one cannot fully appreciate the strength and depth of the knowledge unless one has been exposed to the cultural and physical context that has spawned and nurtured that knowledge from time immemorial. While a legal, rights-based framework clearly has dominated discussions and negotiations in national and international fora to date, support for complementary policies and moral mechanisms is on the rise, particularly the role of voluntary codes of conduct and codes of ethics.[42] In our view, and as the ISE Code of Ethics illustrates, a key strength in approaching issues of appropriation of traditional knowledge through such codes is the ability to design and redefine the values base upon which the discussion and negotiation fora are premised—a significant step towards creating ethical space.

Part II: Philosophical and Ethical Issues: Toward the Creation of 'Ethical Space'

Conrad G. Brunk

The discussion above traces the story of a progressive movement within the global community of scholars, particularly ethnobiologists, but also within the larger corporate and government communities, toward a consensus account of the fundamental ethical principles that need to be respected to avoid what we have called the 'misappropriation' of traditional knowledge. However, arguments continue to be made that these principles constitute an unwarranted attack upon the value of free inquiry and free access to knowledge by anyone and everyone—a fundamental requirement of scientific rationality. Indigenous claims to rights of control over traditional knowledge on the grounds of its intrinsic relationship to land and culture are seen as a pre-scientific, indeed, anti-scientific, and thus 'primitive' understanding of knowledge and truth.

Knowledge and cultural conventions

The many different cultures of the world, those that have evolved through time and those that coexist in the same epochs of time, have understood the concept of 'knowledge' in a myriad of ways. All of them have had to develop criteria for determining *what* counts as knowledge (and its relationship to 'truth') and *who* in the community has the authority to apply the criteria and say when they have been met (the priests, the shamans, the chiefs, the judges, the scholars). All these cultures had to develop rules for determining *how* knowledge gets used in the community, for what benefit, for whose benefit; and *who* gets to *use* it (the medicine men, the religious and technological elites, the guilds, etc.). And, finally, cultures adopted conventions and understandings about the assignment of *responsibility* for the ways in which knowledge was used—for good or ill—in the community.

These different cultural practices are in large measure mere conventions. They are options that need to be exercised about how to assign roles and responsibilities within the community for learning, and for retaining what is learned, for passing it on to others, and ensuring that it serves the community's values and goals. Those values and goals will differ dramatically from culture to culture, and the effectiveness of the conventions around the use of knowledge will, of course, be relative to those goals. There is no one way to do these things.

The understanding of knowledge in the culture of the Judeo-Christian-Islamic world, somewhat inaccurately referred to as 'European' or 'Western' culture, evolved from a primarily religious understanding of knowledge, informed by the Abrahamic monotheism shared by these three religions, into the rationalism of the Enlightenment and the rise of the modern view of science as the paradigm of knowledge. The earlier, religious, view was committed to the idea of knowledge as a universal truth, inherent in the mind of an omniscient deity, and it assigned the various criteria of truth, authorities for application of the criteria, and responsibility for its use largely to religious authorities—priests, monks, popes, bishops and imams—and the religious conflicts of this era were largely over who these authorities should be. Enlightenment rationalism retained the notion of knowledge as an insight into universal truth, but that truth no longer required a divine intelligence. It required only a rational mind and methods for observing the world exactly as it 'really was'. In the new science, knowledge was defined, as in Francis Bacon's famous dictum, as 'power'—that is, the power to manipulate nature in the interests of humanity. If knowledge is the power to control nature for human ends, then the criterion of truth is success in this endeavor, and the authorities with the responsibility for it were no longer the religious authorities, but the secular philosophers, scientists and the engineers.

This Enlightenment view of knowledge as an abstract, universal truth, discernible to anyone trained in reason, logic and the scientific method, now seems self-evidently true to most people in Western culture and increasingly in other technologically advanced cultures around the world. It is the conception that underlies the conventions around intellectual property that are now enshrined, not only in the laws of European and North American countries, but in the system of international law and trade conventions. Within this conception, the idea that any knowledge about the world, being the product of a rationality and methodology available to all people, is the 'common heritage' of all people, also seems self-evident. Within this knowledge paradigm, anyone who claims that a bit of knowledge about the world is their domain, or 'property', over which they have exclusive rights of revelation and control, appears to be claiming the indefensible, if not the incomprehensible. How could anyone claim that some truth about the world is an exclusive right when it is in principle discoverable, and thus knowable, by anyone?

The 'terra nullius' *fallacy*

Of course, when cultures adopt this scientific-rationalist paradigm of knowledge they are left, like all cultures, with the problem of developing conventions and rules to govern the assignment of responsibility for generation, validation and preservation of that knowledge. This includes conventions for motivating and rewarding the discovery of abstract knowledge and its application to problem solving. Not surprisingly, the cultures who adopted this paradigm developed copyright and patent laws based upon not always clear distinctions between 'pure knowledge' (which is the 'common heritage' of all), 'particular expressions' of knowledge (which can be owned via copyright), and 'techniques' for the discovery and application of knowledge to the world (which can be owned via patents). The important thing to recognize is how these distinctions try to reconcile the ownership of knowledge with the basic commitment to the abstract 'common heritage' view of knowledge in the scientific-rationalist paradigm. They do so by invoking another familiar Enlightenment view of property ownership, associated with the philosopher John Locke. On this view, an agent becomes entitled to own something as his or her property when he has 'mixed his own labour' with that thing, and by so doing, has added value to the thing, for which he or she can claim responsibility and thus rights of ownership. Until someone's labour is mixed with a thing, whether an abstract idea, tangible land or material resource, it is not owned by anyone; it is not the property of anyone. It is '*terra nullius*'.

The concept of *terra nullius* is important here because its vital role in the rationalization of colonialist appropriation of lands from Indigenous populations all over the world provides an instructive history for understanding the appropriation of traditional knowledge, where a very similar logic obtains. *Terra nullius* is now widely understood, even in the Western legal culture that invoked it, not only as a highly unjust imposition of the values of one culture over those of another, but even worse, as a cynical and hypocritical violation of the Western value framework itself. The violation consists in the failure, if not the witting refusal, to recognize the now obvious fact that the Indigenous cultures of the colonized world had indeed 'mixed their labour' with the lands they inhabited. The claim that they had not done so, and thus had no ownership of the lands invaded by the colonizers, was defended by pointing out the 'fact' that these Indigenous peoples had no formalized conventions (like those in European legal systems) for the assignment of property rights to individuals or groups, or that they did not settle upon, and cultivate, the lands in the same ways Europeans typically (though not always) did.

Often the *terra nullius* doctrine is cited as an example of the completely incommensurable nature of two different value systems, settled by the sheer preponderance of power held by the colonizers. It is seen as a confirmation of the truth of cultural relativism, and also of the dangers inherent in ethical objectivism or universalism—any form of the belief that there are universally valid moral values and principles. The danger is that those who believe their own values to be universally valid will find it easy to impose them upon others when it serves their own interests, and to see themselves as entirely morally justified when doing so. Thus, sheer power is masked with the self-righteous veneer of 'justice'.

But, ethical relativism also carries the same risk of justifying the cynical application of power in the service of brute self-interest. It does so by simply giving up on the possibility of reaching an ethical consensus across cultures. It is more likely to avoid the self-deceptive self-righteousness that one is actually acting ethically when colonizing others. But it fails to provide any reason for entering the 'ethical space' in which dialogue and listening might actually help to clarify one's own values in relation to the values of others. This is illustrated by the late chapters in the history of *terra nullius*, in which it has become clear that, by the very terms of the European philosophy of property, the lands of Indigenous peoples were never anything close to *terra nullius*. The lands of the Americas, of Australia, of New Zealand and countless other colonized places in the world were the home-lands of people who had 'mixed their labour' with the land in the forms of their own cultural conventions, and these conventions produced a form of 'ownership' that now can clearly be seen. It is not 'ownership' as defined in the Western legal forms, but it is a form of ownership (or perhaps better, of *entitlement*) nonetheless.

Knowledge as 'terra nullius'

The debate about the ownership of the traditional knowledge of Indige-nous peoples and of the resources derived and derivable from this knowl-edge has an uncannily similar character to the *terra nullius* arguments of the European colonizers of land. The similarity lies in the way the academic and corporate appropriators of traditional knowledge use the Western scientific-rationalist paradigm of knowledge to justify the claim that Indig-enous peoples have no valid ownership claims to their knowledge of the ecosystems in which they have lived (and which they have significantly shaped) and of its uses. Essentially, this scientific-rationalist paradigm claims that whatever counts as 'abstract' or 'pure' knowledge is, in effect, *terra nullius*. It is knowledge that is owned by no one, because it is not knowledge that has had 'value added' to it—at least not in the way value is added in the traditional scientific-rationalist paradigm. This knowledge is thus the 'common heritage' of mankind, available for anyone to use and 'mix one's labour' with in a way that creates rights of ownership (e.g., copyright or patent).

The clear assumption in the argument is that Indigenous peoples clearly have not 'mixed their labour' with this knowledge in a way that 'adds value' in the Western sense of the term. The Indigenous understanding that Hoodia works as an appetite suppressant, that Echinacea works to stimu-late the immune system, etc., is pure, abstract knowledge, 'common heri-tage' that cannot be claimed as property without disrupting the whole scientific-rationalist enterprise. Why are the important therapeutic appli-cations of these natural products not considered 'value added' knowledge? It is because their therapeutic effects are not understood *scientifically*—i.e., the traditional knowledge has not identified the 'active agent' in the Hoodia or Echinacea plants. In other words, the scientific-rationalist argument assumes that the 'value added' lies in the scientific explanation of the therapeutic effect, which then allows its incorporation into a technology—a 'product'. Who, then, gets to claim ownership of the hitherto 'unowned' Hoodia and Echinacea? Of course it is those who provide the scientific explanation and on the basis of this knowledge extract the 'active ingredient' in each plant and make a new therapeutic product. This is the labour that counts in the scientific-rationalist paradigm. The *terra nullius* argument justifying the colonization of the traditional knowledge of these plants is now complete. The knowledge can be appropriated, made into a technology (thus mixed with labour for the first time) and first-time ownership can be also be claimed.

This version of the *terra nullius* argument is clearly as strained and self-serving as a rationalization in the context of traditional knowledge appropriation as it was in the context of the colonialist appropriation of land from Indigenous peoples. Just as in the land case it failed notoriously to recognize the cultural conventions by which Indigenous peoples 'mix their labour' with the land and make it their own in ways quite different from Europeans, so also in the case of knowledge appropriation does it fail to recognize the cultural conventions by which Indigenous peoples 'mix their labour' in the creation of knowledge in ways that make it distinctively wedded to, or embedded in, their culture. This is what Indigenous peoples all over the world have been trying to say to the scientific-rationalist appropriators of their knowledge when they claim that the knowledge is no more in the 'public domain', no more a 'common heritage', than are the copyrighted texts or the patented 'techniques' of modern, scientific culture.

They make the point in the language we have seen put forward in the international fora where the codes of ethics for ethnobotanical research and corporate appropriation of traditional knowledge have been hammered out. We recall the claims, for example, that Indigenous knowledge is intrinsically connected to the long history of habitation of a landscape or ecosystem, which has both shaped the knowledge gained from it and been shaped by that knowledge. Thus, the biological resources produced by that knowledge cannot be separated from the knowledge itself. This is not some esoteric claim, understandable only within the framework of some 'primitive' Indigenous metaphysic. It is a claim comprehensible within the Lockean philosophy of property itself insofar as it establishes the sense in which Indigenous knowledge is not simply the sum of abstract concepts or principles by which nature is manipulated, but is the engaged, *practical* understanding of a people on a landscape.

In the scientific-rationalist paradigm, if someone appropriates or uses the abstract knowledge discovered by another, this act does not 'take' anything from the other, since the other is left with the knowledge in its entirety. If nothing has been taken, nothing owned has been stolen or 'misappropriated'. The Indigenous claim is that the appropriation of traditional knowledge is indeed a 'taking from' the culture itself, which leaves it with less than it had before. That 'something less' is, among other things, the security of the culture and the landscape or ecosystem that has been shaped by the culture, and upon which the identity and very existence of the culture and its people depend. The discovery of the biological resources that form part of the traditional knowledge of a people and the appropriation of those resources into an external enterprise constitutes a tangible threat to the culture. In this respect there is a definite 'taking' of something to which the culture has a rightful claim, insofar as it has a right to its cultural identity.

It does not matter much that the nature of this rightful claim will be, and in fact is, disputed among Indigenous peoples themselves. Some are willing to call the rightful claim one of ownership and property. Others are not comfortable with the idea of cultural 'ownership' of knowledge, often out of a legitimate fear that the concept will be co-opted by the dominant culture into justification of its own ownership claims on biological resources. Whether or not knowledge is viewed as property, the point of agreement is that others do not have the right of appropriation and assertion of ownership without the full consent and proper recognition of the legitimate claims and interests of the originators of that knowledge.

The principles enunciated in the ISE Code of Ethics lay out the implications of the validity of this underlying rightful claim to traditional knowledge by Indigenous peoples. The most important of these are:

- The right of community participation in research;
- The right of truly informed consent to research and promulgation;
- The right to cautionary measures in the protection of resources and culture;
- The right to reciprocity, mutual benefit and equitable sharing of benefits;
- The right to continuous and on-going communication and interaction;
- The right to respect for Indigenous research methods and epistemologies;
- The right to acknowledgment and due credit.

All of these, of course, are claims that Indigenous peoples may rightfully assert, although *whether* they are asserted, or the *form* in which they are asserted, remains the right of the particular culture.

The 'ethical space' that is necessary for the just resolution of traditional knowledge and biological resource appropriation is in part achievable by the attempt of persons on all sides of the cultural divides to listen carefully to the claims of the other side. The first order of business in the space is to explore the extent to which the claims of the other can be captured in the terms of one's own ethical understanding. We have argued here that honest engagement in this space can lead those outside the Indigenous cultures— those with an interest in the appropriation of traditional knowledge and its resources—to see the validity of the claims on the Indigenous side within the terms of their own conceptual framework. The differences here are not primarily differences of philosophy or of basic values, but different understandings of how different cultures address similar issues in the terms of their own conventions. What is at issue here is not so much the values as the *facts* about different cultural practices. What is needed in this ethical space is more careful listening, more careful observation, more careful anthropology.

Notes

1. Brown, M. (2003). *Who Owns Native Culture?* Harvard University Press, Cambridge, p. 7.
2. Brown, M. (2003). *Who Owns Native Culture?* Harvard University Press, Cambridge, p. 251.
3. The International Society of Ethnobiology defines 'collective biocultural heritage' as the cultural heritage (both the tangible and intangible including customary law, folklore, spiritual values, knowledge, innovations and practices) and biological heritage (diversity of genes, varieties, species and ecosystem provisioning, regulating, and cultural services) of Indigenous peoples, traditional societies and local communities, which often are inextricably linked through the interaction between peoples and nature over time and shaped by their socioecological and economic context. This heritage includes the landscape as the spatial dimension in which the evolution of Indigenous biocultural heritage takes place. This heritage is passed on from generation to generation, developed, owned and administered collectively by stakeholder communities according to customary law (ISE Code of Ethics, 2006).
4. Howard, A. and Widdowson, F. (1996). Traditional Knowledge Threatens Environmental Assessment. *Policy Options*, November 1996, pp. 34–6;

Widdowson, F. and Howard, A. (2006). Aboriginal 'Traditional Knowledge' and Canadian Public Policy: Ten Years of Listening to the Silence. Paper presented for the Annual Meeting of the Canadian Political Science Association York University, Toronto. June 1–3, 2006.

5. For example, an in depth discussion on terminology for the specific purpose of defining or elaborating the subject matter of traditional knowledge *protection* is found in WIPO, 2002. Traditional Knowledge—Operational Terms and Definitions. Intergovernmental Committee on Intellectual Property and Genetic Resource, Traditional Knowledge and Folklore. Third Session. Geneva, June 13–21, 2002. WIPO/GRTKF/IC/3/9. Available at http://www.wipo.int/edocs/mdocs/tk/en/wipo_grtkf_ic_3/wipo_grtkf_ic_3_9.pdf (last accessed Dec 9, 2008).

6. Bannister, K. and Solomon, M. (2009). Indigenous Knowledges. In *The Prepared Palgrave Dictionary of Transnational History*, edited by Akira Iriye and Pierre-Yves Saunier. Palgrave Macmillan; Basingstoke. pp. 523–26.

7. Brown, M. (2003). *Who Owns Native Culture?* Harvard University Press, Cambridge. Pp. 7.

8. International Cooperative Biodiversity Groups (ICBG) Program, Fogarty International Centre, US National Institutes of Health. http://www.fic.nih.gov/programs/research_grants/icbg/index.htm (last accessed March 10, 2008).

9. Collective Statement of Indigenous Peoples on the Protection of Indigenous Knowledge. Third Session, United Nations Permanent Forum on Indigenous Issues. New York, 10–21 May 2004. Agenda Item 4(e): Culture. Online version (cited from the website of the Indigenous Peoples Council on Biocolonialism) http://www.ipcb.org/resolutions/htmls/pf2004.html (last accessed March 10, 2008).

10. White, A. and Sloane, B. (1937). *The Stapeliae*, 2nd edition. Abbey San Encino Press, Pasadena, California. 3 volumes.

11. Watt, J. M. and Breyer-Branwijk, M. G. (1962). *The Medicinal and Poisonous Plants of Southern and Eastern Africa*. 2nd edition. Livingstone, London.

12. Stephenson, D. (2003). The patenting of P57 and the intellectual property rights of the San peoples of Southern Africa. Commissioned report prepared for First Nations Development Institute and First Peoples Worldwide, Virginia.

13. Wynberg, R. (2004). Rhetoric, Realism and Benefit Sharing: Use of Traditional Knowledge of *Hoodia* Species in the Development of an Appetite Suppressant. *Journal of World Intellectual Property*, **7**(6): 851–876.

14. Bioprospecting (or 'biodiversity prospecting') was first defined by Reid *et al.* in 1993 as 'the exploration of biodiversity for commercially valuable genetic resources and biochemicals.' This definition continues to evolve and there is no universally-agreed definition. Source: Reid W., Laird S., Meyer C.,

Gámez R., Sittenfeld A., Janzen D., Gollin M., and Juma C. (1993). *Biodiversity Prospecting: Using Genetic Resources for Sustainable Development.* WRI: Washington, DC.

15. Scientists and South African San join forces in research project on San use of indigenous plants: Bioprospecting agreement between the CSIR and the South African San Council signed in Upington. Joint media release by the South African San Council and the CSIR, 28 October 2004. http://ntww1.csir.co.za/plsql/ptl0002/PTL0002_PGE157_MEDIA_REL?MEDIA_RELEASE_NO=7233055 (last accessed March 10, 2008).

16. Harry, D. and Kanehe, L. M. (2005). The BS in Access and Benefit Sharing (ABS): Critical Questions for Indigenous Peoples. In Burrows B. (ed.) *The Catch: Perspectives on Benefit Sharing.* Edmonds Institute. Online version (cited from the website of the Indigenous Peoples Council on Biocolonialism) http://www.ipcb.org/publications/other_art/bsinabs.html (last accessed March 10, 2008).

17. An internet search of the combined words 'hoodia' 'weight loss' and 'buy' using Google search engine on March 31, 2007 led to over one million hits.

18. Laird, S. (2000). Benefit-sharing 'best practice' in the pharmaceutical and botanical medicine industries. In Svarstad H. and Dhillion S. (eds.) *Bioprospecting: From biodiversity in the South to medicines in the North.* Spartacus Forlag As, Oslo, pp. 89–99.

19. Wynberg, R., personal communication to K. Bannister on March 10, 2008; Wynberg, R. and Chennells, R. 2009. Green Diamonds of the South: An Overview of the San-Hoodia Case. In Wynberg R., Chennells R., and Schroeder D. (eds.) *Indigenous Peoples, Consent and Benefit-sharing. Lessons from the San-Hoodia Case.* Springer, Berlin.

20. World Health Organization, (2006). Rich and Poor Countries Divided on Patent Treaty. *Bulletin of the World Health Organization.* Volume 84 (5): 337–424. May 2006. http://www.who.int/bulletin/volumes/84/5/news20506/en/index.html (last accessed March 10, 2008); Letter of March 2006 to the ministers responsible in South Africa, Germany, and Switzerland written by the Working Group of Indigenous Minorities in Southern Africa in collaboration with other non-profit organizations http://www.evb.ch/cm_data/Letter_Governments_Hoodia_e_Final.pdf (last accessed March 10, 2008).

21. Convention on International Trade in Endangered Species of Wild Fauna and Flora (CITES). Notification to the Parties. Document No. 2006/047. Geneva, 18 August 2006. http://www.cites.org/eng/notif/2006/E047.pdf (last accessed March 10, 2008).

22. International Institute for Environment and Development (2005). Protection of Traditional Knowledge and Cultural Heritage—the Concept of 'Collective Bio-Cultural Heritage'. Working Group on Indigenous Populations, 23rd

Session. http://www.iied.org/pubs/pdfs/G01067.pdf (last accessed Dec 10, 2008).

23. Forbes, S. (2005). Maori Environmental Management 2005. Unpublished tutor notes, Victoria University of Wellington. On file with author.

24. For example, one of the authors (Solomon) is of Moriori and Maori descent and was taught in New Zealand public school that Moriori people were a myth, despite the fact that his grandfather Tame Horomona Rehe (Tommy Solomon) who died in 1933 was full-blooded Moriori. For a widely accepted history of Moriori people, see King, Michael, 1989. *Moriori; A People Redis-covered*, Viking, Auckland. See also Denise Davis and Maui Solomon. 'Moriori', Te Ara—the Encyclopedia of New Zealand, updated 21-Dec-2006. http://www.TeAra.govt.nz/NewZealanders/MaoriNewZealanders/Moriori/en (last accessed March 10, 2008).

25. Speech presented at Arowhenua Marae, Temuka on November 5, 1989. http://www.gov-gen.govt.nz/media/speeches.asp?type=archive&ID=206 (last accessed March 10, 2008).

26. Cracknell, M. (2006). Which way is up? Paper presented at the tenth Interna-tional Congress of Ethnobiology, Chiang Rai, Thailand. November 5–9.

27. The software was developed by Victor Steffensen, a member of the Balkanu Aboriginal community in Australia. See Traditional Knowledge Revival Path-ways website Homepage http://www.tkrp.com.au/, and About page http://tkrp.com.au/index.php?option=com_content&task=view&id=17&Itemid=2 6 (last accessed March 10, 2008).

28. Brendan, T. (2004). Towards an International Regime for Protection of Tra-ditional Knowledge: Reflections on the role of Intellectual Property Rights. IP Genethics conference paper. University of Cambridge and University of Sheffield.

29. Bannister, K. and Barrett, K. (2001). Challenging the Status Quo in Ethno-botany: A New Paradigm for Publication May Protect Cultural Knowledge and Traditional Resources. *Cultural Survival Quarterly.* **24**(4): 10–13.

30. Posey, D. (1999). Safeguarding Traditional Resource Rights of Indigenous Peoples. In Nazarea (ed.) *Ethnoecology: Situated Knowledge/Local Lives.* Uni-versity of Arizona Press, Tucson, pp. 217–29.

31. Barsh, R. (2001). Who Steals Indigenous Knowledge? *Proceedings of the 95th Annual Meeting of the American Society of International Law*, pp. 153–61.

32. Ermine, W. (2005). Ethical Space: Transforming Relations. Discussion paper commissioned by Canadian Heritage. http://www.traditions.gc.ca/docs/docs_disc_ermine_e.cfm (last accessed March 10, 2008).

33. International Society of Ethnobiology, 2006 (with 2008 additions). Code of Ethics. http://ethnobiology.net/code-of-ethics/ (last accessed March 13, 2011).

34. Posey, D. A. (2002). Commodification of the sacred through intellectual prop-erty rights. *Journal of Ethnopharmacology* **83**: 3–12.

35. History of the International Society of Ethnobiology http://ethnobiology.net/about/history-of-the-ise/ (last accessed March 13, 2011).

36. Vodden, K. and Bannister, K. (2008). Circularising Knowledge Flows: Institutional structures, policies and practices for community-university collaborations. In Lutz J. and Neis B. (eds) *Making and Moving Knowledge.* McGill-Queens University Press, Montreal, pp. 245–70.

37. Bannister, K. and Hardison, P. (2006). Mobilizing Traditional Knowledge and Expertise for Decision-Making on Biodiversity. Commissioned paper prepared for the consultative process towards an International Mechanism of Scientific Expertise on Biodiversity (IMoSEB). German Federal Agency for Nature Conservation. http://www.polisproject.org/PDFs/BannisterHardison%202006.pdf (last accessed March 10, 2008).

38. Convention on Biological Diversity, Article 8(j): Traditional Knowledge, Innovations and Practices. http://www.biodiv.org/programmes/socio-eco/traditional/default.shtml (last accessed March 10, 2008).

39. Convention on Biological Diversity, Access to Genetic Resources and Benefit Sharing. http://www.biodiv.org/programmes/socio-eco/benefit/default.aspx (last accessed March 10, 2008).

40. World Intellectual Property Organization, Intergovernmental Committee on Intellectual Property and Genetic Resources, Traditional Knowledge and Folklore. http://www.wipo.int/tk/en/igc/ (last accessed March 10, 2008).

41. Solomon, M. (2004). Who Owns Traditional Knowledge? Paper prepared for the International Bar Association. Auckland, 26 October 2004. [italics in original; unpublished]

42. Three recent examples are: the 2002 *Bonn Guidelines on Access to Genetic Resources and Fair and Equitable Sharing of the Benefits Arising out of their Utilization.* COP Decision VI/24: Access and benefit-sharing as related to genetic resources. Convention on Biological Diversity. http://www.biodiv.org/programmes/socio-eco/benefit/bonn.asp (last accessed March 10, 2008); the 2004 *Akwé: Kon guidelines* for the conduct of cultural, environmental and social impact assessment regarding developments proposed to take place on, or which are likely to impact on, sacred sites and on lands and waters traditionally occupied or used by Indigenous and local communities. COP-7 Decision VII/16/F. http://www.biodiv.org/doc/publications/akwe-brochure-en.pdf (last accessed March 10, 2008); and 2005 *Elements of an ethical code of conduct to ensure respect for the cultural and intellectual heritage of indigenous and local communities relevant to the conservation and sustainable use of biological diversity.* COP-8 Decision VIII/5/F—Article 8(j) and related provisions. UNEP/CBD/WG8J/4/8 14 November 2005. Convention on Biological Diversity. http://www.biodiv.org/doc/meetings/tk/wg8j-04/official/wg8j-04-08-en.pdf (last accessed March 10, 2008).

8

A Broken Record: Subjecting 'Music' to Cultural Rights

Elizabeth Burns Coleman and Rosemary J. Coombe with Fiona MacArailt

Introduction

Issues involving the appropriation of intangible cultural heritage have attracted new attention in the last decade, becoming the focus of domestic and international law and policy. Ironically, this renewed attention to cultural rights has occurred at the same time as growing concern about the expansion of intellectual property rights and their capacities for stifling creativity, limiting expressive rights, imposing unwarranted forms of censorship and restricting the growth of the public domain. Although most of this critique is quite properly levelled at the corporate cultural industries, one corollary is an intensified suspicion about any new limits being imposed upon cultural production.

This chapter concerns the ethics of appropriating 'artistic content', and draws primarily upon case studies about the loss of rights to musical forms from Canadian First Nations in the Northwest Coast cultural area. These groups have an interest in the history of their own music, particularly in ritual songs, whose performance rights were property in traditional legal regimes and may be unknown to current generations whose only access to them may be via recordings of their ancestors. The request for the repatriation of such recordings may be understood as an assertion of cultural rights; more specifically, it is one of many such claims to collective cultural heritage that look, to outsiders, suspiciously 'proprietary' in nature. In a public sphere in which it is popularly believed that 'information wants to be free', and 'free culture' has become a youth rallying cry for a progressive movement to preserve the public domain, new articulations of cultural rights with respect to cultural texts are unlikely to be welcomed. Some of the fiercest battles are being fought with respect to rights over recorded music, with rights to record, download, sample, and recode musical forms asserted against the recording industries who continue to bring the full force of the law against those they accuse of 'piracy'. (Halbert 2005) This is a difficult context, then, in which to make an argument for restricting rights to music.

Digital technology now enables sounds and images to be 'captured' and manipulated by anyone with a computer. In defense of musical sampling, the band Negativland asserts that

> Artists who routinely appropriate . . . are not attempting to profit from the marketability of their subjects. . . . They are using elements, fragments, or pieces of someone else's created artifact in the creation of a new one for artistic reasons. These elements may remain identifiable, or they may be transformed to varying degrees as they are incorporated into the new creation, where there may be many other fragments all in a new context, forming a new 'whole'. This becomes a new 'original'. (Negativeland n.d.)

Appropriation of music through technological means may be viewed as a continuation of a long Western artistic tradition of musical parody, mimicry and quotation. Even in classical music, 'Bach and Handel borrowed from other composers . . . Stravinski referenced older styles . . . Other classical composers have based compositions on folk music, such as Bela Bartok's works based on Hungarian folk music and Dvorak's 1893 "Symphony No. 9 From the New World", which quotes "Swing Low Sweet Chariot . . ." (Lindenbaum 1999) Within this context, appropriators may consider the sampling of the musical forms of Indigenous people in 'world music' and 'world beat' as a form of artistic homage and even a means of establishing forms of communication and respect across cultural, geographic and territorial divides. (Feld 1996: 15)

One irony of the artistic appropriation of Indigenous music is that, although the musicians who appropriate the music declare their 'fundamental respect, even deep affection for the original music and its makers', their music focuses on a small sample of the repertoire of the originating culture, in turn misrepresenting its musical achievements. (Feld 1996: 26–7) With respect to the appropriation of Forest Peoples' music, anthropologist Steve Feld notes,

The documentary records emphasize a vast repertory of musical forms and performance styles, including complex and original polyphonic and poly-rhythmic practices. Yet what of this diverse musical invention forms the basis for its global pop representation? In the most popular instances it is a single, untexted vocalization or falsetto yodel, often hunting cries rather than songs or musical pieces. This is the sonic cartoon of the diminutive person, the simple, intuitively vocal and essentially non-linguistic child. (Feld 1996: 27)

Contemporary practices of sampling and adaptation may therefore carica-ture the music and the communities for which appropriating artists profess aesthetic respect. Misrepresentation is thus one of the harms that may be done by insensitive forms of cultural appropriation. It is not, however, the only one.

When we frame our topic as one of 'appropriating artistic content' we may already be skewing our ethical considerations because the practice of art as an autonomous realm of individual creative production is a culturally specific framework that leads us to consider matters of appropriation through a lens that is both proprietary and expressive. When we character-ize the ethical dilemma as one of conflict between a right to freedom of expression in artistic practice and a right to restrict the use of content based upon proprietary claims, we have already posed the issue in a misleading fashion that denies many of the equities at stake. Specific questions almost certainly emerge: is copying the theft of creative labor? Is attribution neces-sary? Has a forgery taken place? Does the assertion of rights unduly limit the freedom of expression of others? These are not insignificant questions, but there is no reason for them to wholly orient our moral compass. Indeed, by categorizing the activity of cultural appropriation *as* the appro-priation of artistic content, we may misunderstand the nature of cultural rights claims made by peoples for whom traditional cultural forms do radi-cally different social work.

Articulating cultural rights in terms of a right to artistic forms similarly trivializes the issue at stake. For instance, Jeremy Waldron's argument against cultural rights as human rights characterizes the issue as a claim about artistic form. If a freewheeling cosmopolitan life, 'lived in a kaleido-scope of cultures', is both possible and fulfilling, he argues, 'It can no longer be said that all people *need* their rootedness in the particular culture in which they and their ancestors were reared in the way that they need food, clothing and shelter.' (Waldron 1995: 99–100) He contrasts the cosmopolitanism of Salmon Rushdie's novels and life with the claims by

Will Kymlicka that 'stories' provide people with role models and values that allow them to make meaning of the world, arguing instead that meaningful options may come to us as items or fragments from a variety of cultural sources. Waldron uses as his example a passage from MacIntyre in which he lists recognizable stories from first-century Palestine, the Roman Republic and Germanic folklore. (Waldron 1995:106–7) This celebration of the ethical bricoleur privileges the Western aesthetic assumption that stories are fictions, oblivious to the social networks and/or cosmological ecologies in which many of the world's peoples' 'stories' locate their commitments and obligations.

Anthropologist Michael Brown, a keen observer of the politics surrounding proprietary claims in cultural heritage, notes that 'the rise of the Information Society' has produced 'a diffuse global anxiety around the movement of information between different cultures' and a contemporary 'crisis of cultural heritage' in which culture is now a scarce resource to be defended. (Brown 2005: 42–3) He suggests two main reasons for believing cultural appropriation to be wrong: the first is that appropriation is disrespectful of cultural values and has rarely been agreed to by the source community, and the second is that appropriation subjects the community to material harm by denying it economic benefits or undermining 'the shared understandings essential to its social health.' (Brown 2005: 44) Nonetheless, he argues that academic and advocacy work with respect to intangible cultural heritage must recognize the fact that 'Information answers to its own rules . . . By its nature, the Information Society undermines social norms and institutions.' (Brown 2005: 41, 43)

It is the relationship between social health and cultural forms that we wish to emphasize here. We do not intend to repeat, like a broken record, the assertion that 'Indigenous cultures must be seen as total social systems in which land, the natural environment, social practices and traditional knowledge form a seamless whole.' (Brown 2005: 45) Nor do we assume that any and all cultural appropriation is wrong. We will, however, argue that the appropriation of some recorded music needs to be understood as a violation of cultural rights and its 'repatriation' considered not only a partial means of restitution for historical injuries suffered, but as a provision of unique resources necessary to enable distinct futures to be articulated. Although the emergence of informational capitalism cannot be denied, and does indeed account for 'the meteoric rise of intellectual property rights (IPR) as a matter of global contention', (Brown 2005: 43) it is precisely this reduction of all cultural forms to information that must, we insist, be avoided if issues of cultural appropriation are to be approached ethically.

To make this argument we will proceed historically to understand the dominant conditions under which recordings of traditional music have been made, historical records broken and injuries thereby incurred, and some of the equities involved in rendering their repair. We will suggest that some rights claims to intangible traditional cultural forms challenge modern understandings about tradition, art and the public domain while exposing their limits in societies committed to multiculturalism and or the establishment of pluricultural values.

Tradition and Modernity: Culture, Works and Others

Although arguments about the injuries of cultural appropriation and requests for restitution of cultural forms are not limited to Indigenous peoples, the cultural rights claims made on identitarian grounds that most seem to offend defenders of the public domain are often influenced by the growing international politics of indigenism, which increasingly involves claims based upon tradition. (Coombe 2008) The global position of indigeneity, it is important to emphasize, has no necessary ethnic referent. The international category of Indigenous peoples is, emphatically, a modern and postcolonial one in which human rights are asserted by and extended to ever-emergent groups of peoples who constitute their identities and make their claims by reference to their continuing survival as distinct societies despite their marginalization and oppression by the modern state.

It might be argued that Indigenous peoples are internationally defined as such precisely because of their commitment to their own cultural survival in the face of long histories of domination by others committed to obliterating their cultural traditions. Anthropologist Ronald Niezen suggests that

> [W]hen we look for things that indigenous peoples have in common, for what brings them together and reinforces their common identity, we find patterns that emerge from a logic of conquest and colonialism. These patterns apply equally to people otherwise very different in terms of history, geography, method of subsistence, social structure and political

organization. They are similarities based largely on the relationship
between indigenous peoples and states . . . usually [involving] . . . assimila-
tive state education, loss of subsistence, and state abrogation of treaties.
(Niezen 2003: 87)

These historical injustices are understood by Indigenous communities
to be denials of their specificities as culturally distinct peoples. As Niezen
summarizes, modern state policies of cultural assimilation subjected Indigenous peoples around the world to schools in which their language and
cultural understandings were targeted for eradication and children were
treated as socially inferior because of their cultural difference, which
authorities often viewed as undesirable forms of social backwardness.
Coupled with these efforts were state or missionary endeavors that sought
to destroy Indigenous spirituality, desecrate sacred sites, remove artifacts
and prohibit social rituals and healing systems. State education systems also
upset traditional patterns of mobility and undermined oral knowledge
(and thus the authority of elders) while encouraging children to lose culturally significant connections to ancestral lands. A loss of subsistence due
to modern development and settlement efforts and the intensification of
extractive industry on traditional territories have compounded threats to
Indigenous peoples' identities and autonomy.

A shared history of social struggle against these forces is constitutive
of indigenism as a global movement. For better or worse, given the
dominant ideological climate, 'the notion of belonging to a separate culture . . . [including] language, religion . . . laws . . . technology, art, [and]
music . . . is central to Indigenous peoples' own self-definition.' (Berger
1987: 12) While this may seem 'essentialist' to critical theorists, these claims
of belonging are not adequately understood as asserting proprietary rights;
rather, they express alternative assumptions of and attachments to *obligation* that register an understanding of tradition long suppressed in Western
thought. We are now witnessing a variety of projects that involve 'the
advent of historical consciousness of defunct traditions, the reconstitutive
recovery of phenomena from which we are separated, and which are most
directly of interest to those who think of themselves as the descendants and
heirs of such traditions.' (Phillips, 2004: 9, citing Pierre Nora) The maintenance of cultural difference may well involve resistance to assimilation
and a rejection of certain demands made by the modern state that those
who bear tradition 'modernize' or become extinct. It may also include a
celebration of the traditions that have enabled peoples to maintain their

identities, and efforts to recover expressions of their traditions that were appropriated from them under modern state directives that deemed their 'progress' necessary and their disappearance imminent (for musical examples, see Frisbie 2001 and Gray 1997).

Many contemporary discussions of tradition are still, unfortunately, mired in a dichotomy between progress and backwardness such that traditions are deemed to be static and essentially incompatible with innovation, and any appeal to tradition is alleged to 'freeze' peoples in time. Claims to rights with respect to traditions are often suspect for this reason. Under such prejudices, 'movements for the defense or revival of tradition mark a break in continuity that signals that a tradition must be in the process of becoming an invented one', when, ironically, 'modern history is full of moments in which cultural continuities were in the gravest doubt, and it is also full of spectacular successes for those who struggled, through processes that mixed revival and invention, to renew their languages and cultures.' (Phillips 2004: 6)

Unfortunately, tradition and modernity are so ubiquitously conceived in a dichotomous relationship that it is very difficult to use the terms in new and distinctive ways. Tradition has been understood as the antithesis of modernity, destined to disappear alongside it, and a barrier to national integration within the modern state. As Will Kymlicka points out, in the nineteenth century both liberal and socialist thinkers agreed that progress required a strong undivided nation state and believed the 'great nations' to be civilized carriers of historical development, while smaller nationalities were 'primitive and stagnant, and incapable of social or cultural development.' (1995: 53) For instance, John Stuart Mill claimed it was better for a Scottish Highlander to be a citizen of Great Britain, 'than to sulk on his own rocks, the half-savage relic of past times, revolving in his own little mental orbit, without participation or interest in the general movement of the world (J. S. Mill 1894 cited in Kymlicka 1995: 53). Similarly, Engels saw the subjugation, absorption and assimilation of small national groups as the entitlement of great nations, 'a right of civilisation against barbarism, of progress against stability ...[This] is the right of historical evolution' (cited in Kymlicka 1995: 70). Assuming either the inevitable assimilation or extinction of 'traditional' peoples, state authorities were (and many still are) ill-prepared for the survival of Indigenous worldviews, customs, and values under conditions of modernization. For the longer part of Western history, however, tradition represented a dynamic vision of society in which present generations were reflexive custodians of a legacy that linked the living, the dead and those to be born in relationship. Only in the late nineteenth century did the concept of tradition acquire the negative valences of unthinking obedience to static conventions and become linked to a new distinction between Culture and cultures.

Literary theorist Terry Eagleton suggests that the clash between Culture (capitalized to convey its singularity and its elevation through Western aesthetics) and cultures is central to contemporary world politics (with respect to law see Coombe 1998). It is certainly pivotal to the way we imagine the ethics of cultural appropriation and issues of cultural repatriation. High culture (which we will designate Culture here to avoid confusion and highlight its ideological valences) Eagelton argues, has historically been used as 'the spiritual badge of a privileged group' and the collective works that constitute canons 'are offered as evidence of the timeless unity of the human spirit; . . . of the truth that the individual stands at the center of the universe; . . . and other such modern prejudices.' (Eagleton 2000: 52–3) The point about Culture is it is cultureless; its values are not those of any particular form of life, simply human life as such. (32) The universalist self-understanding of Culture puts it in a relationship of superiority to 'mere cultures' as blatantly historical forms of life that value collective particularity. Culture draws a direct relation between the individual and the universal in Eagleton's view:

> Culture is itself the spirit of humanity individuating itself in specific works; and its discourse links the individual and the universal, the quick of the self and the truth of humanity, without the mediation of the historically particular . . . What else is the artistic canon, a collection of irreducibly individual works which testify in their very uniqueness to the common spirit of humanity? (55)

European intellectual property doctrines reflect this ideology quite clearly. In the rhetoric that legitimates intellectual property, the aesthetic work, be it literary, artistic or musical, both embodies the personality of its individual creator and makes a singular contribution to human civilization, universally conceived. As Geoffrey Galt Harpham astutely suggests, the aesthetic is a concept fundamental to European modernity and its self-description as an enlightened culture. Referring to particular categories of objects and the attitudes appropriate to judging them, it also registers modern understandings of the human faculties of imagination and creation, and the value of freedom itself. (Harpham 1994: 124–5)

Our failure to transcend what might be deemed the prejudices of the modern concept of tradition has left us with little critical vocabulary for appreciating the traditions claimed by others, which are ethnocentrically assumed to be 'the unselfconscious continuance of social institutions and practices.' (Phillips 2004: 18) Only by dissolving the binary of tradition and modernity, however, can we address increasingly important questions about the ways in which the life of cultures is passed on in works of art and religion, or indeed, the ways in which our understandings of 'works' of art and the expressions of cultures have themselves been limited by European modernity and its prejudices. Musicologist Philip Bohlman, for example, suggests that European aesthetic theory has disembedded music from culture by virtue of its refusal 'to admit to the full range of cultural work that music accomplishes.' (Bohlman 2003: 45–56) Similarly, sociologist Simon Frith has pointed out that in many societies, music 'could be described in almost exclusively social terms: music was used in games and in dancing, to organize work and war, in ceremonies and rituals, to mark the moments of birth, marriage and death, to celebrate harvest and coronation; and to articulate religious beliefs and traditional practice. People *might have* enjoyed music individually, but its purpose was not to make them feel good.' (Frith 2003: 98)

During the eighteenth century, music came to refer to a fine art, one designated by the mid-nineteenth century as the finest and most transcendental of the arts. 'Across the century from 1750 to 1850, music lodged itself at the heart of a discourse that pried Europe and its histories apart from non-European lives and cultures'. Music came to counter song, 'not conceived as a European version of worldwide activities, but as a European métier opposed to practices elsewhere.' (Tomlinson 2003: 34) Kant's positioning of instrumental music in his analysis of beauty in the *Critique of Judgment* is an early and influential instance in which 'music' is defined as most valuable when it is without words, serves no ends or purposes and is independent of actually existing social orders. Tomlinson suggests that 'song' serves here as music's implicit 'other', solidifying a philosophical conception of aesthetics in which singing occupies a categorically different and lesser precinct of beauty. Kant, in any case, is understood by musicologists to have prepared the ground for what became a dominant view that 'the achievements of recent European instrumental music could be viewed as the culmination of progressive world history' in which music, dispensing with words, became, in Herder's words, 'a self-sufficient art': (35)

The idea of instrumental music as an autonomous, nonmimetic expressive means, together with the emergent formation of the modern conception of the discrete musical work, invested new and substantial powers in the written form of the work. The notated music came to be viewed less as a preliminary script for performance than as the locus of the composer's intent, the unique and full inscription of the composer's expressive spirit, which was elsewhere—in any one performance—only partially revealed. (39)

The modern aesthetic valuation of music, then, is predicated upon significant forms of abstraction and decontextualization, in which social and creative matrices are denied and music is detached from situation, a 'conception of musical autonomy [that] appears as a powerful philosophical assertion by elite Europe of its own unique achievement and status.' (38) Progressive evolution in music came to be associated with writing, relegating the sonic endeavors of others with oral histories to the lesser domain of folklore, conceived as primitive, static, and incapable of development. (37) Significant forms of delegitimation were thereby accomplished. An ethical consideration of rights with respect to 'music' must reconsider the social capacities of song, if cultures as well as Culture are taken into account and the injuries as well as the accomplishments of modernity are to be acknowledged.

Record Collection and Salvage Paradigms

The study of the world's musical forms can be credited to the invention of the phonograph and the rapid development of sound recording as a scientific tool that could be used for collection in the field and transcribed for study in sound archives. (La Rue 2002) Communications theorist Jonathan Sterne suggests that the history of sound recording is bound up with the Victorian culture of commemorating and preserving the dead. *Scientific American*'s response to news of Edison's invention of the phonograph in 1877, for instance, stressed the possibility that future generations would be able to hear the voices of the dead as its most 'startling' implication; 'speech has become as it were, immortal.' (Sterne 2003: 298) There are many 'messages to future generations found amongst early recordings. For their own purposes, modern peoples imagined the possibilities of cross-generational speech, in which learning could be passed along to descendants. Recording was understood as a pedagogical technology to be put in the service of tradition, in that older sense of transferring knowledge through a handing down to the next generation.

If early recording enthusiasts praised sound recording for its preservative potential, the earliest ethnomusicologists more fully extended the metaphor. While Edison promoted the use of the phonograph to preserve the voices of dying persons, American anthropology justified the use of sound recording to preserve dying 'cultures'. Early ethnography depicted their Native subjects as living in a different temporal zone than modern society and this denial of coevalness has been shown to be a constitutive means by which European modernity dehumanized non-Western peoples. (Fabian 1983) This tendency was particularly acute in the Americas and in Australia, where the extinction of distinctive Indigenous societies was treated, not as the deliberate policy it was, but as the inevitable by-product of the force of civilization and the great historical march of progress. As Fewkes, one of the earliest practitioners of ethnographic and folkloric sound recording, wrote,

> When one considers the changes which yearly come to the Indians, and the probability that in a few years many of their customs will be greatly modified or disappear forever, the necessity for immediate preservation of their songs and rituals is imperative . . . Now is the time to collect materials before all is lost. . . . The scientific study of these records comes later . . . Edison has given us an instrument by which our fast-fading Aboriginal languages can be rescued from oblivion, and it seems to me that posterity will thank us if we use it to hand down to future students of Indian languages this additional help in their researches. (Cited in Sterne 2003: 318)

It was commonly known that Native populations had been in steady decline for over a century (due to disease, alcohol poisoning, warfare and some deliberate acts of genocide) when the earliest phonographic cylinders were being made, so this belief is not surprising, even if it turned out to be short-sighted. It had distinctive consequences for the way these recordings were valued and bears significantly upon the contemporary ethics of repatriation. For decades many anthropologists devoted themselves to producing fixed artifacts—bodily measurements and 'life masks' to document Native physiognomy, and photographs and phonograph records to document 'dying' peoples and their 'dying' cultures. In the process these artifacts functioned to dehistoricize these cultures by presenting a dynamic tradition at a single moment in time so as to produce texts for future study. Recordings were valued primarily for the transcriptions they enabled. Transcriptions, considered the primary analytical basis for scholarly work, were the tools that enabled comparative musical study. Few records were made to preserve the performances of these songs themselves for posterity. A particular performance was of little scholarly interest; only insofar as it helped to reconstruct a paradigm for cross-cultural research that would illuminate a universal human history was it considered significant. (Brady 1999)

There is a fundamental difference, then, between the understanding and valuation of recordings made by and on behalf of modern subjects and those made to document the cultural forms of Indigenous peoples and traditional others. The preservation of phonographic records in dominant societies would enable respected or beloved individuals to speak to future generations and their heirs with their own voices to pass along their wisdom. The actual performances of Native others, however, were considered data, or mere information, to produce records to serve more universal (Western) scholarly purposes. Non-Western and folk music forms, even when they were not regarded as more primitive 'ancestors' of Western music, were deemed destined to disappear under the onslaught of modernity.

The context of understandings in which recordings were made suggests that the Indigenous performers being recorded were not seen as having any legitimate interests in the records being produced; the recordings were made for purposes that made their performances means for the ends of others. They were recorded so that their songs could be preserved and subjected to scrutiny by scholars with a disinterested curiosity about the human past. Indeed, the ethnographic information collected through salvage anthropology is today considered by some curators, anthropologists and Indigenous-rights activists to be as morally compromised as the medical information amassed by the Third Reich in concentration camps. (Brown 2005: 36) While this may be considered an extreme position, we would agree with Scarre (this volume) that to view people and their projects primarily as a 'means' for further research, that is, as objects of study and not also as ends in themselves, is a clear breach of the Kantian injunction to treat people with respect. The collaborations that produced these recordings were, in any case, the product of grossly unequal forms of cultural interchange.

Musical recordings of Indigenous performances of traditional songs, in particular, were collected under conditions of great social stress. In search of pristine and authentic records of 'dying' traditions, representative of western North America's 'disappearing' Indian cultures, salvage anthropologists often erased any reference to the time period in which they were working. In so doing, they represented one of the most traumatic and turbulent periods of Indigenous history as paradigmatic of a timeless Aboriginal culture. (Raibmon 2005: 5) In the Americas, the Northwest Coast was the focus of attention for some of this era's most influential producers of anthropological knowledge and the site of an intense 'scramble' for Indian artifacts. This was the area where Franz Boas, the foundational figure in professional anthropology in North America, conducted his fieldwork. (5) It was also the region where Ida Halpern, a Canadian musicologist of Dutch ancestry, recorded over 400 hereditary Indian songs over four decades from the 1940s.

Like her anthropological predecessors' collections, Halpern's activities were motivated by a desire to preserve First Nations cultures. It might be speculated that as a Jew who escaped Austria when Jewish culture and music were being actively suppressed, she had particular empathy. For Halpern, it would be a 'sin' if the songs and culture were lost; the imperative to record these songs was of supreme importance to her. (Cole and Mullins 1993: 24) Although she collected primarily from the Kwakwaka'wakw (then known as Kwakiutl), Nuu-Chah-Nulth (previously known as Nootka) and Haida nations of the northwest coast of Canada, Halpern also gathered songs from the Bella Bella, Bella Coola, Tsimshian, Coast Salish and Tglingit nations.

The songs Halpern collected were eventually published as records and used in television and radio broadcasts, museum galleries, theatrical productions, films, academic theses and by contemporary composers wanting to incorporate a 'native' element in their works. Her collections also formed the basis of an education study unit for grade 4 students. (34) In 1984 Halpern donated the bulk of her collection (which amounted to over eighty file boxes of textual records, publications, moving images, photographs and sound recordings) to the Provincial Archives of British Columbia and the remainder to the archives of Simon Fraser University. A case study of Halpern's research shows that we cannot always reduce 'cultural appropriation' to acts by bad people, or even acts by good people mistakenly engaged in salvage ethnography. Rather, it shows that cultural appropriation may occur simply through the imposition of dominant aesthetic categories and that perfectly acceptable, indeed laudable activities in one era, may cause harms that affect injuries that we must ethically acknowledge in another.

Preserving Indigenous 'Music': Rights and Responsibilities

Many of the songs Halpern recorded were central to potlatch ceremonies. Potlatch means 'to give' and is a term used to describe ceremonies that mark status-defining events such as marriages, naming of children, memorials to the dead, raising a totem pole, and, most significantly, transfers of rights and privileges. Potlatches were the foundation of Kwakwaka'wakw economic, political, social, spiritual and legal systems, and the means for transferring cultural knowledge to future generations. (Bell *et al.* 2008: 46) Kwakwaka'wakw refers to people who speak Kwak'wala (known historically as the Kwakkewlths by the federal government and as Kwakiutl by anthropologists), whose ancestral territories extend from Comox to the north end of Vancouver Island and the adjacent mainland inlets from Smith Inlet south to Toba Inlet. They consist of a number of distinctive tribal communities with their own names and creation stories. The activity of witnessing enabled the potlatch to affirm status, fulfill chiefly responsibilities and mark significant family events. These ceremonies served, and may continue to serve, 'as a means of sharing and verifying Kwakwaka'wakw history' and the people's connection to their lands; they also connected participants to the spirit world in a way that is often described by contemporary elders as healing. (49) In these ceremonies, 'entitlements to songs, dances, masks and regalia are demonstrated and transferred before witnesses.' (50–51)

The importance of songs to Kwakwaka'wakw and other peoples in the Northwest Coastal cultural area is not limited to the fact that they are held by right and performed in religious and social ceremonies. The songs do not *accompany* or *adorn* potlatch ceremonies. Their performance has a 'performative' value, demonstrating and enacting—indeed constituting—the transfer and possession of those rights which define the central bonds of the society. Similarly, anthropologist Brian Noble's research (2008) shows that the Blackfeet of northern Montana and the Skinnipiikani people of southern Alberta also have orally based performative practices of law. Law is enacted in ceremonial protocols of transfer in which song demonstrates transferred rights in witnessed ceremonies. The transferred song is the seal of right or 'ownership' and transferred songs are spoken of as akin to a credential or a license granted by an authority. (Noble 2008) Although it is outside of the parameters of this paper to demonstrate this, song may well define the 'constitutions' of a number of Indigenous societies.

When Halpern arrived in Canada, bans on potlatch ceremonies (1884–1951) had been in place for nearly sixty years. The purpose of this ban, first introduced in 1884 and revised in 1895, was the cultural improvement, assimilation and, for some, the Christianization of the Kwakwaka'wakw, long viewed by missionaries as the most recalcitrant and uncivilized of Indians. (Raibmon 2005: 17) Although Kwakwaka'wakw had been interacting with Europeans for over a century, few outsiders settled in their territories until the final decades of the nineteenth century, precisely when government and missionary forces began stepping up their assaults on an Aboriginal life-world structured around extended kinship and inherited resource rights and anthropologists began to document their pending 'extinction'. Although performed in more remote locations to escape surveillance, the potlatch proved tenacious.

Amendments to the ban in 1918 made the celebration of potlatch a summary conviction offense so as to avoid the necessity of finding a judge to effect the sentence and enabling local magistrates (such as Indian Agents) to put practitioners in prison. Knowing their ritual significance, officials offered an ultimatum to people, agreeing to lenience and to forego prosecutions if people turned over their potlatch-related regalia. This truce was quickly broken. Following Dan Cranmer's potlatch in 1921, forty-five people were charged, mostly high-ranking chiefs and their wives, for criminal acts of singing, dancing, making speeches and giving and receiving gifts; twenty men and women were sent to prison, the rest receiving suspended sentences after agreeing to give up potlatch artifacts (most of which the Indian Agent, Halliday, personally sold to museum collections). The ceremony was driven further underground, almost disappearing in the next three decades.

During the period that Halpern made her recordings then, the potlatch system was in crisis, as were the social systems of many cultural groups in this region. Halpern, as well as the chiefs and artists with whom she worked, could have been imprisoned for these collection activities. Chiefs who are alive today acknowledge that their laws were not properly followed during this period of crisis and that many sacred possessions were illegally sold or stolen as villages were abandoned and disease decimated populations, making it impossible to mobilize resources to support feasts and fulfill ritual obligations. 'It likely seemed to many that the predictions of the missionaries and government officials of their complete demise as a people was actually coming true.' (Overstall 2008: 99)

Halpern's first collection of songs was made in 1947 with Billy Assu, chief of the Lekwiltok Kwakwaka'wakw. Historians Douglas Cole and Christine Mullins suggest that it was Halpern's ambition to help keep Kwakwaka'wakw culture 'alive' that persuaded Chief Assu to record the songs: ' "What", Halpern asked the chief, "will happen to your songs if you die?" "They will die with me", was his fatalistic reply.' (Cole and Mullins 1993: 21) But once he understood her intention, according to Halpern, he said, 'You come: I give you hundred songs.' (21) Her second singer, Chief Mungo Martin, was also concerned with cultural preservation, according to the historians. He had been influential in persuading people no longer interested in performing the potlatch to pass on their ceremonial materials to the University of British Columbia Museum. Cole and Mullins read this as evidence that the chiefs were 'not so much passing on their culture as a living continuity among their Kwakiutl people but as a memory culture in anthropological literature, in museums, and on Halpern's recording and tapes.' (1993: 24) Thus they interpret the chiefs' intent as consciously supporting and engaging in a process of making a record 'for posterity' in the sense of disinterested study by later scholars. (24)

It is difficult to ascertain if the chiefs' understanding of and interest in 'posterity' dovetailed with Halpern's or if they shared the belief that they were bestowing these materials as a general record for humankind, as Cole and Mullins believe. There are reasons to suspect that the chiefs had other social motivations according to contemporary collaborative research being done with Kwakwaka'wakw partners. (Bell *et al.* 2008) The imperative to pass on songs appears to have been crucial to many First Nations peoples in this region. Songs are connected with lineage, and are subject to rights under customary law. They are also 'evidence' of these rights and associated responsibilities with respect to territory and resources. This is the basis of their law (Overstall 2008: 101), or what we might consider their 'constitution' as a society. For example, elder Solomon Marden testified in legal proceedings that it is one of the Tsimishian and Gitxsan chiefs' main responsibilities to ensure that the *adaawx*, that is, the verbal record of the history of their peoples' origins, migrations, territories and law, is passed on to the next generation. (*Delgamuukw v. The Queen* as cited in Marsden 2008: 118)

Let us consider the possibility that the imperative to pass on the law through the songs they held was one of the most important responsibilities of those people whom Halpern recorded. If, at this time, it was illegal to perform the songs, impossible to hold the ceremonies necessary to teach them to others, and (due to their acculturation in residential schools) the next generation were uninterested in, or due to their illegality, afraid of learning them, the chiefs may have had no other way of fulfilling their obligation to pass on the songs than through the making of these recordings, with the hope that their descendants would, in better times, be able to carry on the tradition. If these were their hopes, they have been fulfilled. Today there is an active cultural revitalization movement among the Kwakwaka'wakw. Seeking recovery of knowledge about the potlatch as well as repatriation of the objects and texts associated with it, they hope to repair the broken record of a tradition whose integrity they believe to be key to the social healing of a community harmed by the history of colonial encounter.

Halpern might be criticized for using First Nations peoples as 'a means', that is, as objects for research, rather than as ends. She might be accused of being more focused on her own reputation than on the needs of the people she studied. She was certainly well recognized for recording and analyzing First Nations music, as well as her other contributions to Canadian musical study. Her work with Indigenous peoples brought her great acclaim, as writer and critic for *Musical Courier*, regional director for the Metropolitan Opera National Council, vice chairman of the Community Music School in Vancouver, a life member of the Vancouver Academy of Music and a counselor for the Society for Ethnomusicology. In 1956, she was made a founding convocation member of Simon Fraser University and an honorary associate of their Centre for Communications and the Arts. The University awarded her an honorary doctorate in 1978, the same year she was named a Member of the Order of Canada. (Chen 1995: 44) But it would be a strange ethics, indeed, that found guilt in Halpern's success or failed to acknowledge the contributions of such risky endeavors to the field in which she so clearly made a contribution.

When Halpern began her collection, the aural cultural forms of these groups were not widely acknowledged to be music, although the Indigenous peoples whose songs she collected had been performing for non-Indian audiences for decades. (Raibmon 2005) Through her study of First Nations music, Halpern freed herself from the cultural assumptions of Western musical superiority with which she had begun with. Whereas the prevailing assumption, influenced by Darwinian evolutionary theory, was that music 'progressed' from primitive to fine art, Halpern was eager to discount prejudices about 'Indian' primitivism and to present North American Indigenous music as developmentally like European art. (Chen 1995: 51; Cole and Mullins 1993: 36) If, as Charles Taylor (1994) suggests, cross cultural recognition and respect involves, at least in part, recognizing the artistic achievements of other civilizations, Ida Halpern's accomplishments were remarkable.

The music she encountered was complex and difficult to understand. The melody and the accompaniment were independent of each other. The vocalization included what were generally considered to be 'nonsense' or 'meaningless' syllables. Her research progressed slowly. Her method of analysis initially involved the separation of the rhythm from the melody, which she analyzed in turn, before she turned to the vocalization. Later research focused on the totality of musical forms and the stylistic elements distinguishing the songs of different groups, the classification of song-types related to different kinds of ceremonies and the comparison between the same songs sung by different generations of singers. (Cole and Mullins 1993: 29–33) She sought thereby to demonstrate the 'complex constructional principles underlying the compositional process' in this music, and her analysis of inter-generational interpretations of the song showed that the performers had 'a full awareness and conscientious respect for compositional principles and techniques [that was] refined over generations and restated, with creativity and regularity'. (33)

Halpern's interest in recording the songs appears, then, to be an interest in preservation in terms of affirming its value as music. This is a different kind of concern than that of the salvage anthropology that preceded her, which viewed such recordings as mere data. Her respect for the music, and the skills and sophistication of the performers, translated into a respect for the sophistication and artistic quality of the region's Indigenous culture. No one, after becoming acquainted with her work, would think that these people did not have art or were not contributors to human civilization. Politically, the very presentation of these songs *as* music, and as sophisticated music at that, brought Aboriginal creativity into the realm of Culture. Moreover, Halpern's research did not 'freeze' this music as a snapshot of an ethnographic past, nor did it obscure its practitioners' own understanding of their music. Her work explicitly focused on change over generations; changes she showed to be intrinsic to the dynamism of these musical traditions. In her liner notes she endeavored 'to foreground her "native experts" as the primary and proper authorities and she kept 'for authenticity's sake the words [and logic] of the informants in the explanations . . . as close as possible to their way of expressing themselves [in English].' (Chen 1995: 54) As one of her biographers points out, this form of ethnographic representation 'would not even be considered by anthropologists until the appearance of Clifford's "On Ethnographic Authority" in 1983' (55) heralded the discipline's postmodern turn.

It would be slanderous, then, to accuse Halpern of using people as means to her own ends, or to infer the full range of her intentions from the general circumstances and attitudes characteristic of salvage anthropology and the dominant function of recording in the ethnography of her era. The making of many other recordings that are now the subject of repatriation claims may indeed be understood in this fashion, but we chose Halpern's recordings as examples precisely because her intentions were more sympathetic. What the example shows is that to focus primarily upon the character and motives of the person who did the original recording obscures a more crucial point about systematic injustice and the cultural losses that Indigenous peoples have suffered. In the mobilization of a universal category such as art, even well-intentioned people may unwittingly do harm. Indigenous music and songs are categorized as 'folk music' because they are traditional—handed down from generation to generation. They cannot be owned under Western legal systems because they lack an identifiable 'author' or creator, and are not 'fixed' in a tangible medium.

Under modern legal principles with respect to the ownership of works of Culture, no one could claim copyright in the music itself and the only copyright would have been created at the time Halpern made her recordings, albeit only in the recordings themselves. She may have assigned her copyright in the recordings to the archives or the university when she deposited them. If so, they may be able to charge a fee for their use, but simply by virtue of controlling these archives they can restrict access to these recordings and thus their use by others, including the descendants of those who originally performed the songs for Halpern. Moral rights, which enable artists to maintain control over a work, even against subsequent copyright owners, are only available to identifiable individual creators in deference to the individual's link to Culture through his contribution to human civilization of an expressive work that, in Hegelian terms, projects their personality. Such moral rights are categorically unavailable to the endeavors of those who have not 'transcended' their immersion in local traditions and projected their individuality into the sphere of the universal.

Legally, however, Halpern is the only individual whose artistry is recognized; the First Nations peoples whose ancestors had songs recorded by Halpern have no rights to them and no other way, it appears, to gain access to songs that formed the basis of their customary laws.

The Harms of Appropriation

Categories do political work. How we categorize something and the priority we give to that categorization have consequences for how we think it ought to be treated, whether it can be owned and how access to it should be governed. Regardless of Halpern's good intentions, her valuation of the music, the creativity and artistry she acknowledged in her Aboriginal informants and the respect she accorded them as expert practitioners in deploying the creative resources of their traditions, Halpern's recordings of their music contributed to the disenfranchisement that the peoples of the Northwest Coast suffered at the hands of the modern state. This disenfranchisement, however, cannot ethically be reduced to a loss of property, nor can the act of restitution be ethically resisted simply in the name of an undifferentiated public domain.

For some First Nations peoples, clearly, songs were and are central to the maintenance of distinct houses, chiefdoms, families and lineages and their rights and responsibilities. Within oral traditions, references for law, jurisdiction and territory are encoded not in statute or treatise, but in mnemonic devices such as songs. Mnemonic devices do not record information in the way that written language does, but provide a code or symbol that serves to remind the user of important historical and legal information. (Goody 1998: 73–94) Gitanyow informant Robert Good, for example, links legally significant crest images to 'a song, a drama, and the *adaawk*, all of which recreate through display and performance the House of Luuxhon's possession of a particular fishing site and of its territories as a whole.' (Overstall 2008: 110) Tsiiwa' wing chief Herb Russell indicates that oral histories, feast names, songs, crests and poles are House possessions; telling the *adaawk* at a feast is the key responsibility of a leader because it demonstrates the necessary familiarity with the history of House traditional territory and thus provides your deed to the land. (104) Given 'the central constitutional role of the protection and display of *adaawk*, crests, and songs, their misappropriation by others is a primary political concern.' (111)

In these societies songs may be a part of a cultural complex that defines a person's responsibilities as a member of a House and in relation to other Houses. The songs held by a House constitute the House as a legal entity amongst the Gitxsan and with respect to wider society. Such songs may therefore be considered essential to the maintenance of a group's social identity as a distinct people (Coleman 2006: 170) and to their self-determination. Historical evidence of the use of songs in Indigenous ceremony suggests they have a similar function in many societies. Within those traditions, such songs should properly be regarded as 'law'. Our 'expressive' rights with respect to the use of such recorded songs should not, we would argue, be permitted to degrade the authority of legal records, or to extinguish a community's political future. To the extent that new regimes of rights pertaining to traditional knowledge and cultural expressions proposed by the World Intellectual Property Organization will acknowledge customary law (Taubman 2005), those laws would appropriately bind others in a future where rights pertaining to tradition were respected. (Coombe 2008)

If certain songs are constitutive of a people's law, it is also the case that the customary rights to territory and resources they represent may be unrecognized by the dominant societies in which they reside. For those without written records, recordings of songs may be the only legal 'records' they possess. However, in many cases, they do not possess them and must seek to retrieve them from others. The capacity of Indigenous groups to make legal claims within Western legal systems may thus be harmed by the unauthorized use of such songs in other contexts, their dissemination to other groups or the failure to provide exclusive rights of access to recordings to the descendants of the original performers. For example, amongst many Aboriginal Australians, songs provide dynamic proof of land ownership and the owners of songs and the ceremonies associated with them also own the land that these songlines trace. Anthropologists used sound recordings to assist in Aboriginal land claims as early as the 1970s. (Koch 1997)

Since the rights of Australian Aboriginal and Torres Strait Islander peoples to hold title to land were finally recognized in 1992, wax cylinder recordings of ancestral song performances from the turn of the twentieth century have assumed even greater significance as forms of proof of customary legal title. They are now used in legal proceedings to help identify the families of Aboriginal people who were removed from their communities, in Native title cases as proof of continuity of cultural practice and in statutory land claims where recorded ceremonies may be accepted as deeds of land. (Koch 1997) The same uses offer hope for others. Gitanyow people, for example, are challenging the Canadian federal government's surrender of traditional House lands to the Nisgaa people under treaty settlement; recordings of their songs would be helpful to their case. It is not entirely clear, however, that judges have the capacity or the inclination to understand the legal function of song. This was illustrated in the case of *Delgamuukw. British Columbia,* in which the Gitxsan of the Tsimshian nation needed a year to perform their stories and songs before a judge in their pursuit of a land claim:

> On one occasion . . . Antgulilibix (Mary Johnson), was telling her *ada'ox* to the court. At a certain point, she said she must now sing a song. Judge McEachern . . . tried to make the plaintiffs understand that this was unlikely to get him any nearer to the truth he was seeking. He asked the lawyer for the Gitskan whether it might not be sufficient to have the words written down, and avoid the performance. Finally he agreed to let Mary Johnson sing her song; but as she was about to start he fired his final salvo. 'It's not going to do any good to sing to me,' he said. 'I have a tin ear.' (Chamberlin 2003: 20)

In the end, Justice McEachern dismissed the case. He claimed that he believed Mary Johnson but not her *ada'ox*. (21) We have suggested that many First Nations songs do not merely record history and rights, but that correct performance, by a person with authority to perform the song, provides a rule for recognition of First Nation law. The song was presented as evidence of legal title. If a law can be 'true' it is not by virtue of correspondence, as history may be, it is true because it is an institutional fact, or has what is known as 'validity'. (Hart 1961: 92) Had the justice been prepared to 'hear' Johnson's song as proof of the validity of the Gitxsan claims about the law, he may well have recognized it as the evidence that it was. His 'tin ear' had nothing to do with his failure to appreciate music, but it does nicely characterize his juridical failure to recognize customary law.

The manipulation, adaptation of and experimentation with songs such as these diminishes their effect as mnemonic and performative devices encoding law for communities. If a constitutive proof of the validity of a law is a song's correct performance by particular people in a particular performance, then its use as a resource in the 'musical' creativity of others strips it of its most significant power. It is not, in other words, information,

and its use is not, in economist's terms, non rivalrous. There is a real difference between the artistic appropriation and adaptation of folk music
generally and the artistic appropriation of the songs of Indigenous societies
in which music functions institutionally as law. Whether artistic appropriation and adaptation is morally acceptable, therefore, bears a crucial relationship to the social role of the cultural form in the society from which it
was appropriated (for a broader discussion, see Walsh and Lopes, this
volume, for presentation of a 'relational model' for considering art objects).
Certainly not all social functions are deserving of deference, but the constitution of a people's rights and responsibilities as a people surely merits
the utmost consideration as a matter of justice and as a matter of human
rights. (Ahmed, Aylwin and Coombe 2008)

Finally, and perhaps most significantly from an Indigenous perspective,
people are harmed when their abilities to fulfill their fundamental obligations to others (past, present and future) are thwarted. Moriori lawyer and
scholar Maui Solomon points out that his own people 'are as much concerned about their obligations to one another and to the natural world at
large as they are concerned with asserting their cultural rights. But without
access to their rights they cannot exercise their responsibilities. Such is the
relationship of respect and reciprocity' that he believes to be true of Indigenous and traditional peoples all over the world. (Solomon 2004: 222) The
loss of Indigenous peoples' capacity to fulfill traditional obligations and to
meet responsibilities that they believe to be bestowed upon them by their
Creator is a form of harm.

We need not define this as a harm that is specific to Indigenous peoples,
or only those people who hold religious beliefs, but, following Paul Bou-
Habib, argue that this is an injury to an individual that derives from a
person's need to maintain their integrity. 'Integrity' in this context may be
defined as 'what is maintained when acting in accordance with one's perceived duties.' (Bou-Habib 2006, 117) The kinds of activities that may
constitute such duties include activities like caring for the elderly and sick,
protecting the environment, preserving cultural heritage and respecting
religious observances—activities that people perceive they are required to
perform 'even if they do not derive happiness from performing them.'
(117) Integrity, Bou-Habib argues, is a basic good but it is not an absolute
good and may be outweighed by other detriments. (121) The good does
not justify the need to accommodate all the perceived duties of people.
However, to the extent that religious duties do not harm others and are
not outweighed by other detriments, it may be argued that they should be

accommodated because the failure to accommodate an individual's perceived religious obligations is a harm that undermines that person's capacity for well-being. If the loss of traditional rights interferes with obligations
to protect and to pass on rights intrinsic to music, to perform ceremonies
or to maintain spiritual heritage, then Indigenous people may be harmed
by a loss of integrity.

Considered as traditional songs, outside of, or at best approaching, the
lesser aesthetic realm of folk music, Aboriginal aural efforts were unable to
attain the full status of music, which enabled anthropologists and musicologists to record and collect them and to claim authorial rights in their
own recording efforts; this effectively also gave them rights to control what
we might call their musical content. Categorized as recordings of public
domain content, it seems utterly appropriate for them to be used as background for films, as advertising jingles and as the basis for expressive
articulations with other musical material. Even if fully valorized as music,
however, these songs have no weight as legal evidence nor as evidence of
a broken social record of peoples and their histories, entitlements and
responsibilities with respect to territories and resources. The harms to
Indigenous people are not simply reminders of historical injuries inflicted
by colonial regimes intent on destroying their cultures. They are systemic;
they result from the imposition of categories that enable these harms to
continue to be perpetuated. In 'appreciating' First Nations' 'musical' contributions to Culture, ironically, we may still fail to recognize First Nations
societies and their cultures. Nonetheless, as Brown implies, it is frequently
assumed that it is now too difficult or, indeed, undesirable to reclaim cultural texts such as Indigenous songs from the public domain. (Ziff and Rao,
1997: 249; Brown, 2005) We beg to differ.

Information Society

Information is not free-floating data without context but the means of
forging and consolidating relations of sociality (Webster 2000), as even the
practices of Creative Commons denizens and other ardent information
society activists are well aware. Feld (1996) suggests that ownership and
control of recording technology creates a new organizational network
for the economy of music. Music, which in Western societies once supported diverse forms of sociality, became repetitive, mass produced and

stockpiled, and in the process enacted a repetitive mass-production of social relations. Musicians, with their ability to copy at will, secure in the knowledge that what they are copying is 'folk music', and convinced of the importance of their artistic creations for civilization, appear to be 'ideologues working alongside powerful technocrats and a knowledge-rich minority.' (Feld 1996: 15)

Brown correctly identifies 'the Information Society' with processes of globalization but fails to consider globalization as anything other than inevitable in its current course. Critics of globalization, however, argue that globalization is not an expression of evolution, but rather a process designed to give primacy to economic values and to aggressively install those values globally. (Struhl 2006) Communications theorist Armand Mattelart (2002) suggests that the idea of the information society was carefully cultivated to represent efforts to Westernize the world as inevitable, depoliticizing this by projecting it as a natural progression of a unilinear development process. A purely instrumental concept of the information society was encouraged to indicate the new destiny of the world; it obscured the interests of those who controlled information technologies and helped to forge the new enclosures of a contemporary informational feudalism. (See Drahos & Braithwaite 2002; Kellner 2002; May 2000)

This reductionist or 'techno-determinist' position unfortunately appears to be adopted by Brown when he assumes decontextualization to be a necessary by-product of digitalization (rather than see it as providing new opportunities for forging contextual relationships, for instance). His discussion of cultural heritage never challenges the legitimacy of the 'knowledge economy' and he comes dangerously close to characterizing those who question the tendencies of the Information Society (which he routinely capitalizes) as Luddites resisting the inevitable. Although Brown argues for a more holistic approach, he places his discussion squarely within a technical framework without questioning the underlying relationships between people and things that animate it. By so doing, he legitimates a political economic structure by repeating its ideologies, and is quiescent in the face of the historic inequalities that are further entrenched by contemporary 'information society' relations.

In the words of Jeremy Waldron, '[T]he world we know is characterized by patterns of injustice, by standing arrangements—rules, laws, regimes, and other institutions—that operate unjustly day by day . . . To judge that establishment unjust is to commit oneself to putting a stop to the ongoing situation; it is a commitment to prevent the perpetuation of the injustice that the law or the institution embodies; it is to commit oneself to its remission.' (Waldron 1992: 14) This suggests, we would assert, a need to reconsider the concept of the public domain. This is a legal term. The fact that something is in this domain on the basis of a legal definition does not make its use morally justifiable. Moreover, it suggests that rights lost through injustice should be rectified, or compensation made. It is not sufficient to say that the past is the past, and nothing can be done about it. Three philosophical arguments may be posited for the restitution of rights in Indigenous or traditional music. The first argues for the restitution of rights and depends on the music being the subject of customary rights within the originating society. The second is also a rights-based argument, but considers rights to be created through the process of recording, as rights arising from an agreement between a performer and a publisher. It does not create a right for the restitution of music, but it creates rights for an audience, and limits the rights of the owner of the recording accordingly. The third argument is consequentialist in nature. It argues that because of the mneumonic power of music, the repatriation of recordings may be an important aspect of the cultural renewal and historical recovery vital to Indigenous self-determination.

Rights-Based Arguments for Restitution and Limited Properties

The Kwakwaka'wakw are today amongst the best organized of Canadian First Nations in terms of their efforts 'to repatriate cultural items, revive cultural practices, and reclaim knowledge, values, laws, principles and beliefs associated with them.' (Bell *et al.* 2008: 33) Of particular significance to them are cultural items surrendered or sold as a consequence of anti-potlatch laws, whose repatriation is 'linked to community well-being and healing through revival of traditions and acknowledgment of injustices suffered at the hands of the Canadian government.' (34) Recovery of objects, stories and songs associated with the potlatch is important for the purposes of reviving a brutally suppressed ceremony that the Kwakwaka'wakw and related peoples consider essential to rights and responsibilities as nations. The U'mista Cultural Society, whose objective is to 'ensure the survival of all aspects of the cultural heritage of the Kwakwaka'wakw' (36), is engaged in repatriating potlatch artifacts and researching the traditional potlatch protocol many community members regard as the historical foundation for their legal system. (46)

The basis of this argument is an historic injustice: the potlatch laws. It makes a claim for rights from which its practitioners have been dispossessed, and seeks the repatriation of cultural artifacts 'surrendered or sold' as a consequence of these laws. One problem with this position is that First Nations peoples sold some of their ceremonial regalia, and, in the case of music, appeared to have agreed to its recording. These agreements, regarded contractually, however, would appear to have been made under conditions of duress or unconscionability, particularly the agreement to forfeit ceremonial objects so as to avoid imprisonment. Moreover, even if the contractual limitations argument fails with respect to the recordings, this does not mean that current generations of First Nations peoples have no moral claim on the recordings their ancestors agreed to have made or that they are not properly asserting their cultural rights when they seek repatriation.

Robert Nozick argues for the rectification of historic entitlement on the basis of two principles of justice, justice in acquisition and justice in transfer, as well as rights against interference (discussed in Thompson 2001: 8). This principle takes into account the best information about what would have occurred, had the injustice not taken place (in this it is similar to the equitable principle of restitution). Claims for rectification are restricted to 'the restoration of expropriated possessions or the provision of an equivalent for these possessions.' (120) The moral claim for repatriation therefore rests on an entitlement, such as the well-recognized rights enjoyed by First Nations peoples prior to colonization.

The potlatch bans, which effectively halted the process of inheritance, are appropriately characterized as an interference with the legitimacy of the transfer of significant property. Thus, to follow Nozick's argument, the sale of objects and the recording of songs would be illegitimate because the legitimate transfer of rights had been precluded, adding to the social situation of duress. The argument from duress is not always available as a general argument for the repatriation of cultural forms from the public domain by Indigenous groups. While similar forms of forced assimilation and outlawing of traditional practices may be found in diverse colonial histories, not all of these will involve interference with the transfer of rights. In other cases, the claim might rest on the injustice of assuming that these songs were part of the public domain as salvage recordings or as folk art. Nozick's argument for rectification makes 'no distinction between dispossession caused by injustice and dispossession that results from a mistake—a belief that something was unowned when this was not so.' (Thompson 2001: 120) This point is significant; it does not require that what was lost was lost as a result of fraud, or theft or even under duress. Rights to music may have been lost because of a belief that songs were not owned, based on the wrongful assumption that, like ancient Greek myth, or European fairy tales, they were not subject to rights within a group.

Some moral philosophers consider Nozick's argument to be beset with a significant flaw: the need to identify rightful inheritors. Jeremy Waldron (1992), for instance, believes that an individual has the right to leave their property to whomever they please. This might be considered a reason for believing that contemporary First Nations people do not have rights to the repatriation of potlatch items that members of previous generations voluntarily sold or to songs they allowed to be recorded. This, however, assumes that property has certain features that are actually far from universal. Inheritance rights based on primogeniture are far more common than those based entirely on individual will, and immediate family members may, and frequently do, make claims against estates when they have not been adequately provided for. (Thompson 2001)

Nonetheless, not all Indigenous groups have the kind of institutionally defined rights to songs for the purposes of transferring social obligation that can be found in Canadian First Nations or Australian Aboriginal societies. A second rights-based argument for the limits to the rights of copyright owners of Indigenous music may be derived from a little known or discussed analysis of the nature of publishing by Kant. (1993: 225–39) Kant is concerned here not with intellectual property rights—the nature of a work or who has property in it—but instead, with the morality of publishing in terms of a speech act. (239) What is particularly important for our argument is how this agreement between the author and the publisher also creates rights for the intended audience of the recording. Kant writes that

> In a book as writing the author *speaks* to his *reader*; and he, who printed it, speaks by his copies not for himself, but entirely in the name of the author. The editor exhibits him as speaking publicly, and mediates but the delivery of this speech to the public. (Kant 1798: 229–30)

Moral rights in this situation are premised upon a series of agreements or promises. The author gives over his manuscript to the publisher in return for the publisher delivering the intended 'speech' to the intended audience. The author, having made this agreement, cannot make agreements with other publishers for the same work. The publisher has the right to benefit from the reproduction of the work, and has the power to make over the publication to another. But this is the limit of the publisher's powers, and the new publisher is also bound by the original agreement. (232) Kant believed that the right to use a manuscript to create copies created rights but rights with respect to the copies could not override the publisher's obligations to respect the rights of the author in the work so copied. Speech acts cannot become 'property', he writes, as they are not 'things existing of themselves, but . . . have their existence but in a person. Consequently these [speech acts] belong to the person of the author exclusively'. (238) Thus Kant insists on what we would now legally consider moral rights of publication, attribution and integrity.

Kant imagined a situation in which the author died before publication; in such a case the publisher could not morally suppress the book as if it were his own property:

> [T]he public has a right, in case of a want of heirs, either to force him to publish the book, or to give up the manuscript to another, who offers to publish it. For it is a business, with which the author had a mind to transact with the public, and which he [the publisher] accepted as a transactor. (235)

Moreover, the manuscript must appear in the author's name, may not be altered and a sufficient number of copies had to be furnished *to the author's public* to convey the author's sentiments. (238)

Many legal jurisdictions have long recognized a right to prevent the unauthorized transmission or dissemination of recordings of live performances without the performers' permission, a legal provision that has indeed been used to prevent the unauthorized sampling and appropriation of traditional music, even when the recording was originally made with the performer's consent. (Coombe 2003, 2005) These laws appear to echo the Kantian argument for moral rights with respect to speech acts because they are not dependent upon whether the material performed is itself protected by copyright. However, the Kantian argument does not provide moral rights merely for the author, but links these to the rights of the public to receive the latter's message.

Kant had in mind the rights of a public who are not merely an amalgamation of intended recipients but a politically vital collective,

privileged as such by virtue of their use of reasoned judgment and its necessary influence upon the state. The circulation of written works played a
particularly crucial role in constituting this public and its capacities; it was
primarily imagined as a reading public. It is not insignificant that Kant's
own publishers thank *das Publikum* in anticipation of their first issue of
the journal that was to publish 'What Is Enlightenment?' and that philosophers of the time declared that they served no prince but only the public.
(Laursen 1986: 587) Publishers had an important role—even a fiduciary
obligation—to assist writers to meet their responsibility to inform the
public and to do so faithfully. In later work, under pressure from authorities, it appears, Kant limited the privileges of free debate and the scope
of the public to a 'learned community' that was smaller than the 'civil
community' and explicitly distinguished between philosophers, on whose
public judgments the state's well-being depended, and other less disinterested men of affairs—clergymen, magistrates, and physicians whose public
use of learning need not be so protected. (Laursen 1986: 591)

Taking Kant's injunctions out of their contemporaneous political
context—and certainly many have found in Kant's works more universal
precepts and principles—we might argue that any speech act belonging to
an author has an intended audience and that the agreement with a publisher must respect the author's intentions as reflected in the nature of the
agreement that constituted the *consent* to publish. The current owner of
the recording is not entitled to any further publication than was intended
and agreed to by the performer or to publish the work in a fashion that
does not respect the integrity of the performance as a speech act. Property
rights in the original recordings cannot authorize re-recordings as pop
music, or as film soundtracks. These would infringe the performer's right,
as well as the audience's right, to the integrity of the work. Distribution is
limited to the intended audience agreed to by the performer, and that
audience has a right against the publisher to receive the author's work
as delivered to and for them. The contemporary law of moral rights has
certainly moved in this direction.

The First Nations chiefs who collaborated with Ida Halpern provided
her with a message for publication in the absence of access to their usual
traditional means of passing along their songs (and thus their territories
and resources) to future generations. It does not follow from this that
current First Nations peoples have a right to possess the music as recorded,
but they have a right to receive the message or speech act that these recordings contained. Halpern, for her part, appears to have met part of this

obligation by publishing the songs and using the chiefs' explanations of them. The current owners of the copyright in the recordings (usually archives) have a duty to provide access to them and to deliver them or faithful copies of them to the generation that seeks to fulfill its obligations as conveyed in these recordings.

The Kantian argument may fail to capture the full moral dimension of the situation for First Nations peoples if the speech act is not simply a message but a 'performative' that brings other social roles, obligations and relationships into being. Current generations of First Nations peoples whose ancestors collaborated with Halpern thus have moral rights to have adequate access to it for these traditional purposes. As a performative that aspired to reach future generations of these songholders' nations (and/or as a proud declaration of identity and territory to non-Indigenous Canadians), the songs inscribed in these recordings create obligations that remain unfulfilled. To the extent that a current generation perceives themselves as having such obligations, withholding the cultural resources that enable them to fulfill them harms their integrity.

A final moral argument for repatriation of music to Indigenous groups involves the capacity of such recordings to enable groups to recover their histories and rebuild their communities under postcolonial conditions. This moral argument need not be based on rights, but on the potential benefits to the recipient community and the social goods thereby realized.

Repatriation and Recollection

During the 1930s potlatches were forced underground and became more sporadic; after this it appears that they became far less frequent. Knowledge of the potlatch system was lost to many people because they were forbidden to speak their language for most of the year and could never fully participate in the traditional legal system. A younger generation now wants to learn the system but their parents and grandparents no longer know the names of their relatives or the songs and dances. The revival of the potlatch has been acknowledged as a place where the Kwakwaka'wakw can reinforce who they are, where people get spiritual connection as well as learn protocols and traditional law. (Bell *et al.* 2008: 60–61) The challenge for contemporary traditionalists is to ensure not only that the songs are protected but that they are reintegrated with the teachings that historically accompanied them so that people can know their history and thus fulfill their responsibilities.

Kwakwaka'wakw peoples are grateful that their ancestors recorded many of their songs and thus that they can now do the research to learn about their traditional responsibilities. They are not interested in 'going back to the past' but in revitalizing their traditions to serve them in the present and into the future. Today, the descendants of those alive when the potlatch was outlawed—and almost extinguished—seek to bring their ancestors' songs 'back to life' and thereby to re-establish their connections to territories and their responsibilities to ancestral homes. Hereditary chiefs were known by their songs and had important roles in performing the oratory necessary to maintain the law in the potlatch ceremonies whereas elders had primary responsibility for maintaining knowledge within families. Although there is now some confusion as to ownership of some songs given the gaps in knowledge and practice over the years in which the tradition was under siege, most people believed that even when songs were 'borrowed' by others in times of hardship, seeking permission and acknowledging ownership remained important. (Bell *et al.* 2008: 65–66)

The existence of recordings of Indigenous peoples' songs in public archives neither addresses nor resolves contemporary claims for their repatriation. With respect to the relationship between archives and power, anthropologist Peter Toner suggests that 'we must lay aside naive assumptions about archival neutrality and impartial guardianship of the truth. In reality, decisions are constantly being made about what kinds of records are worthy of archiving, how they should be described, to whom they should be made available, and under what conditions'. (Toner 2004) Many archivists now recognize that by treating records 'as contested sites of power, we can bring new sensibilities to understanding . . . archives as dynamic technologies of rule which actually create the histories and social realities they ostensibly only *describe*.' (Schwartz and Cook 2002: 7)

If we treat recordings of Indigenous songs as mere records of archaic folk music in the public domain, we arguably ratify a colonial history in which Indigenous peoples were treated as doomed to extinction and deny them the capacity to recover their traditional resources for the purposes of forging their own futures. To the extent that repatriation is often expressed and experienced by Indigenous peoples as a form of healing from the historical traumas of colonization, it may also be understood as a form of restitution. Activities of restitution, moreover, may be both innovative and collaborative. The use of the information society communications technologies in repatriation efforts may, surprisingly, serve *both* contemporary archival and Indigenous social needs, as the following example illustrates.

In the course of the 'Yolngu Music: Anthropological and Indigenous Perspectives' collaborative research project undertaken in the early 2000s, it became clear that songs functioned traditionally as law for Yolngu people. The project involved the digitization and community recovery of audio recordings made in northeast Arnhem Land in Australia between the 1920s and the early 1980s. The recovery of these recordings was considered necessary for the purposes of helping Yolngu peoples to 'remember' their heritage. The issue of memory is particularly important and sensitive for Aboriginal land rights where connections to 'traditional owners' must be traced. These connections are difficult to establish in areas where European ideological conditioning had for decades encouraged Aboriginal peoples to regard their pre-contact ancestors as savage 'wild blackfellows' from whom they should appropriately distance themselves and *declaim* relationship.

Amongst the Yolngu, most sacred religious and ceremonial knowledge was traditionally stored in memory and orally transmitted. Memory, however, is shaped by current needs and concerns and the continuing 'integration of the past within the consciousness of the present' is the way that 'history enters, in an active way, the system of social reproduction.' (H. Morphy and F. Morphy 1984, cited in Toner, 2004) Listening to old recordings, Yolngu participants were stimulated to trace kinship relations as a means of educating youth about their ancestors, to reconstruct social networks, and to recall suppressed matrilineal genealogies. The latter were particularly relevant to the traditional transmission of cultural knowledge; this knowledge helped both to re-establish traditional systems of content management over repatriated heritage properties and to integrate these into contemporary ritual life based on a foundation of ancestral law, itself reinvigorated by the recovery of these songs. Listening to the recordings, people felt they were exposed to a higher level of performative competence, and to key representatives of their group's cultural expressive capacity. Often, people would find themselves performing the appropriate dance and hand movements to accompany the song; memory, it seems, is an embodied phenomena. The recovery of music or other forms of what we might consider 'artistic content' may help to trigger the recovery of other memories relevant to mending broken historical records. In the process new forms of contextual 'metadata' may be collected, making these songs far richer and more meaningful, even as objects for 'universal' study.

(Toner 2004) As Aboriginal peoples become research partners in such processes of repatriation, broken records may be mended by the reanimation of archival objects in new forms of collaborative sociality.

Conclusion

Our consideration of the harms of appropriating artistic content legally considered to be traditional music through usages made of historical recordings has engaged in the anthropological exercise of thick description as well as moral and philosophical argument to forge a richer field of ethical inquiry to guide considerations of cultural rights claims. Some forms of harm from the categorization of traditional cultural forms as expressive work that is either protected or in the public domain are not specific to Indigenous peoples but may be shared by many cultural minorities, such as harms of misrepresentation or caricature. Other harms are more likely to be suffered by those who share particular histories of oppression by modern states that sought to assimilate them and/or welcomed their extinction as distinct nations and races. These are peoples for whom the cultural forms the Western world addresses aesthetically may do other kinds of performative work; their contemporary capacities to meet traditional responsibilities and thus to exercise their territorial, environmental and cultural rights may depend upon access to these cultural forms and require some restrictions on their use. Repatriation arguments may be made for the rectification of historical entitlement based on justice of acquisition, justice of transfer and rights against interference in a speech act; they may also be based upon principles of restitution and self-determination. The ethics appropriate for the reparation of injustice are never simple and are importantly related to patterns of historic dispossession. These cannot be addressed and indeed are likely to be exacerbated by quiescent inclinations to reduce charged issues of cultural access, meaning and appropriation to the inevitable tendencies of 'information', technologically rather than sociologically imagined.

Acknowledgments

Fiona MacArailt's research into Ida Halpern provided the initial impetus for the essay; the authors acknowledge her important work and her role as our critical interlocutor. They would like to thank Nicole Aylwin, Irena Knezevic and Tim MacNeill, graduate students at York University, for assistance with the preparation of this article.

References

Ahmed, M., Aylwin, N. and Coombe, R. J. (2008). Indigenous Cultural Heritage Rights in International Human Rights Law. In: Bell, C. & Patterson, R. (eds.) *Protection of First Nations Cultural Heritage: Laws, Policy and Reform.* University of British Columbia Press, Vancouver, 533–83.

Barsh, R. (1995). Indigenous Peoples and the Idea of Individual Human Rights. *Native Studies Review* **10**(2), 35.

Bell, C., Raven, H. and McCuaig, H. in consultation with Sanborn, A., Cranmer, B. the U'mista Cultural Society, and the 'Namgis Nation (2008). Recovering From Colonization: Perspectives of Community Members on Protection and Repatriation of Kwakwaka'wakw Cultural Heritage. In: Bell, C. & Napoleon, V. (eds.) *First Nations Cultural Heritage, and Law, Volume One: Case Studies, Voices and Perspectives.* University of British Columbia Press, Vancouver, 33–91.

Berger, J. (1987). *Report from the Frontier: The State of the World's Indigenous People.* Zed Books, London.

Bohlman, P. V. (2003). Music and Culture. In: Clayton, M., Herbert, T. & Middleton, R. (eds.) *The Cultural Study of Music: A Critical Introduction.* Routledge, London and New York, 45–56.

Bou-Habib, P. (2006). A Theory of Religious Accommodation. *Journal of Applied Philosophy* **23**(1), 109–26.

Brady, E. (1999). *The Spiral Way: How the Phonograph Changed Ethnography.* University Press of Mississippi, Jackson.

Brown, M. (2005). Heritage Trouble: Recent Work on the Protection of Intangible Cultural Property. *International Journal of Cultural Property* **12**(1), 40–61.

Chamberlin, E. J. (2003). *If This is Your Land, Where are Your Stories? Finding Common Ground.* Alfred A. Knopf, Toronto.

Chen, K. (1995). Ida Halpern: A Post-Colonial Portrait of a Canadian Pioneer Ethnomusicologist. *Canadian University Music Review* **16**(1), 41–57.

Cole, D. and Mullins, C. (1993). The Musical World of Ida Halpern. *BC Studies* **97**, 3–37.

Coleman, E. B. (2005). *Aboriginal Art, Identity and Appropriation.* Ashgate, Aldershot, Hants & Burlington, VT.

Coleman, E. B. (2006). Cultural Property and Collective Identity. In: Herbrechter, S. & Higgins, M. (eds.) *Returning (to) Communities.* Rodopi, Amsterdam & Kenilworth, NJ, 161–71.

Coombe, R. J. (1998). Contingent Articulations: A Critical Cultural Studies of Law. In: Sarat, A. & Kearns, T. (eds.) *Law in the Domain of Culture*. University of Michigan Press, Ann Arbor, 21–64.

Coombe, R. J. (2003). Fear, Hope and Longing for the Future of Authorship and a Revitalized Public Domain in Global Regimes of Intellectual Property. *De Paul Law Review* **52**, 1171–91.

Coombe, R. J. (2005). Cultural Rights and Intellectual Property Debates. *Human Rights Dialogue: An International Forum for Debating Human Rights* **2**(12): 34–6.

Coombe, R. J. (2008). First Nations Intangible Cultural Heritage Concerns: Prospects for the Protection of Traditional Knowledge and Traditional Cultural Expressions in International Law. In: Bell, C. & Patterson, R. (eds.) Protection of *First Nations Cultural Heritage and Law: Law, Policy and Reform*. University of British Columbia Press, Vancouver, 313–63.

Drahos, P. with Braithwaite J. (2002). *Information Feudalism: Who Owns the Knowledge Economy?* Earthscan, London.

Eagleton, T. (2000). *The Idea of Culture*. Blackwell Publishers, Oxford.

Fabian, J. (1983). *Time and the Other: How Anthropology Makes its Object*. Columbia University Press, New York.

Feld, Steven (1996). Pygmy POP: A Genealogy of Schizophonic Mimesis. *Yearbook for Traditional Music*, XXVIII, 1–36.

Frith, S. (2003). Music and Everyday Life. In: Clayton, M., Herbert, T. & Middleton, R. (eds.) *The Cultural Study of Music: A Critical Introduction*. Routledge, London and New York, 92–101.

Frisbie, C. (2001). American Indian Musical Repatriation. In: Koskoff, E. (ed.) *The Garland Encyclopedia of World Music, Volume Three: The United States and Canada*. Garland Publishing, New York, 491–501.

Goody, J. (1998). Memory in Oral Tradition. In: Fara, P. & Petterson, K. (eds.) *Memory*. Cambridge University Press, Cambridge, 73–94.

Gray, J. (1997). Returning Music to the Makers: The Library of Congress, American Indians, and the Federal Cylinder Project. *Cultural Survival Quarterly* **20**(4), 42.

Halbert, D. (2005). *Resisting Intellectual Property*. Routledge, London.

Harpham, G. (1994). Aesthetics and the Fundamentals of Modernity. In: Levine, G. (ed.) *Aesthetics and Ideology*. Rutgers University Press, New Brunswick, 124–49.

Hart, H. L. A. (1961). *The Concept of Law*. OUP, Oxford, 77–120.

Kant, I. (1993) (1798). Of the Injustice of Counterfeiting Books. In: *Essays and Treatises on Moral, Political and Various Philosophical Subjects. Volume One*. Thoemmes Press, Bristol, 225–39.

Kellner, D. (2002). Theorising Globalization. *Sociological Theory* **20**(3), 285–305.

Kymlicka, W. (1995). Introduction. Kymlicka, W. (ed.) *The Rights of Minority Cultures*. Oxford University Press, Oxford, 1–30.

Koch, G. (1997). Songs, Land Rights, and Archives in Australia. *Cultural Survival Quarterly* **20**(4), 38.

La Rue, H. (2002). The Stones Resung: Ethnomusicology and Cultural Property. In: Barkan, E. & Bush, R. (eds.). *Claiming the Stones, Naming the Bones: Cultural Property and the Negotiation of National and Ethnic Identity*. Getty Publications, Los Angeles, 224–42.

Laursen, J. C. (1986). The Subversive Kant: The Vocabulary of 'Public' and 'Publicity'. *Political Theory* **14**(4): 584–603.

Lindenbaum, J. (1999). *Music Sampling and Copyright Law*, www.princeton.edu/~artspol/studentpap/undergrad%20thesis1%20JLind.pdf, viewed July 1 2006.

Marsden, S. (2008). Northwest Coast *Adawx* Study. In: Bell, C. & Napoleon, V. (eds.) *First Nations' Cultural Heritage, and Law: Case Studies, Voices, and Perspectives*. University of British Columbia Press, Vancouver, 114–49.

Mattelart, A. (2002). An Archaeology of the Global Era: Constructing a Belief. *Media, Culture & Society* **24**(4), 591–612.

May, C. (2000). The Information Society as Mega-Machine: The Continuing Relevance of Lewis Mumford. *Information, Communication & Society* **3**(2), 241–265.

Mill, J. S. (1894). *Considerations on Representative Government*. Longmans, Green and Co., London.

Mills, S. (1996). Indigenous Music and the Law: An Analysis of National and International Legislation. *International Yearbook for Traditional Music* **28**, 57–86.

Negativland, N. (n.d). *Changing Copyright*. Available at http://www.negativland.com/news/?page_id=22. Accessed December 16, 2008.

Niezen, R. (2003). *The Origins of Indigenism: Human Rights and the Politics of Identity*. University of California Press, Berkeley.

Noble, B. in consultation with Crowshoe, R. and in discussion with the Kuut-sumatak Society (2008). Poomaksin: Skinnipiikani-Nitsiitapii Law, Transfers and Making Relatives. In: Bell, C. & Napoleon, V. (eds.) *First Nations Cultural Heritage and Law: Case Studies, Voices and Perspectives*. University of British Columbia Press, Vancouver, 258–311.

Overstall, R. in consultation with Napoleon, V. and Ludwig, K. (2008). The Law is Opened: The Constitutional Role of Tangible and Intangible Property in Gitanyow. In: Bell C. & Napoleon, V. (eds.). *First Nations Cultural Heritage and Law: Case Studies, Voices and Perspectives*. University of British Columbia Press, Vancouver, 92–113.

Phillips, M. (2000). *Society and Sentiment: Genres of Historical Writing in Britain, 1740–1820*. Princeton University Press, Princeton, NJ.

Phillips, M. (2004). What is Tradition when It Is Not Invented? A Historiographical Introduction. In: Phillips, M. & Schochet, G. (eds.) *Questions of Tradition*. University of Toronto Press, Toronto, 3–32.

Raibmon, P. (2005). *Authentic Indians: Episodes of Encounter From the Late-Nineteenth Century Northwest Coast.* Duke University Press, Durham.

Schwartz, J. and Cook, T. (eds.) (2002). Archives, Records, and Power: The Making of Modern Memory. *Archival Science* **2**(1–2), 1–19.

Solomon, M. (2004). Intellectual Property Rights and Indigenous Peoples' Rights and Responsibilities. In: Riley, M. (ed.) *Indigenous Intellectual Property Rights: Legal Obstacles and Innovative Solutions.* AltaMira Press, Walnut Creek, 221–50.

Sterne, J. (2003). *The Audible Past: Cultural Origins of Sound Reproduction.* Duke University Press, Durham.

Struhl, K. J. (2006). Is Globalization the Problem? 'Another World Is Necessary' Conference Papers. Centre for Global Justice. Available at http://www.globaljusticecenter.org/papers2006/struhlENG.htm, last accessed October 2, 2007 (5 pages).

Taubman, A. (2005). Saving the Village: Conserving Jurisprudential Diversity in the International Protection of Traditional Knowledge. In: Reichman, J. & Mascus, K. (eds.) *International Public Goods and Transfer of Technology.* Cambridge University Press, Cambridge, 521–64.

Taylor, C. (1994). The Politics of Recognition. In: Gutman, A. (ed.) *Multiculturalism.* Princeton University Press, Princeton, NJ, 25–73.

Thompson, J. (2001). Historical Injustice and Reparation: Justifying Claims of Descendents. *Ethics* **112**(1), 114–35.

Tomlinson, G. (2003). Musicology, Anthropology, History. In: Clayton, M., Herbert, T. & Middleton, R. (eds.) *The Cultural Study of Music: A Critical Introduction.* Routledge, New York and London, 31–44.

Toner, P. G. (2004). History, Memory and Music: The Repatriation of Digital Audio to Yolngu Communities or Memory as Metadata. In: Barwick, L. *et al.* (eds.) *Researchers, Communities, Institutions, Sound Recordings.* University of Sydney, Sydney. Available at http://ses.library.usyd.edu.au/handle/2123/1518

Waldron, J. (1992). Superseding Historic Injustice. *Ethics* **103**(October), 4–28.

Waldron, J. (1995). Minority Cultures and the Cosmopolitan Alternative. In: Kymlicka, W. (ed.) *The Rights of Minority Cultures.* Oxford University Press, Oxford, 93–123.

Webster, F. (2000). Information, Capitalism and Uncertainty. *Information Community and Society* **3**(1), 69–90.

Ziff, B. and Rao, P. (eds.) (1997). *Borrowed Power: Essays on Cultural Appropriation.* Rutgers University Press, New Brunswick, NJ.

9

Objects of Appropriation

Andrea N. Walsh and Dominic McIver Lopes

Introduction

Object appropriation is typically viewed as taking possession of objects for use and exhibition in foreign contexts. Ethics of object appropriation have consequently centered on whether appropriation is permissible or impermissible and how to remedy it within the framework of moral and legal property rights. These discussions rightly probe the intricacies of contested conceptions of property across cultural and legal boundaries. These intricacies are important and absorbing. But the question is rarely asked why appropriation is so hotly disputed in the first place. Why do reasonable people share so little common ground when it comes to the ethics of object appropriation? One possible answer is that the typical view of object appropriation as taking possession is incomplete: it leaves out the power of objects to generate culturally important meanings. We propose to broaden the discussion of appropriation beyond the ethics and law of property. To do this, we consider acts of appropriation by members of Aboriginal communities in Canada in response to monuments whose original purpose was to validate colonialism. A look at acts of object appropriation that do not involve exchanges of property might shed light on acts that do.

Monument as Museum, Museum as Monument

The rotunda of the British Columbia Legislature houses four murals that allegorically depict early moments in the colonial history of the province. The murals, entitled *Courage, Enterprise, Labour* and *Justice*, were painted between 1932 and 1953 by George Southwell as a gift to the province from Provincial Secretary S. L. Howe.[1] Sixty-five years later, the murals became a flash-point over the representation of First Nations. At the heart of this debate was the mural titled *Labour*, which depicted bare-breasted Native women hauling logs to create a colonial fort. In 2000, the First Nations Summit Task Group wrote a letter to British Columbia's Attorney General stating that 'these paintings of bare-breasted Aboriginal women and of Aboriginal persons in subservient positions are, we are sure you will understand, highly offensive, demeaning and degrading to First Nations people in the province.' (British Columbia Legislative Assembly 2001: 7) Some proposed that the murals should be removed or destroyed for their offensive and inaccurate portrayal of historical dress codes and material culture objects.[2] Responding to this proposal, some complained of political correctness, censorship and the dangers of historical revisionism.[3] Suggested compromises included covering the murals with a curtain allowing those who wished to view them to do so, and installing a plaque expressing the province's regret for the treatment of Aboriginal peoples in colonial times with a promise toward positive future relationships (see Letters to the Editor, *Times Colonist* May 3, 2007: A13). Letters to the editors of provincial newspapers expressed overwhelming opposition to the outright removal of the murals.[4] After seven years and a report by a panel of experts, the province decided to plan for the removal of the murals.[5]

This is but the latest of several debates in Canada involving the representation of Aboriginal peoples in monuments. Earlier incidents include two sculptures of the Métis leader Louis Riel in Manitoba and Saskatchewan and a monument dedicated to the explorer Samuel de Champlain at Nepean Point in Ontario (Figures 9.1 and 9.2).

In 1967, Saskatchewan's premier, Ross Thatcher, commissioned John Nugent to create a monument to Louis Riel. Thatcher chose one of two maquettes that Brian Osborne describes as a 'bronze figure in the style of a classical nude, an open Mackinaw-coat partly covering Riel's nudity, his head and right hand thrust upward in a final act of defiance as he surrendered at Batoche in 1885.' (Osborne 2002: 312) Neither the Métis community nor First Nations peoples were consulted, and, when the sculpture was unveiled in 1968 by Prime Minister Pierre Trudeau, no Métis or First Nations people were invited to speak. According to Osborne, 'Thatcher was determined to appropriate their voices for his purposes and his preferred image of Riel was 'assimilated, educated, Europeanized.' And even given Nugent's well-intentioned motives, his work represented 'a

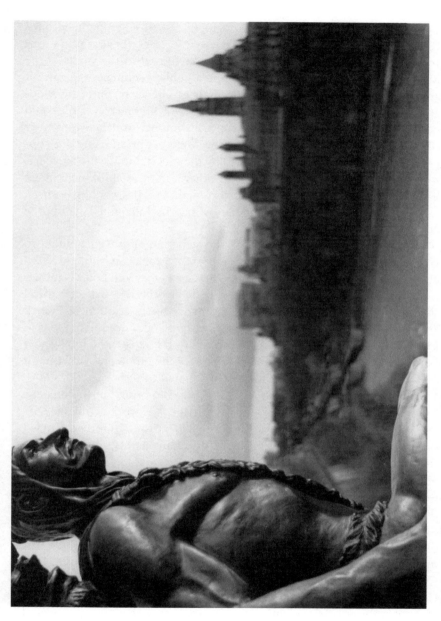

Figure 9.1 Jeffrey Thomas. Indian man and Samuel de Champlain Monument, Nepean Point, Ottawa, 1992.

Euro-Canadian aesthetic and historiography, albeit a sympathetic one.' (Osborne 2002: 313) Over the next twenty years the sculpture was continuously denounced, and in 1991 it was moved to the vaults of the Mackenzie Art Gallery. This also prompted public comment: 'the current government does not have Riel's strength of character' and 'the Métis gentlemen who apparently started all the fuss over our one real statue could not see the grace and dignity expressed in the face and figure of their countryman.' There was praise too: 'the Métis . . . presumably are supposed to feel honoured not humiliated by the Riel statue . . . the move has some merit' and 'if public statues of any other leading establishment figure had been portrayed with his genitalia exposed the artist would have been run out of town, his body black and blue with welts' (all quoted in Osborne 2002: 316).

Also in 1967, the government of Saskatchewan approved funding to erect a monument to Riel on the grounds of the provincial legislature, and an abstract sculpture of Riel created by Marcien Lemay and Louis Gauthier was unveiled in 1971. The sculpture was flanked by two half-cylindrical shells topped with Riel's name and a provocative inscription in French and English: 'I know that through the Grace of God, I am the founder of Manitoba.' (Osborne 2002: 314) According to the artists, the monument portrayed Riel's face in 'anguish . . . to convey the mood and suffering of a man sacrificing himself for his beliefs' (quoted in Osborne 2002: 314). They also explained that Riel appears in a 'cage' to bring out this anxiety. Comments printed in local newspapers described the work as 'misshapen,' 'grotesque,' and 'a monstrosity.' (Osborne 2002: 314) Supporters pleaded under the banner of anti-revisionism: 'Don't remove this statue. It represents a history that cannot be undone or erased' (quoted in Bower 2001: 35). Shannon Bower reports that sentiments like these 'embodied the foremost fear of the Métis: that Lemay's statue would legitimize an interpretation of Louis Riel that they condemned.' (Bower 2001: 35) Like the monument in Winnipeg, the Regina monument also suffered from vandalism. In 1991 the Manitoba Métis Federation and the provincial government agreed to its removal and it was moved in 1995 to the grounds of College St. Boniface.[6] A year later, a new sculpture of Riel was unveiled. Commissioned by the Manitoba Métis Federation and created by Miguel Joyal, it portrays Riel wearing a 'Métis sash, suit jacket, moccasins with Métis pointed toes and wav[ing] a scroll.' (Osborne 2002: 318) This more subdued image also came in for criticism: it 'may well depict any unadventurous insurance agent holding a policy or broker peddling prospectus,' it is 'misleading and intellectually empty' (quoted in Osborne 2002: 318). Bower notes that Joyal's statue is a 'statement as much as a symbol' but it allows for 'relatively few interpretive options.' (Bower 2001: 32) Lemay's sculpture is much more 'ambiguous'. According to Bower, 'ambiguity is certainly not an inherently negative quality. However, given the enduring social context of colonialism, any symbol that did not overtly oppose colonialism was suspected of collusion.' (Bower 2001: 32)

In 1917, several decades prior to the creation of the Riel monuments, a monument to the seventeenth-century explorer Samuel de Champlain was erected at Nepean Point on the Ottawa River at Ottawa. Champlain founded the city of Québec in 1608 and then in 1613 explored the Ottawa River, and the monument, created by Hamilton MacCarthy, commemorates the three-hundredth anniversary of Champlain's second trip up the Ottawa River.[7] The Ottawa *Evening Citizen* reported the day after the monument was unveiled: 'The sculptor represents the great discoverer standing upon this spot of earth, holding in his hand the astrolabe, and looking towards those regions of Ontario into the primeval forests of which Champlain was the first to carry the torch of civilization and flambeau of Christianity' (quoted in *Ottawa Citizen,* October 3, 1996: C1). A campaign to add an Indian Scout with a canoe was launched in 1918 but a lack of funds forced the cancellation of the full plan and the canoe was never manufactured (see Figure 9.1).

For eight decades the Champlain monument overlooked the Ottawa cityscape and the river. However, in 1996 the Assembly of First Nations contacted the National Capital Commission to raise an objection to the monument. AFN Chief Ovide Mercredi stated that the Indian Scout misrepresented Native peoples by portraying them as subservient to Champlain. The complaint prompted spirited debates about how colonial history dominated the Ottawa landscape and how Native peoples were represented in that history. Again, the suggestion of removing the offending part of the monument generated contending opinions. Christopher Hume, writing in the *Toronto Star*, pinpointed a tension between historical monuments and historical revisionism in contemporary politics: 'Such condescension has no place in the official art of the 1990s, but does that mean we should reinvent history?' (October 19, 1996: E3) Some saw the removal of the Scout as an act that would 'deface the history of the city' and damage what 'belongs to the people of Ottawa.' (*Ottawa Citizen,* October 6, 1996: A6) Others opposing the removal of the Scout dismissed the AFN's complaints as 'nonsense' and advised Aboriginal people to 'quit complaining about trivial things and get on with your life.' (*Ottawa Citizen*, October 4, 1996: D3)[8] A member of the Rama First Nation from Orillia, where there is another monument to Champlain, opposed the Scout's removal for different reasons. He wrote that 'removing the figures and storing them in a warehouse like they're doing in Ottawa doesn't make sense. Gee whiz, isn't that what they did to Indians in the first place?' (*Toronto Star*, October 13, 1996: A18)[9] Still others sought a compromise in renaming the monument to reflect the relationship between the two figures.[10] In 1999 a decision was taken to remove the Scout from the base of the monument and relocate it to Major Hill's Park, across the road from the Champlain monument.

Discussions of appropriation in Canada have focused primarily on material objects that were made by members of First Nations and then collected by non-Native institutions or individuals in Canada and abroad. The vast majority of items collected in Canada are held in provincial and national museums such as the Museum of Civilization; only recently have First Nations cultural and heritage centers assumed responsibility for collecting and exhibiting artifacts.

At first glance, monuments which involve representations of members of First Nations have little in common with material objects appropriated from First Nations for display in museums. The Champlain monument is and always has been a public object. It is not an item of personal heritage or provenance. Moreover, the Champlain monument does not have a history of migration: it was created for the place it occupies and it gets its meaning as a monument created for that place. Objects in museums undergo a change in meaning when taken from one context and placed in a context of exhibition.

Yet there remain provocative similarities between the monuments and the appropriation of First Nations artifacts, for both are elements in the visualization of a national narrative of Canadian history. Monuments like the one to Champlain at Nepean Point memorialize people and events so as to lay a claim to nationhood and ownership of the land. (Osborne 2001) This is obvious in the case of the monuments, but appropriated objects, at least when displayed in Canada, also contributed to the narrative of the nation. The objects were visual symbols of Aboriginal identity and even proxies for actual bodies. A display of masks made by peoples from a particular nation symbolically represents those people and the beliefs for which they made the masks. True, the monuments differ from artifacts in museum collections that symbolically represent First Nations peoples because the monuments depict realistic human figures. Looking beyond this difference means that we can understand the contested character of the monuments from the perspective of debates concerning appropriating objects and that we can understand the latter debates from the perspective of the contested character of the monuments. Responses to the appropriation of images of Aboriginal bodies in monuments that mark landscapes and memorialize colonial events can carry over to object appropriation.

Arts of Appropriation

Objects lying at the intersection of Native and non-Native cultures, be they pieces of material culture created by one or the other, are an inescapable and vital element of present-day relations between Indigenous peoples and the dominant society in Canada. The contested nature of these objects certainly has to do with competing conceptions of property and competing property claims. But this is not the whole story if colonial monuments share a place with appropriated objects as elements used in colonial narratives. The contested nature of these objects has something to do with meaning as well as property. This comes through clearly in the work of two First Nations artists, Jeffrey Thomas and Greg Hill. Both Thomas and Hill have voiced their concern that with the removal and relocation of the Scout, history, and Native people's involvement within it, has been erased or rewritten. Their response has been to appropriate the monument to Champlain at Nepean Point.

Thomas, an Onondaga photographer, first viewed the monument in 1992. Says Thomas, 'I found the Indian scout to be a perfect metaphor for the dominant society's ideal of an authentic Indian: nameless, without a voice, and caught in the shadow of a dominant European Explorer.' Thomas's photographs of the monument from 1994 to 1996, before the Scout's removal, are close-up portraits depicting the Scout's panoramic view of the architectural and institutional landscape of Ottawa and Hull (see Figure 9.1). These studies developed into a broader project, now twenty years old, that seeks to locate and document monuments that depict Native peoples in Canadian history. Many photographs in this larger project are portraits of his son, Bear, standing next to or in front of the monument. On rare occasions, Thomas took self-portraits with the Indians on the monument (Figure 9.2). In 2001, three years after the Scout was removed, Thomas put ads in local newspapers inviting the members of the public to have their photographs taken standing or sitting on the empty

Figure 9.2   Jeffrey Thomas. Self-portrait with Indian man at Samuel de Champlain Monument, Nepean Point, Ottawa, c. 1996.

platform once occupied by the Scout. The response was enthusiastic and many showed up to have their photographs taken. The sitters were as diverse culturally, economically and politically as the poses they assumed for their portrait. Recently, Thomas has begun a new series of portraits at the base of the monument titled *Seize the Space* (at http://www.scouting-forindians.com/space.html). This new project includes portraits of both Native and non-Native persons, and several of the non-Native sitters contributed text discussing their experiences of the monument as Jeff shot their portraits.

This engagement of the monument as an active site of intervention is also seen in installation and performance work by Greg Hill, who is a member of the Six Nations. On May 3, 2001, he streamed a live performance piece over the internet from the empty platform of the Scout. Over a period of thirty-nine minutes, Hill cycled through a series of four poses that referenced four Aboriginal figures, both historic and contemporary (Figs 9.3–9.6):

Pose 1. Warrior (Lasagna) from Oka.
Inspired by an original photograph by Galbraith, 1990;

Figure 9.3 Warrior (Lasagna) from Oka. (Greg Hill, *Joe Scouting for Cigar Store Lasagna* performance, Ottawa, 2001. Photo-William Kingfisher.)

Pose 2. Cigar Store Indian.

Figure 9.4   Cigar Store Indian. (Greg Hill, *Joe Scouting for Cigar Store Lasagna* performance, Ottawa, 2001. Photo-William Kingfisher.)

Pose 3. Thayendanegea (Joseph Brant).
Inspired by the original painting by W. Berczy, 1794;

Figure 9.5 Thayendanegea (Joseph Brant). (Greg Hill, *Joe Scouting for Cigar Store Lasagna* performance, Ottawa, 2001. Photo-William Kingfisher.)

Pose 4. Annishnaabe Scout.
Inspired by the Champlain monument by Hamilton MacCarthy, 1915.

Figure 9.6 Anishnaabe Scout. (Greg Hill, *Joe Scouting for Cigar Store Lasagna* performance, Ottawa, 2001. Photo–William Kingfisher.)

Video and photographs taken during this performance were installed at the Art Gallery of Windsor, Ontario in the fall of 2001. He titled the installation piece *For eignation (For a Nation)*. On another occasion Hill installed a life-size cereal box canoe at the base of the monument, in response to the 1918 plan to supply the Scout with a bronze canoe (Fig. 9.7). Hill says his performance was about history and its shaping through public art and monuments. It also responds to the controversy over the representation of Aboriginal people in Canadian history and the subsequent removal of the unnamed Indian Scout from a monument dedicated to memorializing history. Hill has sought to renew dialogue about the controversy through a ritual and conceptual rejoining of the two parts of the monument.

Thomas and Hill engage in acts of appropriation without violating any property right. Through their performances they comment on Champlain's claiming the land for France, on the later role of that claim in the Canadian Crown's claim to the land, and thus on the taking of the land from the Aboriginal nations. But they do not comment on this taking by a property grab of their own. They cleverly appropriate without taking: their appropriations do not trade on property. This does not mean that acts of appropriation never have anything to do with property rights, and it certainly does not mean that an ethics of appropriation should have nothing to do with property rights. It simply means that we must also look beyond property to understand the perils and the possibilities in appropriation. Perhaps looking at acts of appropriation that do not trade on property can shed light on acts that do.

Appropriation, Property and Oppression

Although the ethics of object appropriation ties in to the ethics and law of property, this is only part of the story. And although the ethics of object appropriation addresses histories of discrimination and oppression, this, too, is only part of the story. There is some debate—evident in this volume—about whether appropriation implies blame, so that to appropriate is always to do something wrong. There is also some debate about whether appropriation is an activity reserved for hegemonic groups, so that the idea of members of Aboriginal cultures appropriating from the dominant culture is absurd. Perhaps, however, it is useful to think of members of Aboriginal cultures, including artists like Thomas and Hill, as free to

Figure 9.7 Greg Hill posed in his cereal box canoe, Samuel de Champlain Monument, Nepean Point, Ottawa, 2000.

engage in acts of appropriation. At the very least it makes sense to ask the question whether they are appropriating another culture's property and subverting its history. Why rule out a conception of appropriation which allows us to answer this question by saying 'yes, and for all the better'?

Object appropriation is often plain theft. Valuable objects, ranging from masks, carvings and manuscripts to pots and baskets have been looted by invaders, explorers, colonizers and governors. In each case, some person or community has a right to possess and use an object which is taken by someone who has no right to take it. Taking an object is wrong in these circumstances because it violates rights in property. Thus it seems that the act of appropriation inherits its moral character from the morality of property.

Of course, the suggestion that object appropriation inherits its ethics from the ethics of property does not clear up very much, for it raises plenty of tricky issues. A major complication is the relationship between moral and legal property rights: philosophers and legal theorists hold a range of views about the relationship between moral and legal rights in general and between moral and legal property rights in particular. Further complications stem from the fact that different cultures can have different conceptions of property—for example, some have community property and others do not. This leads first to epistemic complications: members of one culture may not know what moral norms hold in another culture. Thus somebody from a culture who is unfamiliar with the idea of community property may reason that because an item is not claimed as the property of any individual, it belongs to nobody, and so she is not wrong to take it. Unbeknownst to her, the object is community property, so her taking it is seen by members of the community as wrongfully violating a property right. A different complication concerns the content of morality: what moral property rights do we actually have? An outsider may know perfectly well that members of a culture recognize community property, but she may reject the idea of community property as incoherent and so she may refuse to accept claims of community property rights. The distinction between legal and moral rights is grist to her mill. She may acknowledge that the community has a legal system that enshrines a legal right to community property and yet deny that the legal right has any basis in morality.

Object appropriation touches on some of the hardest problems in ethics. Take the epistemic complication first. A visiting collector does not know that the people she is visiting recognize community property, and so she takes what she believes is free for the taking. It does not follow that she does nothing wrong, for ignorance is not always an excuse. It is not an excuse for the collector when it was her duty to know how her trading partners think about property. Thus arises the question of how much morality requires us to know about unfamiliar cultures in a context of contact. We need an ethics of contact. Such an ethics requires a delicate balancing act. After all, the only way to learn about unfamiliar cultures is to make contact, yet contact should not proceed entirely in ignorance of what ought to be known. Second, cultures sometimes have incompatible moral codes in the sense that it is sometimes impossible to comply with the demands of all. Dilemmas arise in such contexts. A collector may assert the correctness of her moral code and deny that there are any collective property rights. Is her moral code correct? A relativist may answer that every code is correct in its social context. But relativism is only a solution for cultural isolates: how ought one to act in a context of contact?

There is a wide range of views about the relationship between moral and legal rights, the ethics of cultural contact and the content of morality. Basic disagreement on these matters helps explain why object appropriation is so contested.

An ethics of appropriation should also attend to the fact that acts of appropriation often occur in contexts of past or ongoing oppression, for such a context is a factor in a property-oriented conception of appropriation. Many acts of object appropriation occur where there is an imbalance of power that puts into question whether property transactions are consensual or whether objects are given up under duress. Many First Nations artifacts in Canadian collections came from communities that had long engaged in trading relationships with outsiders. By the legal standards of all parties, the purchase of some of these artifacts may sometimes have been legitimate. Nevertheless, one might argue that these purchases were in fact a morally impermissible appropriation. Many Indigenous communities suffered under colonial powers that had for many decades drained their resources and destabilized their political and social structures. It could be argued that trades or sales of artifacts would never have been made but for the damage the community has sustained from colonization.

So disputes about object appropriation might to some extent reflect different views about the nature, extent and impact of past and ongoing oppression. Some consider that appropriation occurs in a context of colonialism and oppression that infects trade with an element of coercion.

Others deny that these contexts are ones where non-coercive trade could take place. Denying this can come from refusing to reckon with the wrongs of the past (and present). However, it can also have a positive side. The blanket claim that any contact between more powerful and less powerful groups is coercive implies that members of less powerful groups lack agency and the competence to handle their own affairs—and perhaps that leads, ironically, to a case for paternalism.

The performances of Thomas and Hill add something that we miss by tying appropriation exclusively to property and property under conditions of oppression. Their performances are acts of appropriation that do not trade on property; and neither do they rely on a power imbalance where the appropriators are powerful and the appropriatees are victims. The point is not that Thomas and Hill are victims who pull off an act of appropriation against their oppressors. Perhaps that is true, but the more interesting point is that their performances are empowering because they destabilize the assumed alignment of appropriator with oppressor and appropriatee with victim. The fact that appropriation is about control of meaning as well as control of property also explains why it is so hotly disputed.

The negotiated return of collected First Nations objects is our best attempt to date to remove them from inappropriate foreign contexts. Compromises such as shared stewardship and cooperative exhibition policies (described in detail by Eaton and Gaskell in this volume) acknowledge the multiple meanings of objects for parties with vested interest in the objects. If repatriation and shared collection and exhibition policies are a valid way to resolve issues of appropriation regarding objects in museums, then what should be done about the appropriation of First Nations bodies and images in colonial monuments? The monuments cannot be 'returned' or 'co-stewarded'. So far, the solution has been to remove them from controversial contexts or destroy their original form. Curiously, an alternative solution is not to suppress appropriation, but rather to promote it, using contested objects like the Champlain monument as departure points for visually innovative acts of restitution. 'New' appropriations can layer meanings on to monuments not foreseen by their original builders. This approach to appropriation parallels a part of the agenda of co-stewardship policies for First Nations objects in museum collections, which is to recognize the power of objects to generate culturally important meanings at many complex levels.

Appropriation, Memory and Identity

What is most interesting about the work of Thomas and Hill is how it turns the tables on typical discussions of object appropriation. It is not that they take questions about possession and property off the table in order to start a discussion about the meaning of objects. Some of the meaning of monuments and museum artifacts is inseparable from property claims. What Thomas and Hill do is clear a space to create meaning that is separable from property claims.

Monuments are devices that represent and reinforce a national history. In Canada agencies such as the Historic Sites and Monuments Board and the Champlain Society created statuary like the Champlain monument to cultivate a national identity. In doing so, they appropriated Aboriginal symbols and figurative representations. Osborne maintains that this statuary 'represented the personification of the nation or nationalizing state, the transmission of mythic histories, a material and visual connection with the past, and the legitimization of authority.' (Osborne 2001: 51) The monument at Nepean Point performs this role by transforming the landscape itself. As Denis Cosgrove argued, 'landscape constitutes a discourse through which identifiable social groups historically have framed themselves and their relations with both the land and with other human groups, and that this discourse is related epistemically and technically to ways of seeing.' (Cosgrove 1998: xiv) When objects were moved from Native contexts to exhibition in museums they were also made to contribute to this nation-building story, and in this way they acquired a new meaning.

However, the role of monuments and First Nations artifacts in contributing to national myth does not completely explain the reaction to proposals to move monuments or to repatriate collections. As we have seen, one common reaction to proposals such as these is that they will erase a historical record that should be preserved. For example, the panel deciding the fate of the British Columbia Legislature murals placed priority on living First Nations people over the continuity of the murals' exhibition; and their recommendation provoked charges of historical revisionism. The monuments and objects carry powerful messages, but the messages depend on the continued existence of the objects. Underlying this reaction is an archival conception of history. Pierre Nora has suggested that history in the modern period is understood archivally. On this conception, history 'relies entirely on the materiality of the trace, the immediacy of the recording, the visibility of the image.' (Nora 1989: 13) Having lost faith in memory, we rely on material archives, which form 'an unlimited repertoire of what might need to be recalled.' (Nora 1989: 13) The information recalled from such archives is not born of individual experience, but rather of institutionalized narratives. Thus the loss of visible records like the British Columbia Legislature murals, the monuments to Riel and the massive collections of First Nations artifacts in museums is tantamount to a loss of history.

The work of Thomas and Hill challenges the equation of history-making meaning with archiving and possession. On one hand, it resists the act of moving the Scout. On the other hand, it proposes to change what the monument means. In all of the case studies presented here, the final decision about controversial monuments leaned towards their removal or destruction. Thomas and Hill suggest an alternative, which rebuffs the archival conception of history by changing the meaning of the monument. As James E. Young writes, 'neither the monument nor its meaning is really everlasting. Both a monument and its significance are constructed in particular times and places, contingent on the political, historical, and aesthetic realities of the moment.' (Young 1999: 13) By the same token, decisions about collections of First Nations artifacts have leaned towards co-stewardship agreements or to repatriation to local archives. Do the appropriative strategies of Thomas and Hill suggest an alternative here too?

At the beginning of this chapter we proposed that looking at acts of object appropriation that do not involve exchanges of property might shed light on acts that do. Discussions of appropriation focus on artifacts in museums, where fault is associated with acts of appropriation of Native artifacts by colonial interests. The recent response is co-stewardship, which is seen as a way to start a dialogue about the contested meanings and histories of objects and as a way to redress past injustices. However, co-stewardship agreements give paramount consideration to the 'historical' relevance of artifacts and museums' conservation requirements. The agreements downplay the contemporary significance of the objects to First Nations peoples (and other people, for that matter). How might acts of appropriation by First Nations artists help us push past this barrier in the context of museum collections?

In 2000, Lynn Hill, a curator from the Cayuga First Nation, mounted an exhibition of contemporary art entitled Raven's Reprise at the University of British Columbia Museum of Anthropology. For this show, she invited First Nations artists to appropriate the museum's traditional artifact display space. She wrote,

> This exhibition is unique in that the works have been installed throughout the museum amidst the permanent collection. This placement has enabled the artists to create a visual dialogue between the contemporary and historic pieces. These juxtapositions provide the viewer with visual references and establish the context from which the contemporary works stem. This exhibition is not meant to disclaim past artistic traditions or scholarly explorations, but rather to offer some insight into current art practices that venture beyond an analysis of traditional forms and genres. (Webb 2000: 1)

In response to Hill's invitation, Kwakwaka'wakw artist Marianne Nicolson created a mixed media photo-based installation titled *Waxmedlagin xusbandayu'* (*Even Though I Am the Last One, I Still Count*). The piece incorporated historical and contemporary photography with painted traditional design elements and Kwakwala language words. In her artist's statement Nicolson explains that the piece speaks to her family's relationship and rights to eight Bumblebee masks sold to the museum in the 1960s by her grandfather. Decades later, her uncle recreated the masks for use at a contemporary potlatch, and claimed the rights to the dance associated with the masks now owned by the museum. Nicolson explains the cultural relevance of the dance of the Bumblebee that is performed by children, and she is careful to specifically name the people in her family who hold the rights to this dance today, and from whom they inherited it. This is all information that would not otherwise appear in the display of the masks. She writes,

> though my grandfather was forced to sell these masks in the early 1960s, I created this piece to recognize that the rights and privileges that they embodied are still active and integral to the Musgamagw Dzawada'enuxw people. He sold the masks at a time when the future of our traditional culture was in doubt. It is with great pride that I am able to look back and know that each generation of my family has participated in this dance, and feel assured that the continuance of its practice is now without doubt. (Webb 2001: 16)

Nicolson and Hill installed the contemporary piece in a glass exhibition case with four of her grandfather's museum-owned Bumblebee masks above her work, and the other four below it. In this installation/intervention, Nicolson appropriates both the museum's context and objects. She brings a new line to bear on standard ways of thinking about the appropriation of First Nations artifacts by exercising her power to make culturally important meanings.

Notes

1. *Courage* depicts Captains Vancouver and Quadra at Nootka Sound in 1792. *Enterprise* depicts Hudson's Bay Factor, James Douglas, landing from the Cadboro at Clover Point to select the site for Fort Victoria in 1843. *Labour* depicts the building of Forts Victoria or Langley. *Justice* depicts Chief Justice Sir Matthew Bailie Begbie holding court in Clinton during the Cariboo gold rush of the 1860s.

2. First Nations leaders were most outspoken. Grand Chief Ed John of the BC Indian Chiefs stated that 'what some people will suggest is that whether it is anthropological or historically correct won't cut ice . . . sending it [the decision whether to remove the murals] to a panel of experts is not going to change the repugnancy of those murals.' (*Times Colonist*, June 28, 2007) Bill Wilson, head of the First Nations Summit, the largest Aboriginal group in the province, stated that 'the murals should be removed, but not destroyed . . . have them put in a place where they are reflective of First Nations history . . . they represent an attitude that needs to be remembered but not as the primary center in the parliament buildings [which should] reflect the contributions of all that built this province.' (*Times Colonist*, April 7, 2007) A member of the Chemainus First Nation stated that the lack of clothing on figures in the murals was disturbing to her students, and she remarked that 'First Nations people and communities are striving to improve our relationship with the government. The legislature needs to symbolize this new relationship. A mural that symbolizes colonialism and oppression is inappropriate in a house that is meant to fairly represent all of us.' (*Times Colonist*, April 6, 2007)

3. Titles of articles in the *Times Colonist* include: '"Offensive" Murals to Come Down' (April 25, 2007, front page), 'Preserve History, Don't Destroy It' (April 28, 2007), and 'Politically Correct Gesture a Tragedy' (April 28, 2007). Blair Lekstrom, a Member of the Legislative Assembly who voted against the motion to remove the murals from the Legislature, stated that 'history is not always comfortable. But it's real, and we should not hide it'. (*Times Colonist*, April 25, 2007, front page) A letter to the editor lamented that 'it is sad that we have now come to a place of revisionist history made in the name of comfort.' (*Times Colonist*, April 28, 2007)

4. Many writers defended the murals by likening them to great works of art around the world. One writer argued that it would be to destroy

Michelangelo's *David* if nudity ever came to be an offense to the citizens of Florence. (*Times Colonist*, May 3, 2007) Another wrote of the legacy of colonial occupation in Merida, Mexico. As examples of art born of a violent past, he described two stone statues of Spanish soldiers, 'both in full armour and each with his foot on the head of a Mayan native', outside Government House in Merida. He concludes that 'to remove these murals from our legislature buildings reflects profound ignorance and can only be considered barbaric.' (*Times Colonist*, April 28, 2007)

5. The panel of experts comprised of educators, artists, curators and historians, including some First Nations, was charged with considering 'the concerns raised by the First Nations Summit Task Group; the image and message respecting Aboriginal people that the murals convey, and the historical and artistic value of the murals.' (Archibald *et al.* 2001: 7) The panel determined that

> the debate about historical accuracy, the value of the murals as historic art, and the examination of how one is influenced by societal values and attitudes of particular time periods has been an important exercise. But the concerns of the First Nations Summit and the chiefs of the Lekwammen people are much more than an academic consideration. For many years, many Aboriginal and Non-Aboriginal people have found the image and message of the murals to be not only disturbing, but offensive and hurtful. The value of the art and the historical accuracy of the murals are less important than the hurt they cause. They may have had a function in their time, but, as hereditary Chief Andy Thomas stated, that time has gone. . . . While the perspective of Southwell and others deserves an important place in our understanding, it is no longer the only, or principal, means by which we perceived the history of this province. While the perspective that is presented in the paintings deserves an important place in our understanding of historical attitudes in the province, it is no longer the lens through which we view the history of British Columbia. Exploration and colonization are now understood as processes that created this province by displacing Aboriginal people. Aboriginal peoples' historic contributions to building British Columbia are now being recognized. (Archibald *et al.* 2001: 23–4)

6. Jean Allard, the founder of La Societé Louis Riel, who headed the initiative to have the monument created in the first instance, chained himself to the monument in protest. He said, 'I think it's appalling that a government would be trying to remove it, to try to play the sanitized politics of the day' (quoted in Osborne 2002: 315).

7. Ruth Phillips, citing H. V. Nelles, notes that 'the celebrations repositioned a French colonial hero as a contributor to a triumphal history of British imperialism.' In addition, 'the monument has also become a site for contestations of both Anglo-Canadian and settler empowerment. It has served as a rallying point for the patriotic St. Jean Baptiste Society at its annual celebration of the patron saint of Québec, Ottawa's major public display of French Canadian nationalist and separatist sentiment.' (Phillips 2003: 285)

8. Comments also acknowledged underlying racial discrimination that stereotyped Aboriginal people as either noble savages or contemporary criminals. The Scout does not need clothes because 'he knows how to survive in this harsh country' and 'if the Aboriginal people feel the statue is demeaning, perhaps they can pay to remove it. If the allocation of funds prove difficult, maybe funds donated from the lucrative, illegal Aboriginal gambling and smuggling coffers can remedy the situation.' (*Ottawa Citizen*, October 4, 1996: D3)

9. Dennis Martel went on to say that 'what we would like to do is use the statue and learn from it . . . We want to work with the community of Orillia and write a new plaque that explains the true relationship between Champlain and the Hurons.' (*Toronto Star*, October 13, 1996: A18)

10. The suggestion was made by Madeline Dion Stout from the Centre for Aboriginal Education Research and Culture at Carleton University. She was concerned that the Scout's removal might 'erase our memory of that part of history.' (*Ottawa Citizen*, October 7, 1996, D2)

References

Archibald, J-A, Barman, J., Black, M., Lutz, J. and Tsaqwasupp (Art Thompson) (2001). *A Review of the Depiction of Aboriginal Peoples in the Artworks of the Parliament Buildings: Report of the Speaker's Advisory Panel*. Victoria: Legislative Assembly of British Columbia.

Bower, S. (2001). 'Practical Results:' The Riel Statue Controversy at the Manitoba Legislative Building. *Manitoba History* **42**: 30–8.

Cosgrove, D. (1998). *The Iconography of Landscape*. Cambridge: Cambridge University Press.

Nora, P. (1989). Between Memory and History: Les Lieux de Mémoire. *Representations* **26**: 7–24.

Osborne, B. (2001). Landscapes, Memory, Monuments and Commemoration: Putting Identity in Its Place. *Canadian Ethnic Studies* **33**: 46–77.

Osborne, B. (2002). Corporeal Politics and the Body Politic: The Representation of Louis Riel in Canadian Identity. *International Journal of Heritage Studies* **8**: 303–22.

Phillips, R. (2003). Settler Monuments, Indigenous Memory: Dis-membering and Re-membering Canadian Art History. In: Nelson, R. and Olin, M. (eds.) *Monuments and Memory, Made and Unmade*. Chicago: University of Chicago Press, 281–304 .

Webb, J. (2000). Raven's Reprise. *Museum Note* **36B**. Vancouver: UBC Museum of Anthropology.

Young, J. E. (1999). Memory and Counter-Memory: The End of the Monument in Germany. *Harvard Design Magazine* **9**: 1–10.

10

Do Subaltern Artifacts Belong in Art Museums?

A.W. Eaton and Ivan Gaskell

This chapter concerns the collecting and display of material artifacts in art museums. Our principal question is whether it is ever acceptable for Western art museums to collect and display artifacts produced by and for non-Western cultures, particularly when these artifacts were originally intended and used for purposes remote from those of the art world. We aim to show that this practice can be legitimate and to describe some conditions under which this is so.

First, a few words about terminology. We use the term *artifact* in a non-evaluative sense to refer to any human-made object. Of particular interest to us here are tangible objects. In this sense, Greek temples, Italian Renaissance paintings, Baga masks, shoes, and eating utensils are all artifacts. We recognize that some members of subaltern groups may question this term, for it does not appear to recognize that certain things can be imbued with personhood or the capacity for agency (for instance, as living treasures). (Maui Solomon made this point during the research group meeting [June 20–25, 2006], referring to the Maori concept of *taonga*, or living treasure.) Agency can attend certain Western objects, such as miraculous images. Our use of the term is not meant to exclude these possibilities. Other terms that we use, including *hegemonic* and *subaltern*, are colored by Western usage and are equally contentious. By *hegemonic* we refer to the values of Western societies that sustain their dominance, especially insofar as they place other societies at a disadvantage; by *subaltern*, following the usage established by a number of Indian historians, we refer to groups at a disadvantage to those exercising power within a society.[1] It should be noted that *subaltern* includes many groups often referred to as *Indigenous*; that is, societies that have been in any given place longer than those who consequently came to dominate them. There is clearly significant overlap between subaltern and Indigenous groups, although the two are not coextensive. We use the more inclusive *subaltern* because it captures the feature that is relevant to our inquiry: the systematic and persistent subordination of the group in question. We acknowledge that our use of these terms, and others, inevitably reflects the unavoidably Western conventions within which we, as people of European descent working within American institutions, think and write. However, our decisions about terms are informed by discussions with colleagues from subaltern groups who have made us conscious of at least some of their limitations. Similarly, when discussing *museums* without qualification, we refer to those that James Clifford describes as 'majority museums'—those of the dominant culture—as distinct from those museums run by subaltern groups, which he describes as tribal.[2] Our concern is principally with majority, that is, hegemonic, museums.

Our discussion begins with a consideration of recent changes in (hegemonic) museum practice, particularly with respect to the treatment of subaltern artifacts. Section 2 discusses some ways in which the museum can be understood as an apparatus of power. Section 3 addresses cultural appropriation in the museum context. Section 4 responds to the primary objections to displaying subaltern artifacts in art museums and offers an argument for the legitimacy of such display. Section 5 turns to our two case studies: the display of West African masquerades in the Metropolitan Museum of Art, New York and in the British Museum, London.[3]

1.

Museums that deal with artifacts have undergone and continue to undergo considerable conceptual changes since the time when James Clifford, among others, analyzed their fundamental taxonomic principles.[4] Increasingly, as our case studies will demonstrate, such museums are addressing the products of various societies from various time periods in attempts to be even-handed. The ideal world implied by such changes in museums scholars' practice no longer has a geographical center and a periphery, but is instead acentric. On this view, the urban is no longer accorded privilege over the rural, or the agrarian over the nomadic; and the idea of progress in civilization that accords higher status to those societies that have developed means of acquiring dominance over others is placed in doubt. We term the process towards this ideal of acknowledging fundamental equality among forms of human social organization *decentering*.

The urge to decenter represents a huge change from the days when museums expected to divide humankind between those who use writing and those who do not, assigning the artifacts of the former to art museums, and of the latter to anthropology or natural history museums. However, the institutional structure of museums has not caught up with this change in ideals. Many remain constrained by the character of their collections, in spite of recent large-scale redistributions of institutional collections among certain prominent museums.[5]

The fact that change in museums is occurring encourages us to consider fundamental questions that such changes address, or, more frequently, appear to evade. If one of the key goals of all concerned is to redress the balance between hegemonic and subaltern interests regarding artifacts short of the dissolution of museums, does decentering promise a way forward? We believe that it does and in this chapter offer some justification for this view.

Decentering, though, should be promoted both critically and equitably. In seeking to do so, we must acknowledge, first, that there is rarely a neutral, objective position from which to adjudicate. Each society inevitably sees things from its own vantage point or set of sometimes internally contradictory vantage points. Yet people are not wholly trapped within their own habitual ways of thinking. We are all capable of modifying our views, but to do so requires constant negotiation among societies with unequal opportunities to exercise power and influence whose members' views, furthermore, are not invariably unanimous. Second, the various Western disciplines that take artifacts (whether they be purely utilitarian, artworks, or living treasures) as their objects of study—including anthropology, archaeology, art history, history, museology, philosophy and sociology—while developing and interacting, will continue to provide tools with which Western and subaltern scholars can investigate artifacts. Their means may vary, but each discipline and emergent interdiscipline has something particular to offer all participants. These disciplines, though, far from exhaust the possibilities of address, and Western scholars must be prepared to see their cherished assumptions challenged by subaltern thinkers.[6]

This observation relates to the third and most intractable factor for consideration in the promotion of decentering critically and equitably. One might think that it would be enough simply to pool artifacts from all societies and time periods so as to be able to draw on them freely and equally to explore aspects of human ingenuity and skill within museums. However, the artifacts themselves, as well as ideas and knowledge about them, are not available to all interested people equally. Both art and anthropology museums enjoy the availability of many of the artifacts in their care in large part as the result of the continuing exercise of power. Most collections are more or less tainted by long-term practices of appropriation that have affected and continue to affect a considerable variety of social groups both within and beyond hegemonic societies. As far as this concerns relations between hegemonic and subaltern groups, appropriation and retention of spoils is a particular manifestation of the far larger problem of the asymmetry of long-term power relations among them. Equity obliges Western scholars in museums and elsewhere to work through the consequences of past practices, practices without which their collections would not exist as they do. Those processes of 'working through'—involving challenging and, for Westerners, often humbling encounters with members of subaltern groups—would seem to be necessary for the successful use of artifacts in acentric terms. This inevitably involves such radical steps for Westerners as working beyond not only the physical but also the conceptual boundaries of their own institutions, and learning to accommodate the terms and ideals of subaltern peoples.

In addressing some of the ethical issues pertaining to the collection of artifacts for use in museums, we propose to concentrate on the most publicly visible use that follows upon research and often accompanies publication; that is, display. Recent scholarship on appropriation in museums tends to focus on what one might call the problem of cultural property; that is, questions to do with the legitimate ownership of artifacts. No issue could be more fundamental or important, and museums exercise a degree of control over their collections that is certainly open to challenge. Yet critics have failed to recognize that many museums do not treat their collections simply as chattels, enjoying unfettered rights over them. Indeed, museums already operate within a varying but considerable range of constraints, largely to do with both formal and informal public accountability within their own societies. When considering the wishes of those from whom museums acquired their artifacts, art museums have until recently been generally more solicitous than most anthropology museums, reflecting in yet another register the imbalance of power between hegemonic and subaltern peoples. However, art museum practice can help to provide a modifiable pattern for museum practice more generally. Many art museums have long acknowledged that donors enjoy a perpetual interest in the disposition of the artworks and funds that they have given, and recognize that their descendants inherit this interest undiminished. For example, an art museum almost invariably seeks what amounts to permission from the donor or the donor's descendants in the case of the proposed alienation of an artwork (deaccessioning) in jurisdictions where this is permitted. Even in matters of display, recognized best practice is to notify donors or their descendants of the particular use being made of the artworks with which they are associated. Such consideration is described as stewardship. To apply these principles to relations with those who plausibly assert a continuing interest in a wider range of artifacts is to differ in degree rather than in kind from prevailing art museum practice. Best practice in anthropology museums is also a matter of stewardship, but it incorporates recognition that power relations between such museums and those who, as descendants of the originators of objects in their collections, have a legitimate interest in those objects, are asymmetrical. This imbalance remains the case despite the effects of legislation such as, in the USA, the Native American Graves Protection and Repatriation Act of 1990 (NAGPRA). The issue faced by all museums is how precisely to define and work towards best practice, recognizing and attempting to rectify imbalances, as a matter of political behavior rather than abstract ethics.

Asymmetry of long-term power relations affects every aspect of the museum stewardship of the artworks, artifacts and living treasures of subaltern groups. The first key issue concerns the passage from the latter to the former; that is—from the point of view of the museums—collection or acquisition. What, in any given instance, were its circumstances? Museum scholars should ask searching questions about their institutions' acquisition of artifacts in all cases, and not solely in terms of legal constraints and treaty obligations.[7] Was an object taken, if not by force, then under duress? If neither, did those who alienated the object concerned have the right, within their own society, to do so? If they did have that right, what might their expectations have been of the consequences of the alienation? Did it impose obligations on the receiving party, including, for instance, the eventual return of the object?[8] If obligations exist short of eventual return, has the museum met them, or taken steps to rectify past failure to meet them? (These obligations might include the ritual servicing of an object.)[9] Does a subaltern group have a pre-eminent claim on objects associated with it that outweighs a museum's claim upon those objects not only in their own members' minds, but in the formal opinion of the hegemonic society as expressed in law, such as being necessary to the practice of an Indigenous religion?[10] These are among, but far from exhaust, the *prima facie* grounds for restitution. However, even if museums were to accept and to act upon all of these, they would nonetheless retain vast quantities of objects. In many instances there are no identifiable or viable successors to the groups from which the objects were acquired. Further, there are instances when a subaltern group decides for its own reasons not to pursue a claim. To recognize as much is not to acquiesce in nor to ignore the ethical questionability of museums' possession of such things, but to recognize that in such circumstances no viable or even appropriate alternative to continued stewardship by the museum exists. However, this is not to suggest that museums should enjoy an entirely free hand with those many things that have been irremediably severed from their origins. Subaltern groups are among museums' many constituencies and can have legitimate interests in the treatment and uses of objects even when they have no pre-eminent claim to them. Museums should recognize such interests and act appropriately in their light. The most publicly conspicuous aspect of museum practice in which such considerations should play an inevasible part and on which we choose to focus is gallery display. Even when a museum's possession of exhibited objects is undisputed, subaltern groups and individuals can contribute to stewardship through criticism and collaboration, reminding all concerned that the legitimacy of the continued use of such objects by museums depends on constantly developing best practice.

2.

Museums are commonly considered to be instruments of power.[11] Such language may strike non-postmodern ears as driven by a taste for hyperbole and suspicion as well as patently false. Museums, after all, rely on their patrons, the public and governments for support. They have no ability to wield force and, much as we might like to think otherwise, their social influence is negligible compared with that of popular culture. Is there, then, anything to this notion of the museum as an instrument of power? We think so.

Museums are partially constitutive of the social order and the values of dominant cultures. Art museums prescribe what is to be valued, and proscribe from the artworld what is not. Museums legitimate tastes, behavior and markets, and inculcate self-enforced social discipline. Visitors learn how to comport themselves in museums, no less than they do in other places of public social encounter. The acquisition of self-enforced social discipline is an absolute necessity in hegemonic societies owing to the volume and extent of anonymous public contact that constantly takes place within them. Although museum galleries are often subject to remote video surveillance, and the possibility of active intervention by invigilators is never distant, policing would generally be inadequate to the task of enforcing behavior convenient to the powerful without self-discipline on the part of visitors.[12] Carol Duncan has described the social rituals of enhanced aesthetic attention that museums foster within sanctuary spaces as constitutive of communal identity and civic bodies.[13] Museums may not determine the behavior of people within them, but, no less than places of worship, they sanction certain actions. These include an individual's quiet, contemplative progress through galleries, accepting the premises of the arrangement. Meanwhile they inhibit others, such as the coalescing of impromptu discussion groups in front of artworks, for instance.

Much has been made of museums' propensity to exercise unchallenged authority with regard to the artifacts they display and, by extension, to the societies those artifacts represent. This is effected by two principal means: first, by homogenizing or erasing traces of curatorial authorship of the exhibits so that the result appears inevitable, scarcely questionable and backed by the authority of the institution as a whole rather than appearing the responsibility of identifiable individuals; and second, when one exhibit replaces another, all traces of the earlier display, which might have constituted an alternative perspective using at least some of the same artifacts, are expunged. These are aspects of a strategy of self-presentation characterized by the appearance of disinterestedness and neutrality.

Museums typically exhibit the objects in their collections in a way that appears completely neutral on two levels: first, in the sense that the choices (and the assumptions and values guiding them) regarding presentation of the objects are erased; and second, in the sense of appearing apolitical—not aligned with a political or ideological stance. This neutrality lends exhibitions an air of objectivity—they appear untainted by the distortion of personal feelings, prejudices or interpretations—and hence authority: the exhibition appears uncontestable.

But this appearance of neutrality is false. All exhibits are shaped by values to some degree. Choices informed by value judgments intervene at every step of the exhibition process to guide museum goers' ways of seeing, understanding and appreciating the material presented. Following Svetlana

Alpers, we shall refer to this establishing of the parameters of visual interest and knowledge as the 'museum effect'.[14] Here are just some of the mechanisms of the museum effect:

- Taxonomy;
- Choice of objects: the inclusion of the few, the exclusion of the many;
- Ordering the material (by period, medium, color, style, subject matter, genre, artist);
- Framing and mounting;
- Disposition of the objects relative to one another, and to the viewer (e.g., height);
- Ambient décor (e.g., wall and floor treatments);
- Gallery furniture (vitrines);
- Lighting;
- Describing the material in text panels, chat labels, comparative photographs, accompanying publications and audioguides, telling viewers what is important.

This capacity to order objects and control their appearance is part of what is meant by 'instrument of power': objects are categorized, chosen, ordered, described and displayed so as to direct our visual attention and understanding in specific ways.[15] These ways of seeing and understanding can and often do pertain to politically and ethically charged issues: matters such as racial, ethnic and national identity. Karp puts the point thus:

> Exhibitions represent identity, either directly, through assertion, or indirectly, by implication. When cultural "others" are implicated, exhibitions tell us who we are and, perhaps most significant, who we are not. Exhibitions are privileged arenas for presenting images of self and "other."[16]

There are, then, four aspects to the power of museums. First there is their capacity to categorize and choose objects; second, their contribution to the definition of the scholarly terms in which discussion of the objects occurs; third, their organization of ways of seeing and understanding the material presented, some of which touch on politically charged issues such as racial and national identity; and fourth, the alleged neutrality of exhibition that makes these ways of seeing and understanding appear under the guise of objective truth. Museums can guide our ways of understanding and valuing certain aspects of the world.

Still, one might object, this seems like a relatively innocuous kind of power. When it comes to thinking about cultural appropriation, would our efforts not be better spent worrying about matters like the legitimate ownership of artifacts?

Again, let us insist that cultural property is an extremely important issue urgently deserving attention. But the museum effect is also important for those worrying about cultural appropriation. This is because, as Karp suggests above, when it comes to choosing, studying and exhibiting the artifacts of 'others', museums play a significant role in shaping our sense of others and ourselves and the relations between them. For many people, the museum setting is their first and only contact with the societies whose artifacts are displayed. Museums provide one of the major means by which that relationship of cultural perception is defined, and, for the most part, they do so wholly on the terms of the dominant culture. It is for this reason that many critics insist that museum exhibition must be re-thought from the ground up, as James Clifford insists: 'The relations of power whereby one portion of humanity can select, value, and collect the pure products of others need to be criticized and transformed.'[17]

One question we turn to in the next section is: Who, exactly, are these 'others' and who are 'we'?

3.

The authors take 'we' and 'us' to refer to those of European ethnicity for whom European values predominate, whether in Europe itself or its diaspora (including North America). It is more difficult when addressing the artifacts of 'others' to specify just *whose* artifacts we are talking about. Is the concern directed at the display of any artifacts that originated in a society substantially different from that of the collecting institution? If so, then any curator of art from Europe before, say, the seventeenth century should fall prey to Clifford's injunction since Europe of the Renaissance, Middle Ages and Classical times was very, very different—that is, very 'other' in some sense of the word—from the twenty-first-century European world. Such differences only multiply with temporal distance so that a curator of European medieval art truly can be said to be concerned with the display of 'the pure products of others.' But this is not the sort of 'otherness' Clifford and others have in mind. Twenty-first-century European museums collecting and displaying the artifacts of, for instance, medieval Europe do not count as part of the problem of cultural appropriation, no matter how foreign and unfamiliar medieval Europe is to most people today.[18] This is so because in addressing medieval Europe the perpetuation of asymmetrical power relations to the advantage of hegemonic societies at the expense of subaltern groups is not at stake. The 'others' at issue here are those who have come under extensive European political, economic and evangelical dominion; they are those who are or have been peculiarly vulnerable to slavery, imperialism, colonialism and other forms of exploitation. This is to say that the relevant feature of these 'others' is not their difference from us but, rather, their persistent and systematic subordination, which is why we use the term *subaltern*. With this understanding in place, we can now see why a particular set of concerns about exhibiting artifacts arises in the case of artifacts produced within subaltern groups—henceforth *subaltern artifacts*—that does not arise in the case of artifacts emanating from the European tradition, no matter how foreign that culture is to us today.

Before describing these concerns, we should note that among hegemonic institutions that collect, study and display artifacts there currently exist two types, which we shall call *aesthetic* and *representational*.

Representational museums aim to convey knowledge about artifacts (and other objects) and the societies in which they were originally produced and used. If the objects collected are to serve this epistemic function, more often than not they should be typical of the culture that produced them. In this way representational museums treat the objects they address as *specimens*. Ethnographic museums, natural history museums, science centers, museums of industry and technology, and history museums are all examples of representational museums. Aesthetic institutions, on the other hand, seek to avoid artifacts that typify a society; rather such institutions collect objects that are in some way aesthetically extraordinary.[19] In exhibiting such objects, aesthetic institutions aim to highlight these aesthetically exceptional features, treating the objects they address as *artworks*.[20]

Different worries about exhibiting subaltern artifacts arise in each case. In the case of representational institutions exhibiting subaltern artifacts, the concerns all have to do with selective, misleading or culturally limited presentations that misrepresent subaltern groups in ways beneficial or favorable to hegemonic societies. For instance, museums might mask the oppression of the cultures they supposedly represent. They might misrepresent the culture as, for instance, primitive or otherwise less advanced, thereby offering an implicit justification for their oppression. Museums might also contribute to the fantasy of others as primitive by masking the ways in which these traditions are living—for instance, by concealing any interaction with European culture or not showing any contemporary subaltern artifacts.[21] Further, they might mask the facts about how the objects were acquired, and whether existing groups currently have a claim on them. Equally seriously, museums might treat artifacts in ways offensive to peoples with reasonable claims on them (for instance, exposing to general view artifacts that within the subaltern group would be seen only by initiates). Since displays typically do not draw attention to the partiality of the picture they present, they reveal these distorted versions of others as if they were objective truths, thereby contributing to the perpetuation of some of the myths involved in the continued oppression of these groups. Although we should always worry about distortions when representing any society, this is particularly disturbing in the case of the representation of oppressed groups.

Very different concerns arise in the case of aesthetic institutions. One critique alleges that museums impose their European category of art with its concomitant aesthetic standards on artifacts produced by people who do not share these standards.[22] This begins, so the charge goes, the moment that one considers subaltern artifacts to be artworks, as is implied by their inclusion in aesthetic museums. This can lead, and indeed, critics charge, has led, to several problems.

First, the category of art brings with it criteria of excellence that take artifacts from the European tradition as the standard against which all others are to be measured. The result has been that many subaltern artifacts, which are quite different in significant ways from European artifacts, do not meet this standard and so are vulnerable to assessment as deficient. This is most evident in the relegation of subaltern artifacts to the category of the primitive, a term that all too easily can be taken to imply a lack of development and sophistication.[23] Although we should like to think that use of the term 'primitive' is out of fashion today, it is still widely used, especially in popular culture.[24]

Second, most subaltern artifacts were not intended to be displayed in art museums and appreciated for their aesthetic merits; rather, they had practical purposes in the societies that produced them related to functions and activities—such as hunting, crop cultivation, shelter, childcare, food preparation and addressing ancestors or the spirit realm—that have nothing to do with the categories of European art. Indeed, the artifacts in question *couldn't* have been intended to serve as art since the very concept of art is a modern European one that is foreign to subaltern groups. By treating subaltern artifacts as art, museums (and other institutions of hegemonic societies such as the art market) disregard the artifacts' original functions and instead impose upon them a wholly foreign categorization. One might object, however, that aesthetic museums treat certain European artifacts created prior to the emergence of a recognizably modern notion of art in the fifteenth century in a similarly inappropriate way.[25] The key difference is that the perpetuation of asymmetrical power relations is not at issue when, for instance, a Florentine painted altarpiece is treated as an artwork without adequate acknowledgment of its original ritual function. Critics worry that the practice of valuing, collecting and organizing subaltern artifacts from a perspective that takes European culture as the norm exemplifies the sort of cultural imperialism described most influentially by Edward Said.[26] The worry, then, is not simply that the category *art* is misplaced in the subaltern case because it is artificial, but that the imposition of foreign cultural concepts on subaltern artifacts is one facet of a broader cultural hegemony—an imposition of culturally dominant concepts and values on others—that, in Clifford's words, 'reproduce[s] hegemonic Western assumptions rooted in the colonial and neocolonial epoch.'[27] We may impose our twenty-first-century standards on a Florentine painting but such an imposition is considerably less problematic because the Renaissance Florentines no longer exist, nor were they ever the victims of European hegemony. Critics contend that because one aspect of European hegemony has been its utter disregard for the ways of life of subordinated peoples, aesthetic museums should now make a special effort when displaying subaltern artifacts to present them in ways that are not wholly incompatible with what can be known about how their original makers and users viewed them. (As we discuss in the next section, these original uses may well have included aesthetic considerations.[28])

A variant of this same concern comes from proponents of representational museums and their supporters, namely that an artifact has no viable significance divorced from its original circumstances or some reliable representation thereof. The term often used to make this point is 'decontextualization'. Critics contend that art museums, more than representational museums, wrench artifacts from their original contexts and arrange them in a sterile environment where they lose all significance aside from the artificial ones imposed upon them. This has been a leitmotif of criticism of public art museums since the foundation of the first among them, the

Musée du Louvre, Paris.[29] This problem is exacerbated in those cases where aesthetic attention not only differs from the use by subaltern peoples of the objects concerned, but may be perceived by those who produced them or their descendants to be deleterious to or a trivialization of those original functions. This is especially the case when the artifacts in question concern the sacred realm, or relations with the dead.

Related to the objections of decontextualization and trivialization is the objection that in some societies artifacts with aesthetic characteristics respected within those societies may not be among those most highly valued by its members. Other things that are not so readily amenable to aesthetic attention, either within that society or by others, may be far more important to the people who made and first used them. In subaltern societies the most potent objects may even appear to be among the most abject.[30] In Western society, objects embodying power are often purposefully imbued with impressive aesthetic characteristics. The common Western association of impressive aesthetic characteristics with particular efficacy in other respects can be misleading, causing hegemonic societies to overvalue certain subaltern artifacts and to denigrate others inappropriately and offensively from the subaltern point of view. Furthermore, critics also fear that the invitation to view artifacts aesthetically might divert viewers' attention not only from their other functions, but also from how the objects were acquired by the museum, which might directly or indirectly have amounted to crimes of pillage.

Do subaltern artifacts belong in art museums? As we have seen, there are many reasons to think not. In the next section we address these objections and offer an argument for inviting aesthetic attention to subaltern artifacts even when such attention was not intended by an artifact's original makers or users. Art museums can be appropriate and even auspicious contexts for subaltern artifacts so long, we shall argue, as certain precautions are taken.

4.

This section addresses the objections just raised, and provides a positive argument for according subaltern artifacts aesthetic attention. We argue that displaying subaltern artifacts in art museums is a way to honor them and the cultures that produced them, thereby fostering cross-cultural recognition and respect. This is to say that it is not simply ethically *permissible* to display subaltern artifacts in art museums but that such display, when handled with care, is advantageous to all interested parties.

i.   *Objection:* Collecting and displaying subaltern artifacts in art museums is to treat them as art, thereby imposing categories (and their concomitant standards) on objects from cultures to which these categories and standards are foreign. This is not merely a conceptual error but an ethical problem in that it reproduces hegemonic power relations (i.e., the hegemonic group imposing its ways of seeing, values and concepts on the subaltern group).

Response: First, to claim or imply that members of subaltern groups do not have a concept of art is to subscribe to a rigid and impoverished understanding of the Western category of art, namely one centered on painting and sculpture produced explicitly for art museums. The category of art is considerably broader, more dynamic and complex than this allows. As mentioned earlier, most of the European objects that we treat as art, including many of our most prized works, were made for purposes other than display in art museums. In fact, almost everything made before the mid-eighteenth century was made and used for some other function—whether political, ritual, religious or quotidian—and only later collected and displayed in galleries or museums, yet this does not undermine their status as art.[31] As for contemporary art (whether from hegemonic or subaltern societies), some of it is motivated by the explicit intention to contest the category of art itself and to thwart museum collecting and art markets (for example, found art, performance art, earth works, conceptual art, body art) and is not at all limited to the aesthetically pleasing.[32] Finally, philosophers, historians and theoreticians who continue to challenge rigid traditional definitions from within the hegemonic tradition have placed 'art' under tremendous conceptual pressure. The upshot is that in considering whether subaltern peoples share a concept of art as understood within hegemonic societies, one should keep in mind that this concept is capacious, malleable, continually contested and hardly limited to works designed for galleries and museums.

Second, the claim that subaltern peoples do not share a concept of art as understood within hegemonic societies is often motivated by an underestimating and impoverished understanding of the subaltern group or Indigenous society in question. Consider, for instance, philosopher and art critic Arthur Danto's articulation of the objection:

Primitive art, if indeed primitive in this sense, was not meant for audiences, viewers, dealers and collectors, but for participants and celebrants. The objects are instruments of ritual existence to which the suitable response might be a dance or a howl, not the peering and pointing that goes on in museums. In saying that they are not works of art I do not mean that they cannot be treated esthetically but that treating them so is at odds with their raison d'être.[33]

Never mind that much of what Danto says would be applicable to European artifacts from, say, the Middle Ages. He clearly intends to avoid imposing European standards that would measure subaltern artifacts as deficient. At the same time, Danto manifests a proprietary attitude toward the aesthetic that is typical of this sort of complaint: only (modern) Europeans treat artifacts with aesthetic sensitivity, whereas subaltern people howl at and dance around them and see them as mere means to ritualistic ends. It is not just that this assumption underestimates the diversity of roles that artifacts play in subaltern societies, but it is also patently false.[34] Recent work in the anthropology of art reveals complex and highly nuanced aesthetic, art critical (especially qualitative and evaluative) and art historical concepts, principles and practices in a range of subaltern cultures, from the Yoruba of West Africa to the Yolngu of Australia to the Maroons of Suriname.[35] The art museum may be a modern European phenomenon but aesthetic production and appreciation, which are at the center of the art museum's primary concerns, are far from being the special province of modern European culture. As art historian Robert Farris Thompson points out, it is due to our ethnocentric conviction that we Europeans have mastered all relevant issues that we have missed many legitimate aesthetic systems with histories of their own.[36]

Given these considerations, it is not ethnocentric to suggest that there is a trans-cultural understanding of art that subaltern and hegemonic societies share. Indeed, as Thompson and others point out, it is ethnocentric to assume that only Europeans produce and appreciate objects of aesthetic interest.[37] Such an assumption lies behind the common practice of limiting treatment of subaltern artifacts to the role of specimens in ethnographic inquiry (and anthropological museums) while hegemonic artifacts enjoy exalted status in art museums. This assignment of a lower status to subaltern artifacts goes hand in hand with Eurocentrism of the worst sort: our values are the most virtuous, our beliefs the most truthful, our gods the most holy and our arts the most beautiful. Displaying subaltern artifacts in art museums need not impose utterly foreign hegemonic standards of aesthetic quality in a manner complicit with imperialism, nor patronizingly extend our appreciation to the less fortunate.

The grounds for displaying subaltern artifacts in art museums are a trans-cultural understanding of art. We do not mean to offer a complete definition of this concept here, but some of its noteworthy features are that the artifacts are the result of technical decisions often requiring specialized skills, are made in recognizable styles according to rules of form and composition, are intended to offer aesthetic pleasure and imaginative experience (even if this is not their primary aim) and, finally, that there is an Indigenous critical language of judgment and appreciation of such artifacts.[38] Such an understanding is broad enough to encompass a wide range of artifacts—from New York-based performance art to Yolngu painting—and general enough to accommodate a variety of qualitative criteria and ways of talking about and understanding artifacts. With such an understanding of art in place, we can confidently say that we members of hegemonic societies do share with subaltern groups a concept of art.

ii.   *Objection:* The display of a subaltern artifact in any museum (representational or aesthetic) is illegitimate in cases where this is seen by its producers or their descendents to be harmful to its original function.

Response: We agree that this is a serious problem deserving of serious attention, for which adequate solutions to many cases are still wanting. There have been numerous instances of sacred artifacts being displayed in both art and anthropology museums in manners considered inappropriate by members of the society from which they originate or their descendents. This includes the exposure of artifacts that would normally either remain entirely concealed, or be exposed only on certain ceremonial occasions to initiates, or to members of one gender only. For example, the American Museum of Natural History, New York, persists in exhibiting various High Plains peoples' sacred bundles unwrapped to expose their contents, which would normally only be seen by the individual keepers of such bundles. Some museums, including the Peabody Museum of Archaeology and Ethnology at Harvard University, place removable covers over cases containing sensitive objects accompanied by cautionary labels so that visitors can choose whether or not to view their contents. In some instances such attempts may be adequate to satisfy constituencies sensitive to potential detraction from an artifact's original function, but not in all.

There are clearly occasions when one of two alternative courses of action must be followed. Either the museum concerned must adopt the values of the subaltern peoples whose artifacts it holds to the extent that representatives of those peoples make substantive decisions regarding their care; or the artifacts concerned must be returned to their original owners or their descendants.[39] Some museums have increasingly taken the former course, among the most prominent being the National Museum of the American Indian, with branches in Washington, DC and New York City. The director and many of the staff are Native Americans, and they have made considerable efforts to involve American Indian community representatives in planning the display of items that originated in their communities. This has had the effect of sanctioning the display of certain sacred objects that could not otherwise be shown without disapprobation.[40] Many artifacts have left federally funded museums to be returned to federally recognized American Indian nations under the terms of the Native American Graves Protection and Repatriation Act of 1990 (NAGPRA). Several of those museums have welcomed the opportunity to develop long-term stewardship and research relations with the peoples concerned to the benefit of all. NAGPRA was enacted not as an ethical instrument, but as a means of giving substance to the American Indian Religious Freedom Act of 1978 (AIRFA), and nothing more.[41] Some museums, though, have acted on ethical principle rather than simply in terms of legal compliance. For instance, the Peabody Museum returned the sacred pole of the Omaha, and the New York State Museum in Albany returned twelve wampum belts to the Onondega Nation before the enactment of NAGPRA.[42] With care, the relations opened by negotiations leading to the return of objects can lead to involvement of interested subaltern people in the continuing stewardship of artifacts that remain in hegemonic museums, with far-reaching consequences. Modes of storage, handling, and display all change in ways that can reconcile subaltern groups to the continuing presence of their predecessors' artifacts in such museums.

iii.   *Objection:* Treating subaltern artifacts as art 'decontextualizes' them and empties them of significance.

Response: The influence of social history and anthropology on art history, and the consequent rise of what is often called the social history of art, has led to the contextualization of artworks in much art historical and museological practice. To contextualize a work is to interpret from the viewpoint of 'its time and place,' that is, in the general geographical region where it was created and at the approximate, if not at the exact, time of its creation. The interpreter attempts to understand and value the work as its original makers and users or viewers would have understood and used it. Viewers should then be in a position to see it from the perspective of the people for whom it was originally made.[43] To 'decontextualize' an artwork in the first instance is to remove it physically from its original setting, which many critics claim causes scarcely reparable damage to the possibility of understanding its function and significance.[44] If such removal has already occurred, to fail to attempt to accord interpretive precedence to a mental reconstruction of that original setting, bearing as many cultural and social factors in mind as might be necessary to interpret the artwork convincingly and without anachronism, is to commit a grave methodological error.

Although we are sympathetic to its motivations, we disagree with the stringency of this methodological commitment. Our reason is that artifacts *perdure*: that is, they often continue to exist beyond their original makers and users, and are taken up and used in ways that these makers and users could not imagine. Artifacts are promiscuous, to adopt a term used by anthropologist Nicholas Thomas: they move among cultural domains, taking on new significances and functions without having their identity compromised.[45] To assume that the originally intended function is *the* genuine sole function of an artifact is to give undue prominence to the original makers' and users' intentions—a form of what philosophers call the intentional fallacy[46]—and to ignore the fact that artifacts are often *exapted* for new functions.[47] We consider the appropriation by art museums of subaltern artifacts to be a kind of exaptation, one that, when following constraints we outline in the last section of this chapter, can be salutary for all involved.

We do not mean to deny that it can be interesting and rewarding to attempt to understand an artifact in the context of its creation; we simply deny that this is the only legitimate use to which it can be put. Displaying subaltern artifacts in art museums does *re*-contextualize them, displacing them from their original contexts of production and use and give them a new home in the museum, but there is nothing necessarily illegitimate about this. Indeed, one effect of the so-called contextualization of artifacts (that is, situating artifacts in 'their' time and place) is that the artifact in question inevitably becomes a window on to its maker's culture, thereby assuming a derivative role in one's experience. Just think, for instance, of how the contextual information provided in museums can distract from the artifact itself, so that museum goers spend more time reading or looking at photographs, maps or diagrams than they do *looking* at the objects. If the artifact is one that would repay attentive looking regardless of whether the observer is informed about its original circumstances, such distraction does the artifact and the society that produced it a disservice.

To be sure, displays that emphasize the aesthetic qualities of an artifact at the expense of all else do it a different sort of disservice, since such displays focus attention on just one aspect of its ever-changing life. But this is part of the point about the promiscuity of artifacts: they have rich and multifarious lives and cannot ever disclose all of themselves at a single instant. This is why we think it imperative that subaltern artifacts find a home in both aesthetic *and* representational museums, as well as—and this is an important component in the sort of change we would like to see— European artifacts, especially of the sort that have generally been accepted as art, equally finding a home in both as well.

iv.   *Objection:* Attending to the aesthetic qualities of subaltern artifacts diverts attention from questions of acquisition to the form of the objects themselves, thereby concealing the dominant culture's unethical histories.

Response: We recognize this as a very important concern. While we do not think that such diversion is a necessary feature of fostering aesthetic attention, it is a definite risk. We hope to suggest some strategies for avoiding this in the next section of this chapter.

In this section we have considered some of the major objections to the aestheticization of subaltern artifacts in art museums. While we appreciate many of the concerns raised, we take them as cautions rather than as definitive reasons not to display subaltern artifacts in art museums. Although there are many pitfalls to be aware of, we have yet to see a conclusive argument that subaltern artifacts do not belong in art museums under any circumstances. This is to say that, when taking appropriate care and precautions, it is at least *permissible* to display subaltern artifacts in art museums. But this is still a pace away from answering our initial question; that is, we still have not yet shown that subaltern artifacts *belong* in art museums, that it would be good to house and display them in this context. What, then, is to be said *in favor* of this?

Appropriating subaltern artifacts as art can open hegemonic eyes to many new forms of excellence in expression, skill, style and imagination. This is beneficial not simply because it expands our imaginative repertory, nor simply because it makes us palpably aware that our values are not the highest, nor our arts the most beautiful. Appropriating subaltern artifacts as art does accomplish these things, but its chief virtue lies in the fact that recognizing and appreciating the artistic achievements of others is one important element in cross-cultural recognition and equal respect.[48] To recognize another's material culture as worthy of the highest treatment our society accords artifacts—that is, to consider them art and display them in art museums—is to honor and esteem not just the artifacts but also their makers. James Clifford summed up the point: 'Treatment of artifacts as fine art is currently one of the most effective ways to communicate cross-culturally a sense of quality, meaning, and importance'[49]—*if*, that is, this treatment proceeds with a high degree of sensitivity to the sorts of objections that we summarize here. In turning to our case studies in the next section, we hope to illustrate some of the successes and failures in such an undertaking.

5.

We discern both positive and negative aspects of aesthetic institutions' uses of subaltern artifacts in the example provided by one of the world's leading art museums and representatives of hegemonic culture, the Metropolitan Museum of Art, New York. Among the responsibilities of the Department of the Arts of Africa, Oceania and the Americas (pre-Columbian) is the Michael C. Rockefeller Wing.[50] This part of the museum contains galleries devoted to the societies specified by the department designation, and owes its existence to a hegemonic Modernist aesthetic attitude towards what in the early twentieth century was described in ostensibly positive terms as 'primitive art'. Artists such as Pablo Picasso, collectors such as Nelson A. Rockefeller and museum scholars such as René d'Harnoncourt propounded the liberating effect of 'primitive art' on the modern Western imagination, and helped to free some of the artifacts of at least some subaltern peoples (notably in sub-Saharan Africa) from condemnation attendant on the unqualified disapproval of many Christian missionaries, and the dominant racist agenda of at least some anthropologists and colonial officials. In New York one publicly visible consequence was Rockefeller and d'Harnoncourt's Museum of Primitive Art (1957–75), which, although in retrospect it appears offensively patronizing, presented certain kinds of subaltern artifacts as things of aesthetic and cultural value. Its holdings

were amalgamated in 1978–79 with Nelson A. Rockefeller's personal collection to comprise the Michael C. Rockefeller Memorial Collection,
bequeathed to the Metropolitan Museum to form the core of the current
Michael C. Rockefeller Wing of the Metropolitan Museum.[51] The wing
opened in 1982, yet only in 1990 was the name of the curatorial department
changed from the Department of Primitive Art to its current designation.
Here are galleries devoted to, among others, African artifacts. For the most
part they are presented unequivocally as artworks.[52] Text panels suggest
both the antiquity and perpetual novelty of African cultural products, carefully lending this claim the sanction of Western classical antiquity by citing
Pliny the Elder in a quotation accompanying a large map of Africa: '*Ex
Africa semper aliquod novi* [There is always something new out of Africa].'
A further text panel states: 'Africa is the stage upon which the earliest
human dramas were performed. Today there are more distinct people and
cultures in Africa than in any other continent. This antiquity and diversity
are reflected in Africa's artistic traditions.'

Among the various displays from many parts of Africa is a vitrine
devoted to masquerade artifacts from West Africa. Most are presented as
artworks principally warranting aesthetic attention. Their accompanying
labels give basic information concerning function, origin and materials,
but no description of their original uses. Among them are two painted
wooden objects, striking in their formal qualities that, to an informed
Western viewer, seem to invite or even compel comparison with sculptures
by twentieth-century Western artists, most obviously with celebrated
wooden pieces by the Romanian, Constantin Brancusi, which are among
the icons of Modernism. For viewers of these two serpent headdresses
(described in the accompanying label as '*A-mantsho-ñ-tshol* or *Basonyi*),
made by the Baga peoples of Guinea in the nineteenth or twentieth century,
who are unaware of the implicit comparison, the basis of the invitation
extended to the viewer to value them aesthetically is far from
self-evident.

The implicit and at times explicit subordination of such objects to
apprehension predominantly or even solely in terms of hegemonic norms—
in this instance, twentieth-century Modernism—has been steadily criticized, as we have seen, particularly by museum skeptics who protest against
'decontextualization', and by those who object to the subordination of
subaltern artifacts to the terms of the hegemonic culture alone. One objection often voiced is that by choosing objects such as figurative sculpture
and masks for aesthetic presentation, institutions such as the Museum of

Primitive Art and the Metropolitan Museum confer art status only on those African artifacts that conform most readily to Western fine art norms.[53] Another of the most persistent objections has been that objects such as masks and headdresses have been stripped of their accoutrements—raffia, textiles—that allow them to function as objects worn in ritual dances, so as to make them resemble Western sculpture as much as possible. Responses by art museum scholars have been twofold. In some instances they have restored the attachments that had been removed, while also providing information about 'context' similar to that found in representative institutions (anthropology museums) when similar artifacts are exhibited as specimens. An example is to be found in the very same vitrine as that containing the Baga serpent headdresses in the Metropolitan Museum, for beside them is a Banda mask, of the Nalu peoples, also from Guinea. Like the Baga pieces, it is of painted wood, but its raffia and textile attachments have been reconstructed (in 1995, according to the label). An attempt to meet the claim that context and original use are vital to understanding such an object has been made by the inclusion of a photograph of such a mask being used in a masquerade in 1987.[54] There is a pointed contrast between the uncompromisingly Modernist, aesthetic presentation of the Baga headdresses on the one hand—very much in the tradition of the Museum of Primitive Art—and the quasi-anthropological presentation of the Banda mask beside them. How are we to understand this contrast beyond recognizing a curatorial response to critiques of the aesthetic display of African artifacts in art museums?[55] Comparison with a relatively recent display of similar artifacts in a non-art museum, a museum of cultural artifacts—the British Museum, London—may be instructive.

What were long described as the ethnographic collections of the British Museum were, until 1999, consigned to an anthropological satellite museum, the Museum of Mankind. Only recently returned, selections from the African collection have been installed in the newly conceived Sainsbury African Galleries.[56] They are the responsibility of a department that changed its name from the Department of Ethnography to the Department of Africa, Oceania and the Americas only in 2004. Here museum scholars, attentive to criticism asserting that condescension and distortion attend on the anthropological presentation of such material, have responded by adopting art as the applicable paradigm. They present the artifacts within a chronological continuum, stressing continuity from implicitly pre-colonial times to the present, in which hegemonic influences have been embraced and transformed by subaltern societies into manifestations that remain distinctly African even while indebted to hegemonic conceptions of art. The standing as art of contemporary objects by Africans working as artists in an international context is implicitly projected back upon the artifacts made by their predecessors in quite different circumstances. At the same time, the curators have sought to avoid the criticisms leveled at those art museums, such as the Metropolitan Museum, that have long presented African artifacts as art on Western terms. They have done this by continuing to provide contextual information such as one might find in anthropology museums and, in the case of masks, by retaining the raffia and textile attachments in several instances. For example, a mask, which, like the serpent headdresses in the Metropolitan Museum, comes from the Baga peoples of Guinea, described as a *nimba*, retains its raffia hangings, and is accompanied by a label explaining its use by the *simo* society in crop fertility rituals. The large array of masks is set within an entirety that is grouped by materials rather than by region as is the case in the Metropolitan Museum. The display of masks, of which the Baga *nimba* is but one component, is divided into sections arranged thematically ('wild beasts', 'female masks', 'the dead'), and is accompanied by informative labels.[57] A display opposite shows various Nigerian masks, including recently made examples. Beside it is a video screen showing two of the masks on view in use by members of a Kalabari peoples' society in southern Nigeria as they rehearse their rituals. By this means the museum scholars presumably hope to meet the criticism often leveled at their institutions that masquerade artifacts can only be seen to any effect not only with their raffia and textile accoutrements, but when in motion as they were designed to be seen during ritual dances. Nearby is a contemporary artwork made in 1995: a life-size sculpture in painted wood and metal representing an *Otobo* (Hippopotamus) masquerade, by the prominent Nigerian born British artist, Sokari Douglas Camp.[58]

If the Michael C. Rockefeller Wing of the Metropolitan Museum exemplifies African masquerades in curatorial motion from Modernist art to anthropological contextualization, however selective and muted, the Sainsbury African Galleries exemplify African masquerades in curatorial motion from anthropological representation to a paradigm of artifact as artwork. Anthropological representation still apparently dominates the British Museum display, although the presence of contemporary artworks is prominent, and the immediate organizational armature of the galleries presents the underlying value of the objects in aesthetic terms. Sir Robert Sainsbury, commemorated in the name of the galleries, was no less a patron of Modernism in art and a proponent of subaltern artifacts as 'primitive art' than was Nelson Rockefeller. Further, the Sainsbury African Galleries are dedicated to the most prominent British Modernist sculptor Henry Moore, whose name and the abbreviations of whose honors (OM, CH) are carved in stone above the entrance. A text panel explains the connections among Moore, the Sainsbury family and the former ethnographic galleries of the British Museum. Moore is quoted: 'To discover, as a young student, that the African carvers could interpret the human figure to this degree but still keep and intensify the expression, encouraged me to be more adventurous and experimental.' Moore's Modernist practice, patronized by the Sainsbury family, and recognized by the conferment of two of the British state's highest symbolic honors (the Order of Merit and Companion of Honour) is the ultimate sanction of the presence and presentation of the African objects in the British Museum.

We stated at the outset that subaltern groups and individuals have legitimate interests in artifacts—whether artworks or living treasures— even in those many cases when their presence in museums is uncontested. It is hard to conceive of real progress towards best practice in stewardship if museums fail to engage in profound collaboration with those who know subaltern societies from within. The British Museum has acknowledged this by the appointment in 2005 as head of the African Section of the Department of Africa, Oceania and the Americas of the Malian museum scholar, Claude Ardouin. His extensive experience in African museums includes the directorship of the Musée National du Mali. Part of his brief is to develop collaborative relations between the British Museum and museums in African countries, and he has begun planning the reinstallation of African objects in the Sainsbury African Galleries. Long-term senior appointments of scholars from subaltern groups to leading hegemonic museums, short-term collaborative visits and exchanges, and changes in museum scholar education so that Indigenous people, bringing their own values, can assume positions of influence and authority in hegemonic institutions will all contribute to the enhancement of the stewardship of subaltern artifacts in both hegemonic and Indigenous institutions.

We advocate what would be a major structural change in many museums (though we recognize that it is not present in all): an end to gathering artifacts from subaltern societies together as though they shared characteristics that differentiate them as a group from artifacts from other societies. For instance, the Metropolitan Museum's strategy—to gather all subaltern artifacts together in one Department of the Arts of Africa, Oceania and the Americas (pre-Columbian)—perpetuates the notion that these cultures are all primitive. One particularly unfortunate consequence of this strategy is to consign a belittlingly small display of American Indian artifacts to an obscure corner of the Michael C. Rockefeller Wing, rather than to incorporate them in the currently almost exclusively Eurocentric American Wing. What, after all, do a Maori house-post figure, a Dogon mask and a Navajo blanket have in common with one another that they do not share with a Hadley chest or a Florentine altarpiece? We contend that fostering cross-cultural recognition and equal respect requires, among other things, a preparedness to integrate artifacts from many societies in an acentric manner far more readily than is generally the case at present. Considered in this light, the recent opening of the Musée du Quai Branly in Paris, devoted to primitive art in all but name, is a retrograde step.[59]

6.

So, do subaltern artifacts belong in an art museum? Well, it all depends on what one means by *belong*. We have tried to distinguish our question from related concerns dealing with cultural property; that is, questions of to whom such artifacts belong. The sense of 'belong' at play in our investigation regards the suitability, appropriateness and advantageousness of displaying subaltern artifacts in art museums. In this sense of the word, subaltern artifacts *do* belong in art museums, assuming that appropriate care of the sort described above is taken.

We have discerned a convergence of practices in an art museum on the one hand (the Metropolitan Museum of Art), and a culture museum on the other (the British Museum). As we have seen in the case of West African masquerades, the former has made moves selectively to adapt a mode of display associated with anthropological exhibits rather than retaining its previous Modernist approach uniformly and unequivocally, while the latter has adopted an aesthetic model for the presentation of artifacts without sacrificing important elements of anthropological and historical contextualization (however open to question in their details they may be). This promises to be fruitful for the future, as long as such approaches are applied (with appropriate variations) to the full range of artifacts displayed in either museum in pursuit of an ideal of decentering. This would mean, among other things, at times treating the hegemonic artifacts that have traditionally enjoyed the exalted status of art in an anthropological, contextualizing manner.[60]

The concept of exaptation allows us to understand the variety of uses of artifacts, both synchronically and diachronically, as legitimate. Allowing that functions can be exapted means that a given artifact need not have only a single function, nor that it necessarily has a single use. Further, and of considerable consequence for the use of artifacts in museums where they are shown in various ways over time, recognizing exaptation makes us acutely aware that no object ever reveals all of itself on any one occasion. One particular responsibility of museums, whether aesthetic or representational—of art or anthropology—is to show the same object in different ways on various occasions. To bring out their aesthetic qualities—according to different criteria on various occasions—is not only responsible behavior, but enriching for all involved.[61]

Notes

1. The annual journal *Subaltern Studies* began publication in 1982 in Delhi under the aegis of Ranajit Guha. The term in this sense was coined by Antonio Gramsci.

2. Clifford, J. (1991). 'Four Northwest Coast Museums: Travel Reflections,' in *Exhibiting Cultures: The Poetics and Politics of Museum Display*, ed. Ivan Karp and Steven D. Lavine (Washington, DC, and London: Smithsonian Insitution Press, 1991) 212–54.

3. Masquerades are performances that mark seasonal changes and rites of passage. By wearing and carrying equipment made of various materials (including wood, metal, cloth and raffia) key participants transform into other beings. Western collectors often retained only the facial mask itself, discarding the less durable elements that conceal the participant's body and accentuate its movements. Following current anthropological and art historical practice, we use the term *masquerade* to refer both to the rite as a whole, and to the equipment in its entirety worn by participants, as opposed to the facial covering (mask) alone.

4. Clifford, J. (1988). 'On Collecting Art and Culture,' in *The Predicament of Culture: Twentieth-Century Ethnography, Literature, and Art* (Cambridge, MA and London: Harvard University Press), pp. 215–51.

5. Examples include the reincorporation of the collections of the now dissolved Museum of Mankind within the British Museum in London between 1999 and 2004, and the creation of the Musée du Quai Branly in Paris from the

collections of the Musée des Arts Africains et Océaniens, and the ethnographic department of the Musée de l'Homme, which opened in 2006.

6. An example of such a challenge forming part of the present project is the document 'Meeting notes,' dated June 21, 2006 circulated to all the authors of this volume by Sa'ke'j Henderson.

7. Best practice in museums now entails proactive investigation of artifacts to determine their provenance as fully and accurately as possible in order to avoid the retention or acquisition of artifacts that have changed hands unlawfully or contrary to various national laws prohibiting unlicensed export. The most publicly visible cases have concerned antiquities removed from Italy, and artworks alienated under duress between 1933 and 1945 in Europe.

8. Maori scholars and activists point out that Maoris who presented early British visitors to what was to be colonized as New Zealand (Aotearoa) with living treasures (*taonga*) expected them eventually to be returned enriched by their experiences for the benefit of their societies: this was the subject of a paper by Ngahuia Te Awekotuko at the symposium, 'Crossing Boundaries: Art and Anthropology Museums in Search of Common Ground,' at the Harvard University Art Museums and the Peabody Museum of Archaeology and Ethnology, Cambridge, MA, April 21–22, 2006.

9. This is an obligation recognized in the USA by the Association of Art Museum Directors: 'Report of the AAMD Subcommittee on the Stewardship of Sacred Objects,' adopted June, 2006, posted August 9, 2006: http://aamd.org/papers.

10. See the case, *Union of India and Others vs. Bumper Corporation* in the High Court, London, in 1988 concerning a twelfth-century bronze statuette of Shiva Nataraja surreptitiously excavated and removed from a temple precinct in Pathur, Tamil Nadu, India, and seized in transit in London when on its way to enter a Canadian museum on long-term loan from a Canadian corporation. The Hindu god Shiva was recognized as a plaintiff by the court, and the Shiva Nataraja ordered returned to its temple. Mr Justice Ian Kennedy's trial judgment was upheld by the Court of Appeal and the Privy Council: Richard Davis, *Lives of Indian Images* (Princeton: Princeton University Press, 1997). In the USA the Native American Graves Protection and Repatriation Act (1990), enacted in part to promote the return from museums to American Indian nations of objects required for the practice of their religions, has had far-reaching effects.

11. For example, Ivan Karp, 'Culture and Representation,' in Karp and Lavine, *Exhibiting Cultures*, p. 14.

12. Gaskell, I. (2000). *Vermeer's Wager: Speculations on Art History, Theory and Art Museums* (London: Reaktion), pp. 198–99.

13. Duncan, C. (1995). *Civilizing Rituals. Inside Public Art Museums* (London and New York: Routledge), pp. 7–20.

14. Aplers, S. 'The Museum as a Way of Seeing,' in Karp and Lavine, *Exhibiting Cultures*, pp. 25–32.

15. It is not uncommon to describe the museum as 'controlling' the museumgoer's attention and understanding (e.g. Karp, 'Culture and Representation,' p. 15). We think that this language is too strong. Although museums do guide museumgoers in the ways we discuss here, they do not compel obedience. Critical museumgoers can and do resist the museum effect, although it takes critical awareness and effort to withstand the force of the museum effect.

16. Karp, 'Culture and Representation,' p. 15.

17. Clifford, *Predicament of Culture*, p. 213.

18. We do not mean to suggest that curators of European art are not concerned with the principles governing display: quite the contrary. But this has not provoked anything approximating the apprehension and intense scrutiny that marks the display of the artifacts of 'other' cultures.

19. It should be noted that typically, although not always, the standards for aesthetic excellence are taken by the decision-makers of aesthetic institutions to be self-evident. One major criticism of these institutions is that they are biased in their collection and display of subaltern artifacts in that they employ standards—'European standards,' it is usually said—that the makers of the artifacts do not share. We address this criticism in the next section.

20. These aims are not necessarily incompatible, although, as we shall see they do often conflict, and we do not mean to suggest that some institutions cannot have both aesthetic and ethnographic aims. We mean only to make a conceptual distinction between two very different aims that result in different criteria of selection and different practices of display. For further discussion of some consequences of drawing a distinction between specimens and artworks in art and anthropology museums, see Ivan Gaskell, 'Ethical Judgments in Museums,' in *Art and Ethical Criticism*, ed. Garry L. Hagberg (Malden, MA and Oxford: Blackwell, 2008), pp. 229–42.

21. Clifford, *Predicament of Culture*, pp. 200–202. The considerable anger on the part of subaltern thinkers at such behavior is exemplified by Pakistani-born British artist and theorist, Rasheed Araeen, 'From Primitivism to Ethnic Arts,' in *The Myth of Primitivism: Perspectives on Art*, ed. Susan Hiller (London and New York: Routledge, 1991), p. 172: 'The 'primitive' today has modern ambitions and enters into the Museum of Modern Art, with all the intellectual power of a modern genius, and tells [curator] William Rubin to fuck off with his primitivism: you can no longer define, sir, classify or categorize me. I'm no longer your bloody objects in the British Museum. I'm here right in front of you, in the flesh and blood of a modern artist. If you want to talk about me, let us talk. BUT NO MORE OF YOUR PRIMITIVIST RUBBISH.'

22. For example, Clifford, *Predicament of Culture*, p. 235. For a sophisticated version with a detailed case study (the Baule people of Côte d'Ivoire), see

Vogel, S. M. (1997). *African Art, Western Eyes* (New Haven: Yale University Press and Yale University Art Gallery).

23. Some scholars who demonstrated the extreme complexity exhibited by many subaltern artifacts used the term primitive admiringly, for example, Franz Boas, *Primitive Art* (Oslo: Aschehoug &. Co., 1927). Others, among them artists, exalted the primitive as admirably unsophisticated in comparison with decadent or impersonal modernity.

24. One recent example is the heated discussion generated around the new Musée du Quai Branly in Paris (opened 2006). Although the French government explicitly avoided the term 'primitive' to describe the museum's collections, the museum is regularly referred to as 'the new museum of primitive art' by the popular press in both French and English.

25. Belting, H. (1994). *Likeness and Presence: A History of the Image before the Era of Art*, trans. Edmond Jephcott (University of Chicago Press, Chicago).

26. Said, E. W. (1978). *Orientalism* (Pantheon, New York).

27. Clifford, *Predicament of Culture*, p. 197.

28. For the continuing disregard, even among anthropologists, for subaltern ways of life, see Sally Price, *Primitive Art in Civilized Places*, second edition (Chicago: Chicago University Press, 2001), pp. 108–23; reprinted in *The Anthropology of Art: A Reader*, ed. Howard Morphy and Morgan Perkins, (Malden, MA and Oxford: Blackwell, 2006), pp. 167–85. That specifically aesthetic considerations proper to subaltern artifacts in their own societies can be recognized and discussed by outsiders was most influentially propounded by Franz Boas, *Primitive Art*.

29. Among the most vigorous proponents of this view from the early nineteenth century until the present have been Antoine-Chrysostome Quatremère de Quincy, Paul Valéry, John Dewey, Douglas Crimp, and Didier Maleuvre. For the views of these, and others, see David Carrier, *Museum Skepticism: A History of the Display of Art in Public Galleries* (Durham, NC and London: Duke University Press, 2006), especially pp. 51–73, with references. See also, Irene Winter, 'Change in the American Art Museum: The (An) Art Historian's Voice,' in *Different Voices* (New York: Association of Art Museum Directors, 1992), pp. 30–57, especially pp. 42–7, and Arthur C. Danto, 'Defective Affinities: "Primitivism" in 20th Century Art,' in Morphy and Perkins, *The Anthropology of Art*, pp. 147–49.

30. See the discussion in the case of the Baule people of Côte d'Ivoire by Vogel, *African Art, Western Eyes*, pp. 52–68.

31. Denis Dutton makes a similar point in 'But They Don't Have Our Concept of Art,' in *Theories of Art Today*, ed. Noël Carroll (Madison: The University of Wisconsin Press, 2000), p. 225.

32. Alfred Gell makes this point nicely: 'the worst thing about the "anthropology of art" as at present constituted is precisely the way in which it has inherited

a reactionary definition of art, so that it more or less has to concern itself with objects that would have been classified as "art" or, more likely, "craft" at the beginning of this century, but has little or nothing to do with the kinds of objects (installations, performances) that are characteristically circulated as "art" in the late 20th century': Alfred Gell, 'Vogel's Net: Traps as Artworks and Artworks as Traps,' *Journal of Material Culture,* 1 (1996), p. 35 (reprinted in Morphy and Perkins, *The Anthropology of Art,* pp. 219–35).

33. Danto, 'Defective Affinities', p. 149.

34. Elsewhere Danto clearly acknowledges that subaltern peoples can produce great artworks: Arthur C. Danto, 'Art and Artifact in Africa,' in *Beyond the Brillo Box: The Visual Arts in Post-Historical Perspective* (New York: Farrar, Straus, Giroux, 1992), first published in *Art/artifact: African Art in Anthropology Collections* (New York and Munich: Center for African Art and Prestel Verlag, 1988), pp. 18–32.

35. For instance, Sally Price shows that Maroons have a concept of art history that includes the notion of style and stylistic and technical change, recognized individual creativity and criteria for attribution, and attention to chronological development: Price, *Primitive Art in Civilized Places,* pp. 108–23. Robert Farris Thompson reveals a nuanced and well-defined practice of art criticism in Yoruba culture: 'Yoruba Art Criticism,' in *The Traditional Artist in African Societies,* 2, ed. Warren D'Azevedo (Bloomington: Indiana University Press, 1973), pp. 19–61, 435–454). Jeremy Coote discusses ways in which aesthetics and aesthetic valuations play an important role in the everyday life of the Nilotic peoples of southern Sudan: '"Marvels of Everyday Vision": The Anthropology of Aesthetics and the Cattle-keeping Nilotes,' in *Anthropology, Art and Aesthetics,* ed. Jeremy Coote and Anthony Shelton (Oxford: Clarendon Press, 1992), pp. 245–73. Howard Morphy shows that the 'Yolngu clearly are concerned to produce effects on the senses by which the success of the work can be judged and which Europeans would interpret as aesthetic effect': 'From Dull to Brilliant: The Aesthetics of Spiritual Power Among the Yolngu,' in Coote and Shelton, *Anthropology, Art and Aesthetics,* p. 182. (Thompson, Coote, and Morphy's articles are reprinted in Morphy and Perkins, *The Anthropology of Art,* pp. 242–69, 281–301, 302–20 respectively.)

36. Thompson, 'Yoruba Art Criticism,' p. 19. Sally Price makes a similar point (Price, *Primitive Art in Civilized Places,* pp. 124–26) and argues that it is due to our imagining tribal people as primitive—even when we are reluctant to use that word to describe them—that blinds us to other legitimate aesthetic systems.

37. See, in particular, the work of Wilfried van Damme: *Beauty in Context: Towards an Anthropological Approach in Aesthetics* (Leiden and New York: E.J. Brill, 1996); 'World Philosophy, World Art Studies, World Aesthetics,'

Literature and Aesthetics 9 (1999), pp. 181–92; 'Universality and Cultural Particularity in Visual Aesthetics' in, *Being Humans: Anthropological Questions of Universality and Particularity from Transdisciplinary Perspectives*, ed. Neil Roughley (Berlin and New York: Walter de Gruyter, 2000).

38. This list echoes criteria laid down by both philosophers and anthropologists who argue for a cross-cultural understanding of art. See, for instance, Boas, *Primitive Art*; Dutton, 'But They Don't Have Our Concept of Art'; Richard Anderson, *Calliope's Sisters: A Comparative Study of Philosophies of Art*, second edition (New Jersey: Prentice-Hall, 2003); John Dewey, *Art As Experience* (New York: Perigee Publishing, 1934).

39. Members of subaltern groups, and even some curators in hegemonic museums, have made these points eloquently and repeatedly. For an example of the latter, see Jonathan Haas, 'Power, Objects, and a Voice for Anthropology,' *Current Anthropology* 37, 1 Supplement: *Special Issue: Anthropology in Public* (1996), pp. S1-S22.

40. For example, sacred items are displayed that would normally be concealed in the section of the exhibit 'Our Universes: Traditional Knowledge Shapes Our World,' devoted to the Hupa Tribe, planned with the participation of David Hostler (the elder responsible for ceremonial regalia who is also director of the Hoopa Valley Tribal Museum). Ivan Gaskell is grateful to David Hostler for his gracious hospitality during his research visit to the Hupa Tribe in 2002.

41. See Gaskell, I. 'Ethical Judgments in Museums,' pp. 233–4.

42. See Ridington, R., (1997) *Blessing for a Long Time: The Sacred Pole of the Omaha Tribe* (University of Nebraska Press, Lincoln).

43. Michael Baxandall was the first to give a succinct and compelling account of this view. See Michael Baxandall, *Painting and Experience in Fifteenth-Century Italy: A Primer in the Social History of Pictorial Style* (Oxford: Clarendon Press, 1972), especially chapter 2, 'The Period Eye.' This art historical methodology echoes a view held by anthropologists advocating cultural relativism. Virginia Heyer captures the view well: 'Cultural relativity, to phrase it in starkest abstraction, states the relativity of the part to the whole. The part gains its cultural significance by its place in the whole, and *cannot retain its integrity in a different situation*' (our emphasis): Virginia Heyer, 'In Reply to Elgin Williams,' *American Anthropologist* 50, 1 (1948), pp. 163–6. This precept still holds sway in the anthropology of art today. Jeremy Coote, for instance, sums it up clearly: 'it surely must be essential to any anthropological consideration of art, however conceived, than an attempt is made to see the art as its original makers and viewers see it' (in Morphy and Perkins, *The Anthropology of Art*, p. 283).

44. This argument is made forcefully with examples from sixteenth-century Italy by John Shearman, *Only Connect—: Art and the Spectator in the Italian Renaissance* (Princeton, NJ: Princeton University Press, 1992).

45. Nicholas Thomas, *Entangled Objects: Exchange, Material Culture and Colonialism in the Pacific* (Cambridge, MA: Harvard University Press, 1991).

46. For an excellent summary of the philosophical literature, see the entry 'Intentional Fallacy' by Gary Iseminger in *The Encyclopedia of Aesthetics*, ed. Michael Kelly (Oxford, Oxford University Press, 1998), pp. 515–17.

47. The term *exaptation* comes from evolutionary biology. Exaptations are features 'evolved for other uses (or for no function at all), and later "coopted" for their current role': Stephen Jay Gould and E.S. Vrba, 'Exaptation—a missing term in the science of form,' *Paleobiology* 8 (1982), p. 6. An exaptation is a biological adaptation where the biological function currently performed by the item was not the performance selected for.

48. This is one of the lessons of Charles Taylor, *Multiculturalism and 'The Politics of Recognition': An Essay*, with commentary by Amy Gutmann (Princeton, NJ: Princeton University Press, 1994). Thanks to Elizabeth Burns Coleman and Rosemary J. Coombe for bringing this essay to our attention.

49. Clifford, J. (1991). 'Four Northwest Coast Museums: Travel Reflections,' in Karp and Lavine, *Exhibiting Cultures*, p. 225.

50. The following observations derive principally from our visit to the Michael C. Rockefeller Wing on May 9, 2006.

51. Cole, H. M. (1982). The New Michael C. Rockefeller Wing at the Metropolitan Museum of Art, *African Arts* 15, 2, p. 30.

52. In an article published when the Rockefeller Wing opened, Susan M. Vogel, previously curator at the Museum of Primitive Art and the Metropolitan Museum's first curator of African art, discussed the constraints of conforming to the display conventions of an encyclopedic art museum: 'Bringing African Art to the Metropolitan Museum,' *African Arts* 15, 2 (1982), pp. 38–45.

53. Clarke, C. (2003). 'From Theory to Practice: Exhibiting African Art in the Twenty-First Century,' in *Art and its Publics: Museum Studies at the Millennium*, ed. Andrew McClellan (Oxford and Malden, MA), pp. 166–7. Clarke provides a succinct account of the aesthetic exhibition of African artifacts in the USA in the twentieth century (pp. 167–73) with bibliographical references.

54. In 1982, Vogel explained the reasons for conforming to the aesthetic model prevailing elsewhere in the museum in the display of African artifacts: 'While context photos would be useful in many of the Metropolitan's galleries (what did the rooms look like in which Vermeer expected his paintings to hang?), there are virtually none in art museum galleries.' She described such photographs as distracting because less demanding than artworks: Vogel, 'Bringing African Art to the Metropolitan Museum,' p. 40.

55. Perhaps the most influential critiques have been those associated with exhibitions that probe modes of display, including Susan Vogel's *Art/artifact: African Art in Anthropology Collections* (New York and Munich: Center for African

Art and Prestel Verlag, 1988); Mary H. Nooter, *Secrecy: African Art that Conceals and Reveals* (New York and Munich: Museum for African Art and Prestel Verlag,1993); Mary Nooter Roberts and Susan Vogel, *Exhibition-ism: Museums and African Art* (New York: Museum for African Art, 1994).

56. The following observations are based on Ivan Gaskell's visit to the Sainsbury African Galleries on June 7, 2006.

57. To describe these labels as informative is not to exempt them from criticism on the grounds of questionable factual accuracy or ideological bias: for such criticism, see Ruth B. Phillips, 'Where is "Africa"? Re-Viewing Art and Artifact in the Age of Globilization,' *American Anthropologist* 104, 3 (2002), pp. 944–52.

58. The curators responsible discuss their aims in: Christopher Spring, Nigel Barley and Julie Hudson, 'The Sainsbury African Galleries at the British Museum,' *African Arts* 34, 3 (2001), pp. 18–37, 93. They note that by contriving to show the same mask, the *Otobo* or Hippopotamus (or, properly, tokens of it) in three contexts—'an ethnographic installation, a contemporary artwork interpretation, and an actual multimedia performance'—they are addressing 'three different ideas . . . on where the "art" of African masquerade lies and how it should be experienced—in the carved wood, in the visual aesthetic, or in the multimedia act of performance' (p. 24).

59. Although, as mentioned in note 24 above, despite the fact that the word 'primitive' does not appear in the museum's official name, it is regularly referred to as 'the new museum of primitive art' by the French and American popular presses.

60. Successful practice would have to take full and detailed account of the possibility of misleading disparities existing between artifacts and accompanying material, such as comparative photographs. These include the fact that exhibited artifacts and photographs ostensibly illustrating the original use of similar things were often made many years apart; and that since the nineteenth century, photographs by anthropologists of rituals and performances have regularly been contrived through staging or reenactment: see Clarke, 'Exhibiting African Art,' p. 177, and Christraud Geary, 'Photographic Practice in Africa and its Implications for the Use of Historical Photographs as Contextual Evidence,' in *Fotografia e storia dell'Africa: atti del convegno internationale, Napoli-Roma, 9–11 settembre, 1992*, ed. Alessandro Triulzi (Naples: Istituto Universitario Orientale, 1995), p. 104.

61. We should like to thank the editors and our fellow contributors to the volume for their immensely helpful comments on an earlier draft presented at the authors' workshop in Victoria, BC, June 20–25, 2006.

11

'Nothing Comes from Nowhere': Reflections on Cultural Appropriation as the Representation of Other Cultures

James O. Young and Susan Haley

'I feel some anxiety about the way in which I have appropriated this strange material. But appropriation is what novelists do. Whatever we write is, knowingly or unknowingly, a borrowing. Nothing comes from nowhere.'—Margaret Drabble

Introduction

Subject appropriation occurs when members of one culture (call them outsiders for the sake of brevity) represent members of other cultures (insiders for the sake of convenience) or aspects of insiders' culture. (Subject appropriation has sometimes been called voice appropriation, particularly when outsiders represent the lives of insiders in the first person.) Subject appropriation occurs in two main contexts. It occurs in the arts, when artists from one culture represent aspects of another culture, or people who belong to it. These could be painters, writers, filmmakers or artists working in a variety of other media. Subject appropriation also occurs in the social sciences when investigators examine cultures other than their own, but we will focus on the arts. We believe that it is not possible to generalize about the morality of subject appropriation. Sometimes acts of subject appropriation are morally objectionable, but often they are not. Our intention in this paper is to begin the task of distinguishing between the objectionable and unobjectionable cases.

A few examples of subject appropriation will be helpful. W.P. Kinsella has been much discussed. This white Canadian has set a number of stories among the residents of the (actual) Hobbema Indian Reserve of Alberta. Tony Hillerman, a white American author, has set many novels among the Navajo. The central character of these novels is Joe Chee, a Navajo police-man. In the 1930s, Archie Stansfeld Belaney (Grey Owl), an Englishman who emigrated to Canada, successfully passed himself off (on different occasions) as a full-blooded Ojibway and an Apache-Scottish half-blood. He then wrote about the traditional ways of North American First Nations. One of the authors of this paper, Susan Haley, has written several novels in which Native American points of view are represented. (These include Haley 1999 and 2002.) Not all subject appropriation involves the represen-tation of North American First Nations by white outsiders. Alexander McCall Smith, for example, is also engaged in subject appropriation. This Scottish lawyer has written a series of bestselling novels featuring Precious Ramotswe, a Botswanan private detective. The motto given above comes from Drabble's *The Red Queen*, which appropriates the subject of eighteenth-century Korea.

Is 'subject appropriation' a misnomer?

Subject appropriation is in an important respect different from the other sorts of appropriation considered in this volume. All appropriation involves taking and it is not obvious that those who engage in subject appropriation take any-thing from insiders. Even if nothing is taken by subject appropriation, acts of representing cultures other than one's own can still be morally suspect.

Our claim here is intended to be perfectly general and not restricted to subject appropriation as practiced by artists. One could try to defend artists against an imputation of subject appropriation on the grounds that they produce works of fiction. One might hold that works of fiction do not represent real things. Rather, they create fictional objects. One could con-clude that artists create objects and do not represent anything real. Such a line of argument would be disingenuous. In works of fiction, including novels and films, artists can represent real things, including insiders and their cultures. There is no doubt that the Navajo are represented in Hill-erman's novels, even if Joe Chee is a fictional character. So we are not claiming that novels do not represent real cultural contexts. Rather, our view is that an act of representing is not an act of appropriating in the same way that taking the Parthenon Marbles or singing a song from another culture is an act of appropriation.

One way of putting this is to say that cultures do not own subject matters. One of the themes of this book is to explore the question of what cultures own and what is in the public domain (or the intellectual commons). Usually, subject matters are part of the public domain. Anyone may write about or otherwise represent what falls within his experience or within the ambit of his imagination. An exception to this rule can occur when members of a culture wish that something about their culture remain private. We will return to the question of privacy in a later section of this paper.

The claim that nothing is taken by subject appropriation, and so the claim that the term is a misnomer, may seem to have been unduly hasty. One sometimes hears the claim that, by writing, say, about First Nations, outsiders can appropriate an audience that rightfully belongs to members of First Nations. The suggestion is that the reading public, both among insiders and outsiders, will read books about First Nations by outsiders and the insiders will be left without a readership they rightfully deserve. That is, the potential audience for the material has been appropriated. Lenore Keeshig-Tobias, for example, considers the film *Where the Spirit Lives* (1989). This film, directed by Bruce Pittman, an outsider relative to Aboriginal cultures, is concerned with the experience of Indians who were taken from their communities and forced to attend residential schools. Keeshig-Tobias maintains that this film takes from Native people the opportunity to tell the story of residential schools. 'Even if we had access to financial backers', she writes, 'they would say: "Residential schools? It's been done."' (Keeshig-Tobias 1997: 72) Let us call this the audience appropriation argument.

One problem with this argument is that it is not clear that any public audience rightfully belongs to anyone. The audience for works about, say, Italian-American culture no more belongs to Italian-Americans, qua Italian-Americans, than it belongs to anyone else. A public audience is something that a writer or artist earns by producing something that deserves attention. Just in representing another culture an artist takes nothing that rightfully belongs only to members of that culture. Insiders have the right to represent themselves, but this is not taken from them when others represent them.

The second objection to the audience appropriation argument questions the suggestion that artists are playing a zero sum game. Writers, both literary and academic, might be thought to be in competition. This may be true in some sense. Writers may try to outdo others. More importantly, for present purposes, artists and writers may be thought to be competing for the same market. However, the audience for novels, research or films about a given culture is no more fixed than is the audience for murder mysteries or stories about wizards. If someone makes murder mysteries or wizard stories popular, the market for such books increases. Opportunities for other writers expand. They do not contract. There is a potentially limitless appetite for books about any given culture and it is likely that outsider books open up new markets for insider books.

Certainly, the appropriation of artistic styles provides us with a reason to think that this is so. Consider, for example, Paul Simon's appropriation of the music of South Africa's townships. This led to an explosion of interest in South African music and huge opportunities for musicians from South Africa. Think, for example, of the huge success enjoyed by the Zulu choir, Ladysmith Black Mambazo. Another consideration reinforces this view. It is well known that collectors of Australian Aboriginal-style art strongly prefer to buy works that have been produced by Aboriginal artists. These are regarded as more authentic expressions of the style and it is probable that they will be preferred to artistic representations of the culture produced by outsiders. (This matter of authenticity will be taken up again below.) Similarly, all things being equal, we might expect the reading public will prefer insiders' representations of their culture over those produced by outsiders.

Just as Paul Simon's appropriation of content did not stifle Zulu voices, the appropriation of subject seems not to have hindered other cultures as they have striven to find a voice. On the contrary, we believe that writing about Native people has helped them in a real practical sense to have a voice, in the sense that literary attention has helped them to become published. The fashionableness of Native cultures actually draws attention to their problems and permits the voices of Natives themselves to be heard. It seems obvious to us that the members of some cultures are more likely to find an audience if the public is already aware of their concerns than if they do not even appear on the literary landscape. In Canada, non-Aboriginal authors such as Rudy Wiebe and James Houston have been writing about Natives of the Canadian West and North for some time. We suggest that the work of these writers is at least partly responsible for the strong interest that has been awakened in the work of Native authors such as Thomas King, Thomson Highway and Robert Alexie.

This pattern can be observed in arts other than literature. Consider the movie *The White Dawn* (1974). *The White Dawn* was undoubtedly, in many ways, the progenitor of *Atanarjuat* (*The Fast Runner*) (2001), directed by Zacharias Kunuk and winner of the Camera d'Or at Cannes and an Academy Award for best foreign language film. Unlike its predecessor, *Atanarjuat* had not only an Inuit cast, but an Inuit director as well. *The White Dawn* did not steal the audience of *Atanarjuat*, which won a world-wide audience. Saying that *The White Dawn* did not harm *Atanarjuat* does not give sufficient emphasis to its importance. When *The White Dawn* was first shown in Arctic communities, the audience of Native people found this movie completely gripping because they realized that it was about them. Previously they had only seen southerners represented in cinema and this movie contributed to the recognition that the Inuit could be the subject of successful filmmaking.

This is not to say that members of minority cultures have no difficulties in obtaining an audience. This evidence has sometimes been used to argue against the representation of other cultures. There is anecdotal evidence that publishers have been reluctant to print works by members of Canadian First Nations. Keeshig-Tobias reports that 'publishers have returned manuscripts by Natives with "too Indian" or "not Indian enough" scrawled across them.' Barbara Goddard writes that some publishers have used 'not marketable' as a 'euphemism for concern about the race of the characters.' (Goddard 1990: 186–7) Discrimination against Indigenous artists by publishers or the general public is deplorable, but it is irrelevant to the question of whether artists may represent other cultures. The problem is not with artists who represent other cultures. They are not the ones who harm insiders by denying them opportunities. The claim that publishers or others discriminate is a *non sequitur* in any discussion of whether artists may represent others.

Rosemary J. Coombe's comments on subject appropriation identify some more *non sequiturs*. While considering debate over artists who represent other cultures, Coombe reflects on a whole range of issues. (Coombe 1993) These include government policies that had as their avowed goal the assimilation of Indigenous cultures within the mainstream, laws against the potlatch ceremony, the seizing of ceremonial objects, the suppression of Native languages and many others. Coombe takes these factors to be relevant since they provide the background against which the representation of indigenous cultures takes place. In fact, they have nothing to do with the question of whether artists act wrongly in representing others.

Many government policies and social attitudes have savaged Indigenous cultures. That does not show that artists who represent other cultures have done something wrong.

Coombe suggests that the reading public has 'no interest in hearing Native peoples speak on their own behalf.' (Coombe 1993: 280) This is questionable, given the success of Highway, Sherman Alexie and other Indigenous writers. (Strangely, the Goddard article just quoted notes that *Dry Lips Oughta Go to Kapuskasing*, by the Cree playwright Thomson Highway, was, at the time of Goddard's writing, playing in Toronto to 'packed houses and critical acclaim.' It was one of three plays by Highway produced in Toronto in the year she was writing.) Think, also of the huge popularity of Indigenous painters, sculptors and print makers. It is implausible that non-Native people would be happy to have Natives speak through the visual arts but not through the literary arts. Still, even if Coombe is right, her premise does not show that artists act wrongly in representing other cultures. We might hope that the voices of insiders would also be heard, but that is not a reason for not hearing outsiders.

Subject appropriation and misrepresentation

Let us leave now the question of whether subject appropriation takes anything from insiders. Even if insiders are not deprived of anything by subject appropriation, they could still be seriously harmed by it. The most obvious way in which they could be harmed is by misrepresentation. Misrepresentation can also be profoundly offensive.

The fact that misrepresentation has occurred and continues to occur in the treatment of minority cultures in fiction and film is undeniable. It is easy to identify works of art in which cultures have been harmfully or offensively misrepresented by outsiders. One need only think of old Hollywood Westerns which (mis)represent Indians as duplicitous and cruel. (Lutz 1990) No doubt these movies have harmed members of First Nation cultures. These misrepresentations expose members of First Nation cultures to ridicule and derision. Worse, these misrepresentations doubtlessly foster discrimination against Aboriginal people. Such harmful misrepresentation is unequivocally wrong. Just as it is wrong to slander or libel an individual, it is wrong to misrepresent all members of some culture in a manner that harms them.

The harm a culture suffers from subject appropriation could be more subtle than the previous paragraph suggests. Artworks can perpetuate stereotypes that prevent audiences from seeing members of a culture as the individuals that they are. Janice Acoose takes W.P. Kinsella and Margaret Laurence to task. Both Linda Star (in Kinsella's eponymous story) and Piquette Tonnerre (in *The Diviners*) are intended as sympathetic portrayals of Native women but, Acoose maintains, they are stereotypes. (Acoose 1995: 66) The predicaments of these characters are typical, she claims, their reactions are typical, the way that they speak, dress and do their hair is typical. Stanley Cavell makes a similar point about the representation of African-Americans in movies. He writes that, 'Until recently, types of black human beings were not created in film; black people were stereotypes—mammies, shiftless servants, loyal retainers, entertainers. We were not given, and were not in a position to be given, individualities that projected particular ways of inhabiting a social role; we recognized only the role.' (Cavell 1979: 33) Members of other cultures are, however, misrepresented unless they are represented as individuals and this can be harmful.

However, it must be asserted against Acoose that *The Diviners* was a kind of watershed in Canadian literature. It made it clear to Canadians, perhaps for the first time, that their self-depiction was worthwhile. Once Canadians were depicted, the discrimination and the race and class hatred in rural Canadian society emerged. The representation of the Métis characters in *The Diviners* was crucial in that it picked out for Canadians a great historical injustice as an important subject for Canadian fiction. For this reason, it is not entirely clear what is the matter with the 'typicalness' of the Tonnerres, unless Acoose's criticism is not moral but aesthetic.

It is conceivable that even sympathetic portrayals of a minority culture could be harmful. Consider, for example, the adulatory depictions of Native people contained in such movies as Arthur Penn's *Little Big Man* (1970) and Kevin Costner's *Dances with Wolves* (1990). These films provided a corrective to the view of North American Indians in earlier big screen productions, but did not necessarily depict cultural details accurately. Such works can convey and perpetuate stereotypes of the noble savage that are, in the long run, of no benefit to Indigenous peoples.

One could go further and maintain that outsiders necessarily (or probably) misrepresent insiders. Janisse Browning has written that, 'We persons of color [Browning is a woman of mixed First Nations and African ancestry] have hidden knowledge—a wisdom of experience we embody—that can't be accessed by white people because they have not been forced to continually combat white oppression like we have.' (Browning 1991: 33) Browning concludes that white artists who engage in subject appropriation will inevitably produce work that distorts minority cultures. Hurka has made a similar claim. He maintains that 'if a white treats a Native subject, he or she is likely to get it wrong.' (Hurka 1994: 184) His argument is that there is no significant body of Native writing from which Whites can learn and against which their writings can be judged. Both Browning and Hurka may be said to be advocates of what we will call the privileged knowledge argument.

We ought not to conclude from the reflections of the previous paragraphs that outsiders ought not to represent insiders at all. For a start, let us not forget that harm can be done to a culture when outsiders do not represent it. The American author Wallace Stegner has written a novel, *Angle of Repose*, about irrigation projects in nineteenth-century Colorado. This novel has no major Native characters and does not contain any mention of Indian water rights, even though it is about a subject that deeply concerns their present-day interests and the historical violation of their rights. In fact, Indians scarcely appear in the book except as background figures. Despite this, *Angle of Repose* won the Pulitzer Prize in 1972. This might be described as an outrage. More importantly, for present purposes, this example illustrates that if outsiders always refrained from representing insiders and their cultures, the result would be a misrepresentation of reality. Insiders could be harmed much more by being omitted than by being ignored. This argument does not, however, really tackle the privileged knowledge argument head on.

We can only do that by denying that outsiders must misrepresent insiders. Examples of non-distorting instances of subject appropriation are easy to find. Tony Hillerman's Joe Chee novels come readily to mind. They have actually been recognized by the Navajo as accurately representing their culture. In 1987 Hillerman was awarded the Special Friend of the Dineh (Navajo) award. The citation accompanying this award thanked Hillerman for 'authentically portraying the strength and dignity of traditional Navajo culture.' (Hillerman 2002) The Navajo and other First Nations use Hillerman's books in their schools. Anyone who maintains that outsiders are bound to misrepresent other cultures is also required to defend the position that such prominent outsiders as V.S. Naipaul and Michael Ondaatje necessarily misrepresent the European cultures they represent in their work. If it cuts at all, the privileged knowledge argument cuts both ways.

The aesthetic success of the novels of Naipaul and Ondaatje shows that it does not cut either way.

The success of outsiders in representing other cultures should not surprise us. The best biography is not always autobiography. Similarly, sometimes people with a little distance, a little perspective, on a culture may be in a position to interpret and understand it in a way that insiders cannot. We might like to say, for example, that Canadian criticisms of American political life are sometimes insightful (and, just possibly, *vice versa*). In general, we can learn something about ourselves from seeing how others see us. People within a given culture may not be aware of the significance of some of their own practices. The superstructure of culture is not necessarily apparent to those who live inside it. Outsiders do have some limitations. They may be ignorant of certain aspects of a culture simply because they have not lived as a member of the culture and do not have another source of knowledge. It does not follow from the existence of such limitations that outsiders cannot accurately represent many aspects of a foreign culture in valuable ways.

Edward Said famously argued that members of one culture are apt to create stereotypes about other cultures, but he also maintained that it is possible for members of one culture to understand another. He explicitly denied that 'only women can understand feminine experience, only Jews can understand Jewish suffering, only formerly colonial subjects can understand colonial experience.' (Said 1993: 31) Said justifies his position by denying essentialism about cultures. We must 'acknowledge the massively knotted and complex histories of special but nevertheless overlapping and interconnected experiences—of women, of Westerners, of Blacks, of national states and cultures—there is no particular intellectual reason for granting each and all of them an ideal and essentially separate status.' (Said 1993: 32) Humans, for all of their cultural and other differences, are not so different that they are incapable of understanding each other.

Said recognizes that artists from a given culture can have presuppositions and prejudices when they represent other cultures. He forcefully argues that Conrad (in *Nostromo*) and Kipling (in *Kim*) failed to question imperialism. Kipling never doubted for a moment the necessity and rightness of British rule in India and this shapes his perception of the country. At the same time Said recognizes that both Conrad and Kipling are great artists who, while writing about cultures other than their own, produced great masterpieces, ones that are full of insights into the cultures of others. These writers did not suffer from an aesthetic handicap.

In arguing as we have just done, we may have conceded too much to the privileged knowledge argument. At the heart of this argument is the claim that, in order to write insightfully about something one must have experienced it. To correctly depict a culture, the argument assumes, you must have lived it. But this makes no allowance for the exercise of the creative imagination. Many artists have succeeded in imaginatively entering into the lives of individuals from distinct cultures. *Light in August* was not written by an African-American. Yet Faulkner has the depth of insight, the imaginative capability, to reveal by his art what the experience of being African-American is like in a way that, perhaps, someone who has felt it nevertheless could not. One might compare *Light in August* with, for example, Toni Morrison's *Beloved*. The former is not necessarily a less successful work of art just because the author has not been directly victimised by racism. Faulkner has not had the experience of victimization, but he has fully imagined it, and also has something to contribute to our understanding. Armed with a creative imagination an outsider can even convincingly assume the persona of an insider and write about an insider's experience in the first person. Salman Rushdie makes this very point. Speaking of his experience of being an expatriate Indian who still writes about India, he says that

> There are terrible books that arise directly out of experience, and extraordinary imaginative feats dealing with themes which the author has been obliged to approach from the outside. (Rushdie 1991: 14)

The aesthetic success of *Midnight's Children* is evidence that Rushdie is correct.

Another benefit of subject appropriation is that the perspectives of others can help individuals and whole cultures better understand themselves. Edward Said makes this point about Conrad (*Heart of Darkness*) as well as Kipling (*Kim*). Even though both of these great writers were limited by their European perspective, a whole new way of looking at a country and a people (in Conrad's case the Belgian-occupied Congo and in Kipling's case, the Native cultures of India) originated with their work. (Said 1993)

Said identifies another benefit that ought not to be overlooked. The novels of these outsiders opened out a literary field which is being mined by Native insiders to this day. This is especially and obviously true of *Kim*. Probably all Indian writers detest this book's imperialist assumptions. At the same time it is beloved by most Indians and, in many ways, Kipling's work is to be found at the heart of the explosion of Indian literature in English which is going on at the present time. *The God of Small Things* by Arundhati Roy, winner of the 2001 Booker prize, owes a great debt, for example, to *The Jungle Books*.

Said's view is that great literature can have the salutary effect of spawning other works both in imitation and in rebuttal. He sees the world of literature as a kind of giant global stage upon which works of art strive with one another in a huge free market. It is evidently his opinion that misrepresentation, at least of the type of which Conrad and Kipling were guilty, was the source of more great literature. Of course, it is undeniable that colonialism first, and now globalization, have resulted in the worldwide extinction of culture. Said's point is only that the voices of the best artists set up a counter-current to these forces. They do so, first of all, by awakening an audience to the whole idea of a different culture, and secondly, in creating cultural revival even in cultures other than their own.

Cultural Appropriation and Assimilation

In the previous section we considered the possibility that outsiders could, by engaging in cultural appropriation, put some cultures in an unfavourable light, and the further possibility that this could harm a culture. Perhaps the mechanism by which cultures are harmed by cultural appropriation was not properly captured in the argument of that section. Several writers have expressed the fear that certain small, often Indigenous, cultures will be overwhelmed if outsiders engage in cultural appropriation. A culture could be overwhelmed (and assimilated) by subject appropriation, if insiders begin to see themselves as others see them.

Hurka is among those who have argued that a culture could be distorted if outsiders engage in subject appropriation. He is particularly concerned about the danger that small, Indigenous cultures will be overwhelmed by the voices of outsiders. He considers the case of a White author who writes about a First Nation culture and, though ignorance, distorts the culture's symbols. 'If the white's novel is read by Natives, they too may understand the symbols inauthentically. The Native artist then can't speak even to his or her own people.' (Hurka 1994: 184–5) Native artists will have lost some of their cultural identity. They and, perhaps, some of their audience have been partially assimilated into the majority culture. This strikes Hurka (and us) as unjustifiable harm. We will call this argument the assimilation argument. Note that the argument is asymmetrical. Members of minority cultures will not similarly hurt majority cultures by acts of cultural appropriation since members of majority cultures have enough access to accurate representations of their cultures.

The assimilation argument must be taken seriously since it correctly identifies the single most important threat to minority cultures: destruction by assimilation. While assimilation is the greatest danger facing minority cultures, the assimilation argument under consideration is not very persuasive. It depends on an unsupported empirical claim: that exposure to novels (or other works of art) will be sufficient to mislead insiders about their own culture. This is certainly possible, but insiders have many other sources of information about their culture. The insiders can check the outsiders' representations of their culture against their own experience and the inherited knowledge of other members of the culture. If insiders are worried about being harmed by artworks produced by outsiders, they can simply decline to be part of the audience for these works. We cannot absolutely refute the claim that artworks produced by outsiders will distort and overwhelm some minority cultures. The probability that this will happen is difficult to calculate. We think that it is small and that the threat of assimilation does not come from artists who engage in cultural appropriation, but we could be wrong.

The mere fact that outsiders might, in representing a minority culture, contribute to its assimilation is not enough to establish that subject appropriation is wrong. The fact that it is possible that insiders can check any representations of their culture by outsiders is sufficient to undermine the assimilation argument. Insiders bear the primary responsibility for the perpetuation of their culture. They can be expected to take reasonable precautions to ensure that their cultures are protected. Insiders are able (and probably easily able) to avoid being harmed by any artworks produced by outsiders. Consequently, outsiders cannot be held responsible for any assimilation that results from their cultural appropriation. Here cultural appropriation is analogous to playing one's stereo at a reasonable volume. The neighbours might be disturbed, but only if they do not take care to close their windows. (We assume that there is no good reason, in this case, to keep the windows open. For example, it is not a hot or humid evening.) The analogy is not a perfect one. Indigenous cultures are at risk because outsiders have (if we may continue with the same conceit) squatted next door to the insiders, pulled open the insiders' windows and turned on their stereos. Still, the annoyance caused by the music next door is easily avoided. The artists who turned on the stereos are not the real culprits. The real problem is that the outsiders squatted next door.

Harm and Accurate Representation

We have just considered the possibility that misrepresentation of a culture can be harmful and wrong. One might argue that, even when outsiders accurately represent a culture other than their own, they can do so in ways that are harmful and wrong. Consider, for example, a novel that does not misrepresent a culture (and, consequently, is not wrong on this ground) but still puts the culture in a bad light. Some cultures are plagued by serious problems. Colonization disrupts cultures and causes a series of problems such as high rates of violence and substance abuse. A novel may accurately represent this reality. One might think that when outsiders (accurately) represent the culture, its members may be stigmatized. Discrimination against members of the culture may be reinforced and perpetuated. In this way the insiders could be harmed and, one might conclude, even the accurate representation of insiders by outsiders is wrong. It might seem that it is more often wrong to represent other cultures than we have suggested. It might seem that the insiders have a right not to have their dirty laundry exposed to the world.

This is really an argument against the representation of a culture by anyone and not an argument against representations by outsiders. Representations of a culture by insiders could air dirty laundry just as surely as any representation by an outsider. Presumably these representations could be just as harmful as any laundry-airing representations by outsiders. They may even be more harmful, because they are seen as more credible. Furthermore, the argument is not a general one against all subject appropriation. Even if successful, it would only show that some instances of subject appropriation, those that revealed flaws in a culture, were wrong.

These responses do not, however, reveal the full problem with the argument at hand. It is premised on the claim that it is wrong, in certain instances, to reveal the truth and this is something about which we are skeptical. There may be a high rate of HIV infection in a given culture. The correct response is not to ignore this fact. Any accurate representation of the social problems faced by a culture will reveal the sources of these difficulties. It will show when they have been externally caused and when they are not the responsibility of insiders. It will show that the appropriate response to these difficulties is understanding, compassion and assistance. The correct response is not discrimination. If problems are ignored, nothing can be done about them. It is better that artists have the opportunity to present social difficulties in a responsible and compassionate manner.

Privacy

Privacy is extremely important and the individuals who make up a culture have a right not to have their privacy violated by outsiders. It can be painful to be misrepresented and intrusive prying can be deeply offensive. The issue of privacy can be particularly sensitive when we are dealing with the representation of small cultures. Some Indigenous cultures are often very like extended families. Certainly some subject appropriation is wrong because it violates the rights to privacy of individual members of a culture. (Sometimes, all of the privacy rights of a culture's members are violated at the same time.) This is a delicate matter; it is a case where it may be appropriate to ask permission. Where permission may not be gained, or when there is no obvious way to seek it, it may not be clear at all what the right course is for the author. Still, we believe that the right of a culture's members to privacy does not rule out all representation of other cultures.

It is easy to see that representations that violate the privacy of a culture's members are wrong. It is clearly wrong for someone to record surreptitiously an individual's cell phone conversations and then write about them. Artists who obtain information about a culture by violating the privacy rights of individuals and then write about the culture act wrongly in precisely the same way that the recorder of private conversations does. Their actions are more wrong in that the privacy rights of more individuals are violated. The privacy rights of everyone who belongs to a culture are violated. So, for example, Richard Burton acted wrongly when, in 1853, he became the first Englishman to visit Mecca in the company of Muslim hadji. Non-Muslims were forbidden to take part in the pilgrimage to

Mecca. As it happens, Burton wrote a narrative account of his journey, but he would have acted just as wrongly had he written a novel about his experiences. Burton acted wrongly because he violated the privacy of individual Muslims. Muslims did not wish to have non-Muslims present and this wish should have been respected.

In determining the morality of any representation of another culture, a crucial issue must be addressed. This is the issue of how outsiders have obtained information about the culture they represent. We must ask whether any of the information gained by an artist was obtained surreptitiously, deceptively or coercively. Information ought not to come through the sort of stealth employed by Burton. Nor ought it to come deceptively, as it would if someone were to represent himself as an insider in order to obtain information. Neither should any form of coercion be employed. This is a point to which we will return in a moment. Outsiders can obtain information without violating insiders' privacy. The information outsiders possess about insiders may have been obtained in the open interaction between cultures or through the free communication of authorized insiders. When this is the case (and the insiders' culture is not harmfully misrepresented) the representation of other cultures in art is not wrong.

In the previous paragraph, we referred to authorized members of the insiders' culture. Sometimes information about a culture may only be shared with the approval of properly authorized members of the culture. Sometimes this may be individual members of a culture, but sometimes permission ought to be sought from some institutional authority, such as a band council. It is the responsibility of outsiders to ensure that any information that they use in representing a culture other than their own has been shared with the proper authority.

We have said that information outsiders use in representing cultures other than their own ought not to be obtained by coercion. Here coercion ought to be understood in a broad sense. Colonization has coerced Indigenous cultures in a wide variety of ways. Consider, for example, the documentation and photography of the religious ceremonies of the Hopi by the Mennonite missionary H.R. Voth. There is some evidence that he physically forced his way into religious ceremonies. (Talayesva 1942: 252; for a discussion see Brown 2003:11–15) More likely, the Hopi were simply afraid to exclude him because they felt that, as a White man, he was under the protection of the government. If the Hopi allowed Voth to observe and document their religious practices out of fear, they were effectively coerced.

In general, the colonization of Indigenous cultures is a coercive process. Consequently, any representation of a colonized culture may be ethically suspect.

Artists and others who represent other cultures face a difficult problem when others have violated the privacy of members of some culture. Let us assume that Voth obtained information in a manner that violated the privacy rights of Hopis. Voth published the information that he obtained and it is now widely disseminated. His photographs are easily accessible. It would certainly be wrong for a novelist, say, to obtain information in the way that Voth is assumed to have done and then to write a novel set among the Hopi that draws up this information. It is less clear that the novelist acts wrongly in using this same information once it has entered in to the public arena. On the one hand, it seems reasonable to expect outsiders to refrain from using intrusively obtained information for as long as the insiders object to its use. On the other hand, one might think, the damage caused by the violation of privacy has been done. Moreover, using the information, the outsider might be able to write sensitively and produce a work of real value about the culture whose privacy has been violated. The work might even benefit the insiders. This is a difficult issue and we leave it unresolved.

Authenticity and Subject Appropriation

One might object to works of art that represent other cultures on the grounds that they are inauthentic. In this context, to say that a work of art is inauthentic is to say something like that it is not a genuine expression of a culture. The implication is that since subject appropriators will produce works that are inauthentic, these works will suffer from an aesthetic flaw. We want to grant the premise but deny the conclusion. There is a sense in which every artwork that involves the representation of other cultures is inauthentic. Inauthenticity, as the word is used here, is not, however, an indicator of an aesthetic flaw. A work that is inauthentic in the present sense can be vitally authentic in another sense.

Every work of art is authentic in some sense. A work by Grey Owl is inauthentic in that it is not an authentic expression of Ojibway culture. On the other hand, every literary work by Grey Owl is an authentic Grey Owl. It is an authentic product of Grey Owl's peculiar cultural perspective.

Outsiders cannot produce authentic expressions of insiders' culture. Even when outsiders are thoroughly acculturated in a new culture, they generally retain their previous culture and their perspective is not identical to that of a monocultural insider. Nevertheless, outsiders can produce authentic expressions of their own culture. As authentic expression of their author's culture, works involving subject appropriation are often works of literary or, more generally, aesthetic merit.

The authenticity of a work of art is relevant to its evaluation. There is an empiricist tendency within aesthetics that denies that nothing is relevant to the aesthetic value of a work of art besides its observable properties. On this view, the provenance of a work of art is irrelevant to its aesthetic value. Advocates of this view hold that whether a painting was executed by van Meegeren or Vermeer is irrelevant to its aesthetic value. All that is relevant is how the painting looks. In recent years, however, many philosophers of art have argued against this empiricist approach to aesthetic value. In order to evaluate the work, these philosophers have argued, one needs to know the category to which it belongs. This trend in philosophy of art can be traced at least as far back to a classic paper by Kendall Walton. (Walton 1970) He argued that, for example, one cannot determine whether a painting is gaudy without first determining its category. If a painting belongs to the category of Impressionist still lifes in the style of Fantin-Latour we might come to the conclusion that it is gaudy. If we decide that it belongs to post-Impressionist still lifes in the style of Matisse, then we are less likely to judge it gaudy. Works of art are never, on this view, gaudy *tout court*. In determining the category to which a work of art belongs we take into account a wide variety of factors. Among these factors will be knowledge about the artist and his intentions.

This is relevant to our present concerns because, in evaluating a work of art, we may very well need to know the cultural background of the person who produced it. We may very well need to know the culture of which it is an authentic expression. Consider, for example, a novel set among slaves in the antebellum American south. A given passage might appear poignant if we believe it to be written by a freed slave. The very same words might seem callous if we know that a slave owner wrote them. (Whites wrote a number of books that were represented as the works of escaped slaves.) This is not to say that the slave owner could not write a novel of considerable literary merit. Outsiders can enter imaginatively into the lives of insiders. It is just to say that information about the cultural background of an artist can be relevant in the evaluation of their works.

Or, to put the same point in another way, in evaluating a work of art we need often to know the culture of which it is an authentic expression.

Since the evaluation of a work of art can depend on information about the cultural background of the artist who created it, artists ought not to pass themselves off as members of cultures other than their own. Over the years many artists have perpetrated this sort of fraud. We have already mentioned the case of Grey Owl. Others include Forrest Carter, author of *The Education of Little Tree*. Carter, like Grey Owl, was a White man who passed himself off as an American Indian. The fraud which these artists perpetrated has a moral dimension. It is a form of lying and, consequently, morally suspect. Here we are concerned with the aesthetic dimensions of the fraud. We have here cases of people who pass off as authentic expressions of a culture works that actually express quite a different cultural perspective. This hinders and distorts the interpretation, evaluation and appreciation of these works. The fraud is akin to that of which forgers are guilty. In order to determine the merits of artworks we need to know the categories to which they belong. Determining the category will involve knowing the culture of which they are authentic expression.

The conclusion of this section is that works that involve representation of other cultures are, in a sense, inauthentic. They cannot be authentic expressions of the culture of insiders. This inauthenticity does not make a work an aesthetic failure. It will still be authentic in some other way and potentially possessed of considerable aesthetic value. The representation of a work of art as an authentic expression of some culture, when it is not, is morally wrong and also a transgression against aesthetics.

Envoy

So far in this essay we have not challenged the accepted perspective on how debates about cultural appropriation are addressed. In this framework, there is a clear and even essential difference between insiders and outsiders. Insiders fully understand the rules of their culture. Outsiders cannot. Insiders have privileged epistemic access to their culture. This view is closely aligned with cultural relativism, the view that we have no overarching standpoint from which to examine different cultures. We can only look at other cultures from inside our own. Viewing other cultures from within our own, they will appear fundamentally differently than they appear to insiders. (The view that we have just described is not entirely consistent. One cannot really say that insiders have a privileged perspective on their own culture, if this means that their understanding is objectively right. One could only say that insiders have a different perspective that differs from that of outsiders.)

Cultures are much more porous than this picture allows. A culture is not like a windowless monad. As Said notes, we ought not to be essentialists about culture. So the idea that one is either in or out, that one either has all the cultural information, or else cannot properly be said to have any of it, is mistaken. In point of fact all cultures are in a more or less perpetual state of flux, and all of them historically have impinged to a lesser or greater degree upon one another. These facts about cultures render the accepted perspective on cultural appropriation highly suspect. Once we reject essentialism about cultures, the possibility emerges for avenues of communication between cultures that the essentialist does not recognize. Insiders and outsiders are likely to have a great deal more in common than the essentialist allows.

In the course of all this change and movement great historical wrongs have been perpetrated against individuals and groups of individuals through religious and racial hatred. None of these events should be forgotten or even perhaps forgiven; but somehow, as human beings, we have to try to understand what happened. We cannot possibly do that if we do not undertake to try to exchange cultural information. In fact, we risk perpetuating the misunderstanding and hatred if we do not. Exchange and communication are not really possible on the accepted perspective. Each of us lives in his or her own cultural monad and each monad is incommensurable with the others. Or, to vary the metaphor, we are condemned to aesthetic and cultural apartheid. Fortunately, we believe, this perspective on cultures and communication between them is wrong.

In the process of communication between cultures, literature has a vitally important moral role to play. It is through literature that readers undertake to imagine what it would be to be someone else, someone perhaps completely different. Just as women can understand and imaginatively identify with a male character from the inside and *vice versa*, so can members of other cultural communities. Literature is a crucial purveyor and carrier of social information, both the rules for what one should do, and the models of what one should be; and also the subversive information about a society, which shows us how our rules are wrong and our models bad.

As between societies, literature is the main tool we have for understanding one another. It is not, in the famous example of Thomas Nagel, as though in following a work of fiction about a member of another culture, we were trying to imagine what it would be to be a bat. This character is human, he or she functions in a society; and literature places us in a position to better understand what that is like from the inside. It is a tremendously powerful and useful moral tool, which promotes mutual understanding and respect and which could serve to keep humanity from future holocausts.

The most terrible thing about globalization is the disappearance of culture, and the more or less hopeless subjection of a vast multitude of people to the forces of global capitalism. One of the few good things about globalization is that literature cannot completely be commodified and purveyed. Literature keeps breaking out of bounds and being carried here and there about the world. Writers are seizing upon the giant power of the global information systems to make their voices heard. The last thing we want in this sort of situation is to stifle the voices.

In *Culture and Imperialism*, Edward Said sees a kind of great stage upon which great, agonistic works of literature coming from all parts of the globe arrive and duke it out, new literary voices from subjected minorities are heard refuting the assertions of the colonial writers, but also building upon the fact of their achievements. In this arena, as we said, Kipling has spawned a whole generation of superb South Asian writers who hate/love his work; while what we could hope for in North America would be a whole generation of Native American and Black writers to take up the great themes of White settlement and slavery and turn the assumptions of previous writers upon their heads.

But this can only happen if writing upon these themes is open to all. The mimsy, fearful view that writing about culture is impossible does literature a great disservice. It is only in the attempt to imaginatively understand one another across the barriers of sex, race and culture that great literature is created. And even more, the view that this cannot or should not be done harms humanity as a whole. If we cannot make the attempt to cross those barriers and try to understand each other, we are condemned to repeat over and over, and possibly sometimes in megatons, the mistakes of the past.

Conclusion

We have argued in this paper that merely calling something an example of subject appropriation is not a reason to think that it is morally objectionable. Some examples of subject appropriation are in fact harmful, but the story of how and why needs to be presented. We have tried to examine some of the types of cases where subject appropriation is problematic. However, we have concluded that in general literary fiction and film are appropriative by their very nature, and this can be a good thing.

References

Acoose, J. (1995). Iskwewak—Kah' Ki Yaw Ni Wahkomakanak: Neither Indian Princesses Nor Easy Squaws. Toronto: Women's Press.

Brown, M. F. (2003). Who Owns Native Culture? Cambridge, MA: Harvard University Press.

Browning, J. (1991). Self-Determination and Cultural Appropriation. Fuse, 15.4: 31–5.

Cavell, S. (1979). The World Viewed. Cambridge, MA: Harvard University Press.

Coombe, R. J. (1993). The Properties of Culture and the Politics of Possessing Identity: Native Claims in the Cultural Appropriation Controversy. Canadian Journal of Law and Jurisprudence, 6: 249–85.

Goddard, B. (1990). The Politics of Representation: Some Native Canadian Women Writers. Canadian Literature, 124–5: 183–225.

Haley, S. (1999). The Complaints Department. Wolfville, N.S.: Gaspereau Press.

Haley, S. (2002). The Murder of Medicine Bear. Wolfville, N.S.: Gaspereau Press.

Hillerman, T. (2002). Tony Hillerman. Canku Ota: An Online Newsletter Celebrating Native America, issue 75, November 30, 2002.

Hurka, T. (1994). Should Whites Write About Minorities? In: Principles: Short Essays on Ethics. Toronto: Harcourt Brace and Company.

Keeshig-Tobias, L. (1997). Stop Stealing Native Stories. In: Ziff, B. and Rao, P. V. (eds.) Borrowed Power: Essays on Cultural Appropriation. New Brunswick, N.J.: Rutgers University Press: 71–3.

Lutz, H. (1990). 'Indians' and Native Americans in the Movies: A History of Stereotypes, Distortions, and Displacements. Visual Anthropology, 3: 31–48.

Rushdie, S. (1991). Imaginary Homelands: Essays and Criticism 1981–1991. London: Granta.

Said, E. (1993). Culture and Imperialism, New York: Knopf.

Talayesva, D. C. (1942). Sun Chief: The Autobiography of a Hopi Indian. New Haven: Yale University Press.

Walton, K. (1970). Categories of Art. Philosophical Review, **79**: 334–67.

Index